see Joshua 1:9

AMERICAN HEROES

★ ★ ★ ★ ★ ★ ★ ★ ★ ★ ★ ★ ★

IN SPECIAL OPERATIONS

OLIVER NORTH

EDITED BY CHUCK HOLTON

FIDELIS
BOOKS

Nashville, Tennessee

ISBN: 978-08054-4712-5

Published by Fidelis Books,
a division of B&H Publishing Group
Nashville, Tennessee

Dewey Decimal Classification: 355.3
Subject Heading: TERRORISM \ MILITARY PERSONNEL

1 2 3 4 5 6 7 8 9 10 11 12   14 13 12 11 10

For Betsy

The best shadow warrior of all

Ray —

My bat!

Dad

I swear he wrote "bat" instead of
Dad - LOL - Hope you enjoy!
Love
you!

Staff Sgt Aaron Holleyman, Green Beret medic
and recipient of the Silver Star.
Killed in Iraq on 30 August 2004.

THE SPECIAL FORCES CREED

I am an American Special Forces Soldier!

I will do all that my nation requires of me.

I am a volunteer, knowing well the hazards of my profession.

I serve with the memory of those who have gone before me.

I pledge to uphold the honor and integrity of their legacy
in all that I am—in all that I do.

I am a warrior.

I will teach and fight whenever and wherever my nation requires.

I will strive always to excel in every art and artifice of war.

I know that I will be called upon to perform tasks in isolation,
far from familiar faces and voices.

With the help and guidance of my faith,
I will conquer my fears and succeed.

I will keep my mind and body clean, alert and strong.

I will maintain my arms and equipment in
an immaculate state befitting a Special Forces Soldier,
for this is my debt to those who depend upon me.

I will not fail those with whom I serve.

I will not bring shame upon myself or Special Forces.

I will never leave a fallen comrade.

I will never surrender though I am the last.

If I am taken, I pray that I have the strength
to defy my enemy.

I am a member of my Nation's chosen soldiery,

I serve quietly, not seeking recognition or accolades.

My goal is to succeed in my mission—and live to succeed again.

De Oppresso Liber

CONTENTS

★ ★ ★ ★ ★ ★ ★ ★ ★ ★ ★ ★

"At the office" in Afghanistan

ACKNOWLEDGMENTS

CAMP LEATHERNECK
HELMAND PROVINCE, AFGHANISTAN

Keeping company with heroes is a precious privilege. Over the last nine years of this long war against radical Islamic terror, it has been my great blessing to cover and report on tens of thousands of young Americans who volunteered to serve our nation in harm's way. Those with whom I served in a long-ago, far away war called "Vietnam," inspired me then. So do the Soldiers, Sailors, Airmen, Guardsmen, and Marines—and their CIA and DEA counterparts—in this book. They should inspire you as well.

There are no greater American Heroes than those who serve in Special Operations. War is an inherently dangerous undertaking. It is especially so for those who conduct small unit actions deep in hostile territory, far from the nearest "friendlies." Such operations are usually highly classified, even after they are completed. Therefore, the participants rarely receive the recognition they deserve for the risks they take, the skills they employ, or the sacrifices they make.

This book and companion reporting by our FOX News "War Stories" unit are aimed at letting the American people have an inside look at who these remarkable young men and women are and what they do—without divulging to our enemies, things they don't need to know. The stories here are by no means exhaustive—but they are certainly representative.

It is important for readers to know that before accompanying or interviewing any of the Special Operations units or personnel identified in this book, we agreed not to reveal the names and faces of under-cover operatives or describe tactics, techniques, or equipment that would benefit America's adversaries. Therefore, some of the images in this book have been blurred to protect identities and some names and places have been changed. I am most indebted to all who gave us permission to accompany them on missions and trusted us with interviews. Some of their names and pictures are in this book. Most are not. They truly are American heroes. For the opportunity they gave us to let them tell their stories, I am eternally grateful.

It would not have been possible to document these extraordinary young Americans but for the vision of FOX News president, Roger Ailes and Brad Waggoner, president of B&H Publishing Group/Fidelis Books. Their collaboration made possible this salute to America's "Shadow Warriors."

Gary Terashita, my friend and Executive Editor at Fidelis Books, somehow managed to pull all this work together. Former Army Ranger Chuck Holton is not only a talented writer, editor, and friend—he put himself in harm's way more often than I can count to "shoot" many of the images in this book and our companion FOX News reports from the field of battle.

A work of this kind is the task of many: War Stories Senior Executive Producer, Pamela Browne; field producers and cameramen Mal James, Chris Jackson, Rich Harlow, Griff Jenkins, Greg Johnson, Ayse Wieting, Andy Stenner, and Martin Hinton all helped make it possible for me to show you the special operators in this book.

My friend and counsel, Bob Barnett and his counterpart, Dianne Brandi at FOX News made this book a reality. And Bill Shine, my boss at FOX News, gave me the latitude (and travel authorizations!) to "deploy when necessary" with our "Shadow Warriors."

And as they have for more than two decades, Marsha Fishbaugh, my incomparable executive assistant and Duane Ward at Premiere had to make all my travel fit with what needed to get done to complete this chronicle of courage.

At Fidelis Books, Executive Editor Gary Terashita, Marketing Vice President John Thompson, and Sales Vice President Craig Featherstone kept this project moving forward when I was "hard down" with treatment for cancer. But in the end, it was Art Director Diana Lawrence and Managing Editor Kim Stanford who saved the day and ensured that the eye-witness accounts and images in this work went to print in time to be preserved for posterity.

And, as she has for four decades, Betsy, my wife and best friend, patiently waited and prayed for my safety while I kept company with America's heroes in faraway places. Without her love, support and encouragement—and that of our children, their mates, and our twelve grandchildren, this work would not have been possible.

Semper Fidelis,
Oliver North

A NOTE ABOUT TERMINOLOGY

The world of Special Operations is nebulous and full of mystery and so it isn't surprising it is easy to become confused by some of the terms you will read in this book. In order to make some sense of it, here is a short primer on the proper use of the names of Special Operations forces in America. Understand as you read this that it is not meant to be a comprehensive list—for security reasons, there are other units not mentioned here. Many of these units overlap each other in some way—making them even more difficult to decipher. This primer is meant to make reading this book more informative and comprehensible for those unfamiliar with the shadowy world of Special Ops.

SOCOM

First, understand that the terms "special forces" and "special operations" are not interchangeable. "Special Operations" is a blanket term that covers all units within the Special Operations Command, or SOCOM. "Special Forces," on the other hand, refers only to the Army soldiers commonly known as "green berets," made up of highly trained men who specialize in unconventional warfare tactics and are normally

organized into companies of six "A-teams," also known by the term "Operational Detachment Alpha," or ODA.

So while the Special Forces are definitely part of the Special Operations community, they are joined by other units, such as SEALS and Rangers who do not go by the Special Forces moniker. USSOCOM oversees and coordinates between the Special Operations forces of all services.

USASOC

The United States Army Special Operations Command is the umbrella organization that brings together all special ops units within the Army as a whole. This includes the 75th Ranger Regiment, The Special Forces, as well as a Civil Affairs Brigade and Psychological Operations group within the Army.

JSOC

The Joint Special Operations Command is an activity within SOCOM, which directs and supports training and operations between various Special Missions units, specifically those units designated with "Tier 1" status. JSOC units include the Army's fabled counterterrorist unit, the "1st Special Forces Operational Detachment— Delta," also known by various

other names, such as Delta Force or Combat Application Group, the Navy Special Warfare Development Group (DEVGRU) and the Air Force's 24th Special Tactics Squadron, among others. Tier one units represent the top rung of the Special Operations ladder and are made up of some of the most highly specialized warriors on the planet.

While Tier 1 units represent the most secretive and elite units in the Special Operations universe, their work is, by necessity, done in the shadows. As such, while members of these units have most likely played an important part in every phase of the war on terror, they will receive much less credit in this book than they deserve, though that is just the way they like it.

MARSOC

Not to be left out, the United States Marine Corps instituted the United States Marine Corps Forces Special Operations Command in 2005. This newest member of SOCOM was born from what had been Marine Force Reconnaissance—elite Marine units that had heretofore existed outside of SOCOM. Based on the Special Forces ODA concept, Marine Special Operations Teams are made up of a dozen or so highly trained Marines who are capable of direct action, counterterrorism, training foreign nationals, and special reconnaissance. In practice, these teams are often paired with their Army counterparts to form Special Operations Task Forces (SOTF) that train and fight together in Afghanistan and Iraq.

Rangers

Army Rangers, as pertains to the Special Operations community, refers to men who belong to the elite 75th Ranger Regiment, headquartered at Fort Benning, Georgia. Because the Army's premiere leadership course is called "Ranger School," and because graduates of this course may also go by the term "Ranger," it is easy to confuse a graduate of the school with a member of the Special Ops unit. But this is not always the case. Many graduates of Ranger school hail from and go back to their regular army units; and while graduating Ranger school is quite an accomplishment that earns a man the right

to wear the coveted Ranger Tab, it does not, in and of itself, qualify a man as a special operator. There is an age-old saying among men of the 75th Ranger Regiment that illustrates this important difference: "The tab is just a school. The scroll is a way of life."

Night Stalkers

Based at Fort Campbell, Kentucky, the 160th Special Operations Aviation Regiment is, simply put, a unit of the world's best helicopter pilots. These talented men must have years of experience and thousands of hours of specialized training before being selected to this prestigious unit supporting nearly all U.S. Special Operations around the world. Trained on a variety of aircraft, Night Stalkers gained national recognition during the battle of Mogadishu in 1993 when two 160th helicopters were shot down, resulting in

a pitched, eighteen-hour battle that became the basis for the book and movie *Black Hawk Down*. Since then the Night Stalkers have continued to take on every mission given them, virtually all of which are high-speed, low-level, short-notice night missions with no room for error. Without fail, every mission proves this elite unit's motto: "Night Stalkers don't quit."

SEALS

Born out of the Underwater Demolition Teams trained to breach obstacles and perform beachhead reconnaissance in World War II, today's SEAL teams are more likely to be found kicking in the door of a Taliban kingpin or taking down a pirated vessel. The U.S. Navy's Sea Air and Land forces are capable of working hand in hand with all other special operations units in the areas of counterterrorism, counterinsurgency, direct action, and even counter narcotics. They form the Navy's premiere Special Operations unit, undergoing some of the most rigorous and physically demanding training available in the military today. The SEALs are divided into two main units—one stationed on the East Coast and the other on the West Coast. In addition to their unprecedented abilities on, in, and under the water, these stealthy professionals spend a great deal of time working on land alongside their brethren from other Special Operations units.

AFSOC

Air Force Special Operations Command (AFSOC) has its headquarters at Hurlburt Field, Florida. The Air Force component of U.S. Special Operations Command, AFSOC consists of not only specialized air power, but also specialized ground forces like Combat Controllers, Joint Tactical Air Controllers, units specializing in airborne radio and television psychological operations, pararescuemen, and even Special Operations

Weathermen. While these units may not be well known outside the Special Ops community, their operators are universally respected by the units they complement. That's because AFSOC warriors bring some highly valued skills to the battlefield, and for that reason are heavily represented in this book.

AFSOC has approximately thirteen thousand active-duty, Air Force Reserve, Air National Guard, and civilian personnel, organized under two active duty wings along with a Reserve and a National Guard component.

DEA FAST

Under the heading "the other Special Operators," you'll find that not everyone in the Special Operations Community belongs to the Armed Forces. For example, the Drug Enforcement Administration (DEA) fields very competent and capable teams of special agents whose training and mission capabilities put them on par with any Tier 1 Special Operations unit. These Forward deployed Advisory and Support Teams

(FAST) travel the world training and equipping host nation counter-drug units to take down narco-traffickers and destroy their operations. These missions put the FAST operators into some of the most dangerous hot spots on the globe and I was privileged to accompany them on missions from Afghanistan to Latin America.

SPECIAL FORCES PRAYER

Almighty God, Who art the Author of liberty and the Champion of the oppressed, hear our prayer.

We, the men of Special Forces, acknowledge our dependence upon Thee in the preservation of human freedom.

Go with us as we seek to defend the defenseless and to free the enslaved.

May we ever remember that our nation, whose motto is "In God We Trust", expects that we shall acquit ourselves with honor, that we may never bring shame upon our faith, our families, or our fellow men.

Grant us wisdom from Thy mind, courage from Thine heart, strength from Thine arm, and protection by Thine hand.

It is for Thee that we do battle, and to Thee belongs the victor's crown.

For Thine is the kingdom, and the power and the glory, forever.

AMEN

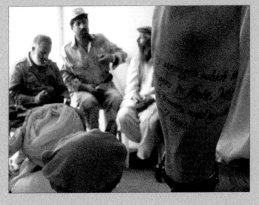

★ ★ ★ ★ ★ ★ ★ ★ ★ ★ ★ ★ ★ ★

Their mottos inspire allies and intimidate adversaries: *"De Oppresso Liber,"* Latin for "Free the Oppressed," the slogan of the U.S. Army's Special Forces; the SEALs, "Ready to Lead, Ready to Follow, Never Quit"; "First There . . . That Others May Live" for U.S. Air Force Special Operations units; and the U.S. Marines' Special Operations Command, "Always Faithful, Always Forward."

Those who know these slogans best are the Soldiers, Sailors, Airmen, and Marines of U.S. Special Operations Command—the tip of the spear in the war against radical Islamic terror. They have all been subjected to rigorous selection, screening, and qualification and then uniquely trained and equipped to become masters of unconventional warfare.

From the jungles of the Philippine Archipelago, to the deserts of Iraq to the shadows of the Hindu Kush, they undertake daring missions in some of the most difficult and dangerous places on this planet.

Modern Special Operations units trace their lineage to 1675 when Captain Benjamin Church recruited and led a force comprised of New England Militia "Rangers" and Native Americans during "King Phillip's War." Less than a century later, in the midst of the French and Indian War, Major Robert Rogers raised and led a formation of colonial irregulars that came to be know as "Rogers' Rangers." His twenty-eight-point "Standing Orders for Rangers" are still part of the U.S. Army training.

Today, Special Operations units are an indispensable part of American military strategy. U.S. Special Operators have been constantly deployed and engaged on the "bleeding edge" of the fight against radical Islamic terror since America was attacked on September 11, 2001.

Though many of the missions conducted by these "Quiet Professionals" remain highly classified, U.S. Special Operations Command has permitted our FOX News "War Stories" team to accompany them on more than a dozen deployments that literally span the globe. We have been with them in the southern Philippians on operations against Abu Sayef and Jemaah Islamiah; in Iraq while they pursued Baath, al Qaeda, and Shiite Militia high value targets (HVTs); and in Afghanistan as our Spec Ops units chased down Taliban kingpins and narcoterrorists.

Activated in 1987, the U.S. Special Operations Command, or SOCOM, now numbers more than fifty thousand unconventional warfare specialists from the Army, Navy, Air Force, and Marines. These extraordinary fighters undertake some of the most sensitive, high risk, missions in the world. And though technology has revolutionized the battlefield, the human component—the warrior—is still the most important element in determining the outcome of a fight.

After a mission with the special mission unit at Shindand

WHAT MAKES THEM SO SPECIAL?

Above and beyond the combat fundamentals taught to every member of our Armed Forces, Special Operators must also master an additional set of skills—call it an "Advanced Degree" in war fighting. They train to fight as small, independent units—often for months at a time. They must adapt to and blend into foreign cultures in which they live, train, and fight.

While Spec Ops personnel are justifiably described as elite, they also know dealing with host nation forces often requires real humility, tempered with the mental toughness to take quick, violent action when necessary. They are trained and equipped to operate in harsh and unpredictable conditions, far from friendly forces for extended periods of time, and their physical conditioning often rivals that of Olympic athletes. Instead of contending for a gold medal, these modern-day gladiators compete for the loyalty of oppressed people by offering to shine the light of liberty into the world's darkest places.

Wherever Special Operators are deployed, it comes at great sacrifice. More than three hundred members of SOCOM have lost their lives since 9/11/01. Two of them—Navy SEALs Michael Murphy and Mike Monsoor—are among the five Americans posthumously awarded the Medal of Honor in the global war on terror. Their valor indicates the true nature of a hero—one who goes into harm's way for the benefit of another.

Because of the highly classified nature of many of their missions, these "masters of chaos" rarely receive the credit warranted for their successes. For example, the highly-publicized capture of Iraqi dictator Saddam Hussein in December 2003 was initially attributed to the 4th Infantry Division, for Saddam was captured in 4th ID "battlespace." But those responsible for pulling the deposed Iraqi dictator out of the hole where he was hiding were members of Task Force 20, a Joint Special Operations Task Force comprised of Delta Force operators, SEALs, and CIA officers from the Special Activities Division who had been tracking High Value Targets (HVTs) across Iraq since the invasion in early 2003.

But these men aren't in it for publicity. In fact, the assignment criteria for the United States Navy SEALs, arguably one of the most elite Special Operations units in the world, specifies that they want warriors to volunteer for this duty because they are seeking "experiences that are both personally and professionally rewarding."

What are those experiences? It's flying through the night on a blacked-out helicopter fifty feet off the ground at 150 miles per hour. It's kicking in the door of a suspected high value target and bringing him to justice. It's raiding an opium bazaar in a remote Afghan village, or treating malaria and providing urgently needed medical care to people who have never seen a doctor. It is knowing that what you are doing matters—that you are a force for good in a world full of evil.

It's being part of the dangerous, demanding, and ultimately rewarding existence that is USSOCOM today—a remarkably trained, equipped, and capable group of warriors, honed to a razor's edge and committed to doing more than their fair share to win the war on terror.

This book is about *those* exceptional Americans—past and present—as a tribute to the sacrifices so many of them have made since 11 September 2001.

America didn't start this fight, but the warriors of SOCOM are determined to be the ones who will end it. These are their stories.

2 0 0 1

22

For government is God's servant for your good. But if you do wrong, be afraid, because it does not carry the sword for no reason. For government is God's servant, an avenger that brings wrath on the one who does wrong. —ROMANS 13:4

11 SEPT 01

THE WAR ON TERROR

NEW YORK CITY, NEW YORK, USA

The date will never again pass unnoticed on the calendars of America. The evil committed against her people on that day in 2001 not only rocked the world by its sheer malevolence, it signaled the end of an era. Terrorism would never again be something that happened to unfortunate travelers outside U.S. borders—never again something Americans simply read about in the news before going back to sleep. America's apathy died that day, along with almost three thousand of her citizens. Things would never be the same.

September 11 was also a beginning. For the first time in decades, there was near agreement across the land. The emotion was almost universal, a knot in our collective gut as people stood in line to give blood, sat glued to the news, or attended memorial services across the country. And even as we grieved, we wanted justice. Something had to be done. This fresh determination galvanized the free world in the belief that safety would only come when the perpetrators of this evil were sought out and destroyed.

Those dispatched first to deliver America's response all belonged to an elite group of warriors—the members of United States Special Operations Command. No matter their branch of service, or their unit designation, every one of them knew this crisis was the one for which they had been preparing all their lives.

Within days, American intelligence services collected a mountain of evidence implicating Osama bin Laden—a Saudi-born radical Muslim whose al-Qaeda terrorist organization had declared war on the United States during the Clinton administration. Unfortunately his previous strikes against U.S. citizens and property were all but ignored. But if it was attention al-Qaeda wanted, they would surely have it now.

For nearly a decade, bin Laden and his radical Islamist allies exported their particular brand of hatred from terrorist training camps first in Sudan and then, Afghanistan. In Kabul, the Taliban regime was rewriting the rogue-state rule book on repression—and quickly became al-Qaeda patrons and protectors.

Above: Emergency response at the Pentagon

Below: Osama bin Laden

Before all the remains could be recovered from the rubble at "ground zero" in New York, a handful of American Special Operators from the CIA and the U.S. military were on the ground in Afghanistan, intent on hunting down bin Laden and removing the Taliban from power. Working quickly and quietly with a fractious coalition of anti-Taliban militias and tribal warloads dubbed the "Northern Alliance," the U.S. teams began the difficult and dangerous task of seizing enemy strongholds—while scouring the landscape for bin Laden and his minions. It took them less than a month to launch the largest covert operation since World War II. The story of their success is the stuff of legend.

7 OCT 01

OPERATION ENDURING FREEDOM

AFGHANISTAN

★ ★ ★ ★ ★ ★ ★ ★ ★ ★ ★ ★ ★

Just twenty-five days after the 9/11 attack, U.S. aircraft and cruise missiles launched the first air strikes aimed at eliminating the Taliban's capacity for command and control. Within forty-eight hours, enemy radar, communications and nerve centers in Kabul, Kandahar, and Jalalabad were elimated. Soon afterward, U.S. special operators—military and civilian—were heading into battle—sometimes mounted on horseback beside their new Afghan allies.

Despite all the high tech weaponry available to our forces, in Afghanistan sometimes they had to resort to more traditional means of transportation.

Among them were men like, then Captain Jason Amerine, commanding officer of ODA (Operational Detachment Alpha) 574 of the 5th Special Forces Group. On September 11 he and his "A-Team" were deployed in Kazakhstan, on a training mission for the former Soviet satellite country's counterinsurgency forces. When news came that terrorists had attacked America, Amerine had no doubt what was coming.

"We knew immediately it was war," he says. "I was definitely certain that this war was going to take place in Afghanistan."

Amerine had been preparing for this moment since he was fourteen years old. He joined JROTC in high school, then after graduation applied and was accepted to the United States Military Academy at West Point. There he focused on cultural and language studies with an eye to someday becoming a Special Forces soldier. When he completed his degree in 1993, he was nearly fluent in Arabic—a skill he would put to good use in the years to come. He paid his dues for several years in conventional units, then upon being promoted to Captain, he volunteered for Special Forces Assessment and Selection (SFAS), which he describes as less a school and more a rite of passage.

"When you're in SFAS, the Green Beret cadre run you through the ringer to see how well you operate in a team, see how well you operate individually, and in the end the cadre assess if they want you to go on to the Special Forces Qualification Course."

Almost a year of highly focused training followed, after which Amerine proudly donned the Special Forces green beret and reported to the 5th Special Forces Group at Fort Campbell, Kentucky.

By September 2001 Amerine's ODA had been working in Kazakhstan for nearly a year. But when four planes were hijacked half a world away, the men of ODA 574 knew their deployment would be a whole lot longer.

Assigned to support an Afghan opposition unit, days and nights of intense preparation for ODA 574 followed. On 14 November, Amerine and his ten-man team, augmented by a USAF Combat Controller (CCT) to rain destruction on the Taliban from U.S. aircraft overhead, flew into Afghanistan for the first time.

The small band of Afghan freedom fighters and CIA officers ODA 574 was ordered to guide and protect was being led by a relatively unknown Pashto, whose father was murdered by the Taliban. His name: Hamid Karzai.

Karzai struggled unsuccessfully against the Taliban regime for years. But on the night of November 16, aided by ODA 574, Karzai's handful of Afghan freedom fighters took Tarin Kowt, the capital of Uruzgan Province, in the heart of Taliban territory north

Maj Amerine (2nd from right in back row) with ODA 574 and Hamid Karzai.

of Kandahar. Intelligence gathered there warned Taliban forces were en route, intent on retaking Tarin Kowt from the south and wiping out Karzai's bid for Afghan freedom before it got started.

Working urgently through the night, Amerine prepared his men for a showdown at the south end of the city. Using satellite radios, he and his CCT flashed messages back to higher headquarters that the team would need nonstop air support in order to survive. The American soldiers and a few of their Afghan counterparts moved to a scrub-covered hilltop at the edge of town from which they could observe the enemy's approach.

They didn't have long to wait. Shortly after daylight the Taliban assault force came rolling across the valley below. "It looked like a scene from *Mad Max*," Amerine recalls. The Taliban were riding in pickups with machine guns bolted to their roofs along with a motley assortment of armored vehicles and heavy trucks carrying troops, ammunition, and even anti-aircraft artillery. The ODA feverishly pinpointed targets for the bomb-laden aircraft circling above, using laser target designators to mark where the guided munitions would have the greatest effect. The results were spectacular. One by one, the Taliban advance evaporated in flame and flying

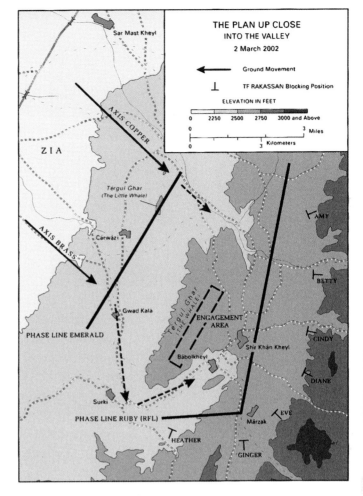

A portable laser designator being used by a Special Operations captain in Afghanistan 2001 directing Air Force and Navy bombs.

debris. The concussion of the bombs was so intense that some of the Afghan freedom fighters, unaccustomed to such a display of firepower, dropped their weapons and ran for their lives.

Maj. Amerine in the streets of Afghanistan

Forced to scramble back to the village, Amerine held a hasty council of war with Karzai—urging him to have his countrymen rejoin the Americans in the fight before the Taliban could mount a second attack. It was imperative they stop the enemy advance before they entered the village, at which point all the American air power in the world would be useless. The American was blunt: "If the Taliban get past us, we've lost the town."

The tough talk worked. Karzai's tribesmen regrouped and joined the Americans on a hilltop closer to the capital. For the next eight hours ODA 574 and their newly invigorated Afghan allies fended off wave after wave of enemy attacks, both with precision guided munitions and their own weapons. When the smoke cleared, the Taliban force was routed, leaving hundreds of dead fighters and scores of wrecked vehicles on the battlefield.

The 17 November victory at Tarin Kowt was decisive. ODA 574 and the American airpower they brough to bear set the stage for further advances by Karzai and his growing column of Pashtun irregulars, culminating with the Taliban surrender at Kandahar on 5 December 2001.

For his actions leading ODA 574 during this crucial time, Major Jason Amerine was awarded the Bronze star with "V" device for valor. In an interview several years later Amerine called his service, "The greatest privilege of my life." Then he added, "In Afghanistan, I commanded American and Afghan soldiers, each fighting for his own nation and his people, yet united in a common cause as they entrusted one another with their lives. There is no greater courage than for people to fight side-by-side against the terrible odds they faced with such impenetrable faith in one another."

Maj Amerine receives the Bronze Star with "V" device for valor.

25 NOV 01

THE BATTLE OF QALA-I-JANGI

MAZAR-I-SHARIF, AFGHANISTAN

While Americans at home were prepared to celebrate Thanksgiving, a desperate situation was developing in northern Afghanistan, near the city of Mazar-i-Sharif. Hundreds of foreign fighters, mostly Arabs and Pakistanis, surrendered to U.S.-backed Northern Alliance troops. Lacking a suitable place to sequester nearly five hundred prisoners-of-war, the Northern Alliance general, Abdul Rashid Dostum, transferred them to a nineteenth-century fortress he used as a headquarters. In the chaotic environment surrounding the surrender of so many, some of the prisoners were not properly searched. It proved to be a costly oversight.

BLU-82 "daisy cutter" bombs, like this one, evened the odds for vastly outnumbered Special Operations troops on the ground in Afghanistan in 2001.

On 25 November several members of the CIA's ultra-secret Special Activities Division arrived on the scene and began preliminary interrogations of the prisoners. One of the CIA officers, Johnny Michael Spann, had served as a U.S. Marine Captain. As he and his team sorted the enemy detainees, they discovered an American, John Walker Lindh. Lindh was a twenty-year-old convert to Islam from Silver Spring, Maryland, whose life choices were as treasonous as Spann's were patriotic.

When one of the detainees detonated a grenade hidden in his clothing, the blast killed a Northern Alliance commander and violence erupted throughout the compound. Suddenly, hundreds of prisoners rushed their guards. In minutes they seized control of the makeshift prison, capturing arms stored in the fortress and trapped the CIA team inside. According to Afghan doctors who witnessed the scene, Spann "held his position and fought using his AK rifle until out of ammo and then drew and began firing his pistol." Though Spann was killed when he again ran out of ammunition, his selfless courage enabled all but one of his teammates to escape. A CIA officer named "Dave" was still barricaded inside.

Twenty-five kilometers away, Major Mark Mitchell of the 5th Special Forces Group was busy setting up an aid point to deliver humanitarian assistance to displaced Afghan civilians when a Northern Alliance soldier breathlessly told him about the uprising at the fort. Mitchell, a veteran of the first Gulf war, quickly organized a rescue force from the only allied troops available: sixteen American and British personnel.

When he arrived at the fortress, Major Mitchell grabbed his weapon and climbed to the highest point on the wall to assess the situation. From this vantage point he could see the prisoners had armed themselves with rifles, grenades, RPGs, rockets, and even mortars from stockpiles found in Dostum's headquarters. Mitchell and his men immediately engaged the enemy with small arms fire, and eventually, by calling in strikes from U.S. aircraft overhead.

By the morning of the 26th, it was clear the previous night's bombing did little to quell the uprising. Though vastly outnumbered by the now-heavily-armed prisoners, Mitchell continued to press the attack until an errant U.S. bomb landed almost on top of his position, wounding half his men. Shaken and exhausted from two days of heavy fighting, the Major turned his attention to his injured comrades, working for most of the day to stabilize and get them evacuated for treatment. He then went back to killing the enemy.

Throughout the second night he directed more air strikes and coordinated the action of Northern Alliance forces. They eventually brought in a tank to punch holes through the ten-foot-thick walls and rescued those still trapped inside.

When the smoke of battle cleared on the morning of the third day, all but eighty-six of nearly five hundred Taliban fighters were dead. Those who lived surrendered only after the Northern Alliance diverted a stream to flood them out of their hiding places in the fort's ancient dungeon. One of the survivors was John Walker Lindh, who was eventually sentenced to twenty years in federal prison for his treasonous actions.

In stark contrast, Major Mitchell became the first recipient of the Distinguished Service Cross since the Vietnam War.

Soldiers from the 5th Special Forces Group using a laser target designator to call in aerial bombardment while Northern Alliance soldiers look on.

One of the rescuers, Chief Petty Officer Stephen Bass, a U.S. Navy SEAL, was attached to a British Special Boat Service unit. The citation for the Navy Cross awarded to Stephen Bass offers another perspective on the desperate fight to rescue the two CIA officers.

NAVY CROSS: STEPHEN BASS, CHIEF PETTY OFFICER, UNITED STATES NAVY

For services as set forth in the following citation: For extraordinary heroism while serving with the British Special Boat Service during combat operations in Northern Afghanistan on 25 and 26 November 2001. Chief Petty Officer Stephen Bass deployed to the area as a member of a joint American and British Special Forces Rescue Team to locate and recover two missing American citizens, one presumed to be seriously injured or dead, after hard-line al-Qaeda and Taliban prisoners at the Qala-i-Jangi fortress in Mazar-i-Sharif overpowered them and gained access to large quantities of arms and ammunition stored at the fortress. Once inside, Chief Petty Officer Bass was engaged continuously by direct small arms fire, indirect mortar fire, and rocket propelled grenade fire. He was forced to walk through an active anti-personnel minefield in order to gain entry to the fortress. After establishing the possible location of both American citizens, under heavy fire and without concern for his own personal safety, he made two attempts to rescue the uninjured citizen by crawling toward the fortress interior to reach him. Forced to withdraw due to large volumes of fire falling on his position, he was undeterred. After reporting his efforts to the remaining members of the rescue team, they left and attempted to locate the missing citizen on the outside of the fortress. As darkness began to fall, no attempt was going to be made to locate the other injured American citizen. Chief Petty Officer Bass then took matters into his own hands. Without regard for his own personal safety, he moved forward another three hundred to four hundred meters into the heart of the fortress by himself under constant enemy fire in an attempt to locate the injured citizen. Running low on ammunition, he utilized weapons from deceased Afghans to continue his rescue attempt. Upon verifying the condition and location of the American citizen, he withdrew from the fortress. By his outstanding display of decisive leadership, unlimited courage in the face of enemy fire, and utmost devotion to duty, Chief Petty Officer Bass reflected great credit upon himself and upheld the highest traditions of the United States Naval Service.

Special Operators calling in fire at Qala-i-Jangi fortress

DISTINGUISHED SERVICE CROSS: MAJOR MARK E. MITCHELL

The Distinguished Service Cross is awarded to Major Mark E. Mitchell, Headquarters and Headquarters Detachment, 3d Battalion, 5th Special Forces Group (Airborne), for extraordinary heroism in action during the period of 25 to 28 November 2001, while engaged in combat operations during Operation Enduring Freedom. As the Ground Force Commander of a rescue operation during the Battle of Qala-i-Jang: Fortress, Mazar-i-Sharif, Afghanistan, Major Mitchell ensured the freedom of one American and the posthumous repatriation of another. His unparalleled courage under fire, decisive leadership, and personal sacrifice were directly responsible for the success of the rescue operation and were further instrumental in ensuring the city of Mazar-i-Sharif did not fall back in the hands of the Taliban. His personal example has added yet another laurel to the proud military history of this nation and serves as the standard for all others to emulate. Major Mitchell's gallant deed was truly above and beyond the call of duty and is in keeping with the finest traditions of the military service and reflects great credit upon himself, the 5th Special Forces Group (Airborne), the United States Army, and the United States of America.

Author's note: Major Mark Mitchell has served in the war zone for a total of five deployments since 2001.

12–19 DEC 01

THE BATTLE FOR TORA BORA

TORA BORA, AFGHANISTAN

On December 7, 2001, Taliban rule in Afghanistan officially ended. By then, they had been driven out of Mazar-i-Sharif, Kabul, Kunduz, and Kandahar and tens of thousands of Taliban and their foreign allies were dead, captured, or fled into Pakistan. But not all were ready to concede.

Since mid November, the CIA had been warned about enemy forces gathering along the Pakistan border in the White Mountains south of Jalalabad. The locals, including former Mujahadeen fighters who opposed Taliban rule, called the place *Tora Bora*. SAD Paramilitary Operations Officers already on the ground in the region reported on al-Qaeda and Taliban fighters taking refuge in fortified caves and fighting positions used during the Russian occupation of Afghanistan decades earlier. It turned out to be an uphill battle—in more ways than one.

Tora Bora, known locally as Spiøn Ghar, is a cave complex in the White Mountains (Safed Koh) of eastern Afghanistan.

Dug-in al-Qaeda fighters occupied the high ground, so an attacker was always at a disadvantage. And while the local warloads were enthusiastic about the copious amounts of cash being handed out by the CIA, the men under their command were considerably less fervent about fighting fellow Muslims, especially after dark or when the weather was bad. This reticence would likely have blossomed into outright mutiny had the United States committed large numbers of conventional forces to the region, given the long local memories of the 1980's Soviet occupation.

As the weather turned colder, the CIA advisors watched in frustration as tribal fighters fought tit-for-tat battles with al-Qaeda and Taliban holdouts without measurable progress. In early December, they convinced tribal elders to allow a select few U.S. commandos to join the fight in early December. Fewer than one hundred American soldiers were engaged, mostly Delta Force operators and men from the 5th Special Forces Group.

This tiny band was given the daunting task of doing what the entire Soviet army failed to do—dislodging a determined foe from the steep slopes of Tora Bora. Chief among those to be targeted: the terrorist who started the war on 9/11/01—Osama bin Laden.

Accompanying these elite warriors were a handful of USAF Special Operators—Combat Air Controllers (CCTs) and Joint Terminal Attack Controllers (JTACs). Their job was—and is—to bring to bear the most powerful weapon the United States had in the fight—air power.

In the special operations community, Joint Terminal Attack Controllers (JTACs) are admired for their ability to call down fire from above. They aren't Old Testament prophets—just highly trained and equipped U.S. Airmen who can summon bombers, fighters, unmanned aerial vehicles, evacuation helicopters, and gunships to support a unit on the ground. JTACs specialize in putting heavy ordnance on ground targets with pinpoint accuracy, often while under fire and inside the

Calling in fire during the opening stages of Operation Enduring Freedom

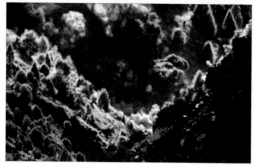

U.S. airstrikes on Tora Bora

"danger close" radius of their own munitions. They carry the same personal weapons as the Special Operators they accompany into battle. But their most valuable weapon is the radio they wear on their backs.

Nowhere was the effectiveness of the Combat Air Controller more evident than Tora Bora. For days on end small teams of three or four operators would occupy observation points on windswept ridgelines and work the airwaves, lining up dozens of attack aircraft and guiding their munitions onto enemy fighting positions and cave entrances. The citation for the Silver Star awarded to USAF Tech Sgt Michael Stockdale for action during the Tora Bora fight exemplifies what they endure—and what they can do.

In one sense the battle for Tora Bora was an unqualified victory—the U.S. Operators neutralized thousands of al-Qaeda fighters and destroyed most of their mountain stronghold. But tribal double-dealing by local commanders compounded by the fog of war caused a failure of the stated mission—to kill bin Laden. By the time fierce winter forced an end to the operation in Tora Bora, nobody could be sure whether he'd escaped or survived.

Members of some SOCOM units yet to be deployed to Afghanistan lamented their misfortune at having "missed out" on the war. What no one knew then was that there were many more Special Operations missions ahead—including one that would etch in history the name of an obscure mountaintop in southeastern Afghanistan: Takur Ghar.

SILVER STAR: TECHNICAL SERGEANT MICHAEL C. STOCKDALE

The President of the United States of America, authorized by Act of Congress July 9, 1918 (amended by an act of July 25, 1963), takes pleasure in presenting the Silver Star to Technical Sergeant Michael C. Stockdale, United States Air Force, for gallantry in connection with military operations against an armed enemy of the United States from 6 December to 20 December 2001. During this period, Sergeant Stockdale excelled in multiple missions where he was directly engaged in combat actions against Taliban and al-Qaeda forces. He provided surgical terminal attack control of close air support aircraft at a volume and accuracy not yet seen until this major offensive in the Tora Bora region of Afghanistan. Sergeant Stockdale volunteered to move to the forward most lines of battle to assist the local Afghan opposition group's assault on the key enemy fortified stronghold. While moving to the front, he came under heavy machine gun and eighty-two-millimeter mortar fire as close as twenty-five meters. Though the other government forces stopped, he continued to press forward with complete disregard to his own personal safety. Positioned in front of the most forward troops, Sergeant Stockdale directed numerous close air support missions against the enemy dug-in positions while under intense two-way direct and indirect fire. His actions rallied the other government forces and directly resulted in their most successful single day advance of fourteen hundred meters, seizing the previously impenetrable key enemy stronghold. Sergeant Stockdale expertly controlled well more than three hundred close air support aircraft sorties of multiple F-15, F-16, B-1, B-52, F-14, AV-8B, and the full combat munitions expenditure of five AC-130 gunships. He skillfully ensured the pinpoint delivery of an incredible six hundred thousand pounds of munitions on enemy targets. In this three-day period he averaged thirteen hours of uninterrupted close air support control daily, an amazing display of dedication, expertise, and deadly destruction. By his gallantry and devotion to duty, Sergeant Stockdale has reflected great credit upon himself and the United States Air Force.

An AC-130H/U Gunship aircraft from the 4th Special Operation Squadron

SPECIAL OPERATIONS WEATHERMEN

Not your everyday meteorologist.

The term weatherman might sound like the furthest thing from the shadowy world of special operations. But the Air Force has a few Special Operations Weather Technicians (SOWT) who represent some of the most highly trained Special Operators in the U.S. arsenal.

Originally known as "air commando weathermen," these Air Force meteorologists have participated in every conflict since World War II. They went ashore on D-day in Normandy. They set up clandestine weather stations in the jungles of Southeast Asia during the Vietnam war. Their advice has literally changed history—invasions pushed up or missions successfully executed because of time-sensitive weather intelligence provided by the SOWT.

Today, Special Operations Weather Technician candidates must complete two and a half years of training before becoming qualified. They are then deployed with other Special Operations units to war zones across the globe, where they gather, assess, and interpret vital weather intelligence data to assist commanders in mission planning. They also train members of host nation countries to do the same. And because they have all trained in special tactics and advanced skills, these

A SOWT checks wind readings in a sandstorm during a Special Forces mission in Afghanistan. Air Force Special Operations Weathermen are the only career field in the Department of Defense that provides Special Forces with meteorological data in support of SOF missions.

operators do more than just predict the weather. They train alongside other Special Operations forces in airborne school, survival school, and even learn to pilot unmanned aerial vehicles.

All this specialized training makes the Special Operations Weather Technician one of the rarest creatures in the Special Ops community. Worldwide, there are fewer than a hundred currently serving today.

A SOWT pilots a RQ-11B Raven, an unmanned aircraft system, that provides real-time reconnaissance of the local environment, such as rivers, at a forward operating base in Afghanistan.

2002

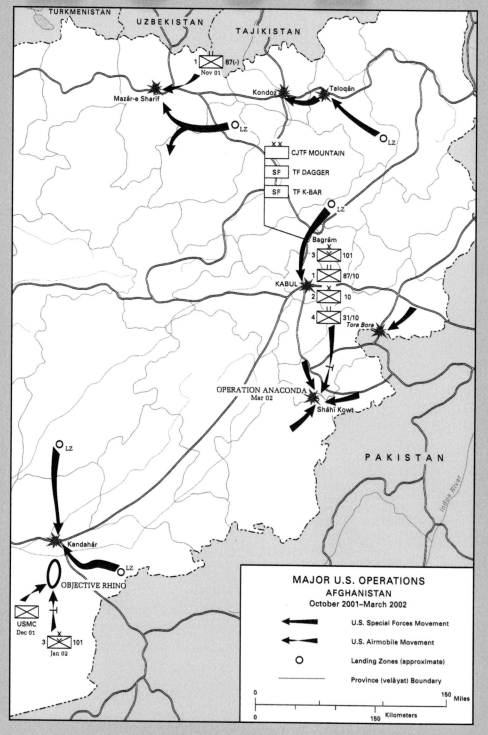

CJTF MOUNTAIN

SF TF DAGGER

SF TF K-BAR

1 87(-) Nov 01

3 101

1 87/10

2 10

4 31/10

OPERATION ANACONDA
Mar 02

USMC Dec 01

3 101 Jan 02

OBJECTIVE RHINO

TURKMENISTAN

UZBEKISTAN

TAJIKISTAN

PAKISTAN

Indus River

Mazār-e Sharīf

Kondoz

Taloqān

Bagrām

KABUL

Tora Bora

Shāhī Kowt

Kandahār

LZ

MAJOR U.S. OPERATIONS
AFGHANISTAN
October 2001–March 2002

➡ U.S. Special Forces Movement

➡ U.S. Airmobile Movement

○ Landing Zones (approximate)

— Province (velāyat) Boundary

0   150 Miles

0   150 Kilometers

42

OPERATION ANACONDA

TAKUR GHAR, AFGHANISTAN

4 MAR 02

★ ★ ★ ★ ★ ★ ★ ★ ★ ★ ★

The beat of the helicopter's rotor blades cutting through the thin air over Takur Ghar's ten-thousand-foot peak echoed through the predawn darkness. Standing in the back of the MH-47E Chinook, a Special Operations Forces (SOF) reconnaissance team clung to the red nylon webbing covering the interior of the aircraft. It was no easy thing to stay balanced as they checked their gear one last time.

Infiltration is one of the most dangerous parts of any Special Ops mission. Helicopters, the most frequent means of insertion, become large, slow-moving targets as they hover over a landing zone.

On this mission, Petty Officer Neal Roberts, a Navy SEAL, was positioned to be the first to exit the aircraft, squatting on the ramp at the rear of the helo, hoping to make the "infil" as fast as possible. Outside, the snow-covered peaks glistened in the moonlight, jutting jagged and harsh into the thin night air.

U.S. intelligence officers had been monitoring a sizeable pocket of al-Qaeda and Taliban forces in the area near Gardeyz for weeks and a military operation, code named Operation Anaconda, was planned to wipe them out. It would represent the first large-scale commitment of conventional U.S. Forces in the war on terror. The 10th Mountain Division and 101st Airborne encircled the valley in a classic "hammer and anvil." But the enemy put up stiff resistance and stood their ground in heavily fortified positions. The decision was made to put "eyes on" the end of the Shah-i-Kot Valley where the battle raged. The mountaintop known as Takur Ghar was identified as ideally suited for that purpose, so SOF teams could report on enemy movements and engage them with indirect fire.

The Chinook approached Takur Ghar and the designated landing zone (LZ) in a small clearing just below the summit of the mountain. As the big helicopter neared its touchdown point, the crew chief spotted a scattering of goat skins—and human footprints in the snow. The mountaintop was already occupied.

He called over the intercom to the pilots, members of the Army's elite Task Force 160—the *Night Stalkers:* "Looks like our insertion may be compromised."

The answer crackled back. "Do we have enemy contact?"

"No, but there are definite signs of activity here. Looks like someone had the same idea we did."

As the pilot flared the helo to slow it down, he could see what those behind him in the aircraft had observed.

"Roger, abort mission," came over the Chinook's intercom.

Before anyone could acknowledge the command, something like a small meteor— an RPG—struck the helicopter, blazing through the aluminum skin, throwing flame and shrapnel around the cargo bay, puncturing hydraulic and fuel lines, and wounding one of the crew. The helicopter lurched to one side as the pilot fought to maintain control.

Hydraulic fluid and fuel instantly turned the deck of the cargo compartment into a surface more slippery then a hockey rink. A crewman lost his footing and plunged off the ramp as a machine gun on the ground began peppering the wounded Chinook, invisible fingers of death stabbing holes in the thin exterior, looking for flesh inside.

Tethered to the aircraft by his safety harness, the crewman dangled a few feet below the ramp. But Petty Officer Roberts had no safety harness; he too lost his footing on the slippery ramp and flailed unsuccessfully for a hand-hold to keep himself onboard. In an effort to gain altitude in the thin mountain air, the pilot jerked violently on the collective. The action nearly stood the chopper on its tail and Neal Roberts slid

out the rear door. His buddies watched him fall about ten feet to the snowy outcropping below.

As the Chinook wheeled away from the mountain, the rest of the team watched helplessly as Roberts came under heavy enemy fire. The last they saw of him, he was returning fire with his squad automatic weapon, attacking a superior force and going it all alone.

The helicopter crash-landed about seven kilometers north of where Roberts fell. An unmanned aerial vehicle (UAV) was diverted to observe Takur Ghar and it sent back video of Petty Officer Roberts fighting off the enemy for nearly an hour, first with his automatic weapon, then his sidearm until he expended all his ammunition, and grenades. He was finally overrun and killed, becoming the first Navy SEAL to die in the war on terror, and the first to be killed in action since the invasion of Panama in 1989.

The tragic chain of events continued. An Air Force AC-130 gunship overhead—capable of annihilating much of the enemy presence on the mountaintop—never received clearance to fire and was diverted elsewhere. Meanwhile Neal Roberts's teammates were clamoring to get back to Takur Ghar and rescue the downed SEAL.

"Although I sacrificed personal freedom and many other things, I got just as much as I gave. My time in the Teams was special, for all the times I was cold, wet, tired, sore, scared, hungry, and angry, I had a blast. If I died doing something for the Teams, then I died doing what made me happy. Very few people have the luxury of that "

—Neal Roberts, in his "open in the event of my death" letter

They boarded a second helicopter in Gardeyz, which flew to the mountain but it too was hit by intense ground fire. The Night Stalker air crew was able to land long enough to insert five SEALs and Air Force Combat Controller John Chapman. The team, led by Senior Chief Petty Officer Britt Slabinski, had the call-sign "Mako Three Zero."

Once on the ground, Mako Three Zero immediately went on the offensive, killing several enemy fighters in a bunker on top of the hill. But when a hail of gunfire erupted from another bunker, two SEALs were hit and Tech Sgt Chapman was mortally wounded. As the volume of fire increased, Slabinski made the decision that the team would have to pull back from the summit and make use of the air assets at their disposal to engage the numerically superior enemy force.

Withdrawing wasn't easy. The team was under continuous fire and with three badly injured team members, each surviving man had to carry a wounded comrade as they slogged through waist-deep snow. For more than sixteen hours, Mako Three Zero engaged in the highest-altitude gunfight in U.S. military history.

For his heroic leadership during the battle, Chief Slabinski was awarded the Navy Cross.

NAVY CROSS: SENIOR CHIEF PETTY OFFICER BRITT SLABINSKI

The President of the United States takes pleasure in presenting the Navy Cross to Britt Slabinski, Senior Chief Petty Officer, United States Navy for services as set forth in the following citation. For extraordinary heroism as Sniper Element Leader for a joint special operations unit conducting combat operations against enemy forces during Operation Anaconda, Shah-i-Kot Valley, Afghanistan, on 3 and 4 March 2002, in support of Operation Enduring Freedom. On the evening of 3 March, Senior Chief Petty Officer Britt Slabinski led his seven-man reconnaissance team onto the snow-covered, ten thousand foot mountaintop known as Takur Ghar, to establish a combat over-watch position in support of U.S. Army forces advancing against the enemy on the valley floor. As their helicopter hovered over the mountain, it was met by unrelenting rocket propelled grenade (RPG) and small arms fire by entrenched enemy forces. As a result of several RPG hits, a member of Senior Chief Petty Officer Slabinski's team was ejected from the helicopter into the midst of the fortified enemy positions. The badly damaged helicopter conducted a controlled crash, at which time Senior Chief Petty Officer Slabinski immediately took charge and established security on the crash location until the crew and his team were recovered to a support base. At this point, Senior Chief

Slabinski, fully aware of the overwhelming, fixed enemy forces over the mountain, but also knowing the desperate situation of his missing teammate, now reportedly fighting for his life, without hesitation made the selfless decision to lead his team on an immediate, bold rescue mission. He heroically led the remainder of his SEAL element back onto the snow-covered, remote mountaintop into the midst of the numerically superior enemy forces in a daring and valiant attempt to rescue one of their own. After a treacherous helicopter insertion onto the mountaintop, Senior Chief Petty Officer Slabinski led his close-quarter firefight. He skillfully maneuvered his team and bravely engaged multiple enemy positions, personally clearing one bunker and killing several enemy within. His unit became caught in a withering crossfire from other bunkers and the closing enemy forces. Despite mounting casualties, Senior Chief Petty Officer Slabinski maintained his composure and continued to engage the enemy until his position became untenable. Faced with no choice but a tactical withdrawal, he coolly directed fire from airborne assets to cover his team. He then led an arduous movement through the mountainous terrain, constantly under fire, covering over one kilometer in waist-deep snow, while carrying a seriously wounded teammate. Arriving at a defensible position, he organized his team's security posture and stabilized his casualties. For over fourteen hours, Senior Chief Petty Officer Slabinski directed the defense of his position through countless engagements, personally engaging the enemy and directing close air support onto the enemy positions until the enemy was ultimately defeated. During this entire sustained engagement, Senior Chief Petty Officer Slabinski exhibited classic grace under fire in steadfastly leading the intrepid rescue operation, saving the lives of his wounded men and setting the conditions for the ultimate vanquishing of the enemy and the seizing of Takur Ghar. By his heroic display of decisive and tenacious leadership, unyielding courage in the face of constant enemy fire, and utmost devotion to duty, Senior Chief Petty Officer Slabinski reflected great credit upon himself and upheld the highest traditions of the United States Naval Service.

Back at Bagram Airbase, Ranger Captain Nate Self was alerted that the SEALs were in trouble on Takur Ghar. Three hours later he and a nineteen-man Ranger Quick Reaction Force (QRF) were inbound on yet another CH-47 Chinook helicopter to the embattled mountaintop. Communication problems that bedeviled the SEALs now struck the Rangers. Neither they nor the pilots flying them into the right received the map coordinates for an alternate landing zone.

As the big helo attempted to land on the mountain, it too was hit with an RPG while it was still twenty feet in the air. Small arms fire killed the right door gunner, Sgt Philip Svitak and brought the Bird down. Incoming fire tore the downed helicopter to shreds and as the QRF tried to exit the wreckage, three Rangers were killed and several more wounded, including Cpt Self. Though shot through the thigh, he continued fighting and along with the rest of the survivors, took cover and began "giving back" to the enemy.

The Rangers and remaining SEALs were still clearly outnumbered and at midday, the enemy launched an assault, concentrating their fire on the casualty collection point holding all the American wounded. During the attack, Air Force Pararescueman Specialist Jason Cunningham, the medic, was severely wounded. Despite pain and loss of blood, Cunningham steadfastly continued to administer aid under fire and is credited with saving the lives of at least seven men.

After losing three helicopters, commanders were reluctant to risk more aircraft during daylight hours, even though there were several "urgent surgical" wounded who needed immediate evacuation. The difficult decision to wait likely cost Pararescueman Specialist Jason Cunningham his life. He succumbed to his wounds two hours before medevac helicopters arrived at 2000 hours.

Pararescueman Spec Jason Cunningham

AIR FORCE CROSS: (POSTHUMOUS) TO JASON D. CUNNINGHAM

The President of the United States of America, awards the Air Force Cross to Senior Airman Jason D. Cunningham for extraordinary heroism in military operations against an opposing armed force while serving as a pararescueman near the village of Marzak in the Paktika Province of Afghanistan on 4 March 2002.

On that proud day, Airman Cunningham was the primary Air Force Combat Search and Rescue medic assigned to a Quick Reaction Force tasked to recover two American servicemen evading capture in austere terrain occupied by massed al-Qaeda and Taliban forces. Shortly before landing, his MH-47E helicopter received accurate rocket-propelled grenade and small arms fire, severely disabling the aircraft and causing it to crash land. The assault force formed a hasty defense and immediately suffered three fatalities and five critical casualties.

Despite effective enemy fire, and at great risk to his own life, Airman Cunningham remained in the burning fuselage of the aircraft in order to treat the wounded. As he moved his patients to a more secure location, mortar rounds began to impact within fifty feet of his position. Disregarding this extreme danger, he continued the movement and exposed himself to enemy fire on seven separate occasions. When the second casualty collection point was also compromised, in a display of uncommon valor and gallantry, Airman Cunningham braved an intense small arms and rocket-propelled grenade attack while repositioning the critically wounded to a third collection point. Even after he was mortally wounded and quickly deteriorating, he continued to direct patient movement and transferred care to another medic.

In the end, his distinct efforts led to the successful delivery of ten gravely wounded Americans to life-saving medical treatment. Through his extraordinary heroism, superb airmanship, aggressiveness in the face of the enemy, and in the dedication of his service to his country, Senior Airman Cunningham reflected the highest credit upon himself and the United States Air Force.

Members of the U.S. Air Force Honor Guard transport the coffin carrying the remains of USAF Senior Airman Jason Cunningham to its final resting place during the graveside funeral service held at Arlington National Cemetery, Arlington, Virginia.

By the time the fight was over, more than a hundred Taliban and al-Qaeda fighters were dead on the mountaintop. But the American death toll—seven Special Operators killed in action—made it the bloodiest battle for the coalition to that point in the war—and the deadliest day for Special Operations since the debacle in Somalia in 1993.

"The Battle of Takur Ghar" painting by Keith Rocco

Capt Nate Self

For his courageous leadership on Takur Ghar, Captain Nate Self was awarded the Silver Star, the Bronze Star, and the Purple Heart. Nearly every member of his QRF and the SEAL team that went to rescue on what came to be called "Robert's Ridge," were decorated for bravery under fire. Excerpts from their award citations paint a vivid picture of the battle.

All the citations on the following pages end with the following words: *The gallantry displayed . . . during eighteen hours of combat is in keeping with the highest standards of valor.*

SILVER STAR: STAFF SERGEANT ARIN K. CANON

Staff Sergeant Canon led the support element during the initial assault on an enemy fortified position. His leadership was instrumental in suppressing the objective and pressing the assault against the enemy. Immediately following this action, he coordinated the defense of the entire objective, placing personnel and key weapon systems that enabled the platoon to defeat two enemy counterattacks.

BRONZE STAR WITH "V" DEVICE: SPECIALIST CHRIS M. CUNNINGHAM

Specialist Cunningham was an integral member of the assault force that attacked a fortified enemy position to relieve the pressure on Chalk 1, who had been fighting the enemy for over two hours.

BRONZE STAR WITH "V" DEVICE: SPECIALIST OSCAR J. ESCANO

Specialist Escano was an integral member of the assault force that moved over two hours through arduous terrain to destroy an enemy fortified position. Additionally, Specialist Escano assisted in providing security for aid and litter teams during two counterattacks by enemy forces.

BRONZE STAR WITH "V" DEVICE: SERGEANT PATRICK GEORGE

The gallantry displayed by Sergeant George during eighteen hours of combat is in keeping with the highest standards for valor.

BRONZE STAR WITH "V" DEVICE: PRIVATE FIRST CLASS DAVID B. GILLIAM

While serving as a M240B machine gunner during Operation Enduring Freedom, Private First Class Gilliam immediately exited the aircraft and suppressed the enemy. Private First Class Gilliam played an integral role in the entire operation by providing suppression on enemy positions to facilitate the capture of the high ground, the defeat of two enemy counterattacks and the consolidation of friendly wounded.

BRONZE STAR WITH "V" DEVICE: SPECIALIST JONAS O. POLSON

While serving as a squad automatic weapon gunner, Specialist Polson's actions, in particular during a battle on 4 March 2002, contributed immeasurably to the tremendous success of a Task Force. Specialist Polson moved under direct and indirect enemy fire to link up with Chalk 1, which was under enemy fire for over two hours.

BRONZE STAR WITH "V" DEVICE: SPECIALIST OMAR J. VELA

The assault force movement culminated in an assault on an enemy fortified position where Specialist Vela was integral to suppressing the enemy. Specialist Vela assisted the aid and litter teams and provided security under a withering enemy counterattack.

SILVER STAR:
SERGEANT MATTHEW LAFRENZ

While serving as a Platoon Medic in support of Operation ENDURING FREEDOM. In five separate occasions, Sergeant LaFrenz exposed himself to enemy fire while providing medical support to casualties. Sergeant LaFrenz was able to consolidate all casualties within four hours providing aid to nine casualties in an exhausting frigid environment.

SILVER STAR:
SPECIALIST AARON LANCASTER-TOTTEN

While exiting the aircraft, Specialist Lancaster-Totten was severely wounded by shrapnel. With total disregard for his own well being, Specialist Lancaster-Totten continued to engage the enemy from a covered and concealed position. His ability to provide suppressive fire enabled the assault element to break contact from the enemy.

SILVER STAR:
CAPTAIN NATHAN E. SELF

While exiting the aircraft, Captain Self was severely wounded in the thigh. With total disregard for his well being, he fought to the first covered and concealed position, engaged the enemy with his weapon, gathering remaining combat effective Rangers, and began calling close air support on enemy locations.

SILVER STAR:
SERGEANT ERIC W. STEBNER

Sergeant Stebner organized an assault against an enemy fortified position. He led all aid and litter teams under withering enemy counterattack fire during consolidation of all casualties. This action took over four hours during which Sergeant Stebner personally exposed himself to enemy fire at least five times in order to save his fellow comrades.

SILVER STAR:
SERGEANT JOSHUA J. WALKER

Sergeant Walker immediately exited the aircraft and destroyed an enemy soldier who was shooting at his aircraft. He was able to suppress the enemy with his M4 carbine, an M249 squad automatic weapon, and an M203 grenade launcher. Sergeant Walker was an integral part of a four-man assault force that moved up a deep slope, in knee-deep snow, through a hail of enemy fire in broad daylight.

SILVER STAR:
STAFF SERGEANT HARPER WILMOTH

Staff Sergeant Wilmoth's valorous actions while in direct contact with enemy forces and in the face of extreme duress during the successful rescue of Special Operators contributed immeasurably to the success of the mission and to the saving of additional lives. Staff Sergeant Wilmoth coordinated the linkup with Chalk 1 over arduous terrain, at an extremely high altitude, and under enemy direct and indirect fire. After the linkup, Staff Sergeant Wilmoth organized the assault on an enemy fortified position.

AF-PAK border

When it was all said and done, the fierce firefight at Takur Ghar was but one part of Operation Anaconda. The fight raged for twelve days and cost more than one hundred American lives. Taliban and al-Qaeda losses were estimated to be nearly eight hundred fighters.

To keep the pressure on Taliban and al-Qaeda elements taking refuge in the mountainous regions along the AF-PAK border, Operation Mountain Lion was initiated in May. By then, a handful of Afghan National Army units were partnered with Green Berets in an effort to clear the enemy from areas around Gardeyz and Khowst. For U.S. Special Forces personnel it was "back to the future"— a return to their classic mission of mentoring indigenous forces to fight for their own country.

The operation was characterized by coalition forces fanning out across the mountainous region in dozens of small patrols—challenging any enemy in the area: Come out and fight.

During one such engagement, a U.S.-Afghan unit came under heavy machine gun fire in a remote area near the border with Pakistan.

The Special Operators responded with quick and decisive action, killing one enemy fighter and driving off the rest, but suffered two friendly casualties in the process. One of them was an Afghan soldier, the other Green Beret Staff Sergeant Gene Vance, a ten-year veteran of the Special Forces who canceled his honeymoon to make the Afghan deployment with his brothers-in-arms. Vance was trained to speak Farsi, and his skills as a linguist and Intel officer made him highly valuable to his comrades in arms.

Staff Sgt Gene Vance

A quiet man, Vance was a citizen-soldier, a member of the 19th Special Forces Group of the West Virginia National guard, one of only two reserve Special Forces units. He'd been decorated for valor once already in 1993, though the details of that medal are still classified. Vance's death in combat marked the first time a guardsman was killed in direct action since Vietnam, and the first time a West Virginia guardsman was killed since World War II.

A memorial service for the thirty-eight-year-old Vance was held in Morgantown, West Virginia, on Memorial Day 2002 and more than 750 of his friends and neighbors attended. Today, the Special Operations compound at Bagram Air Force Base in Afghanistan, is named Camp Vance in his honor.

I've been there. W.S.

Camp Vance

NAMED IN HONOR OF SSG GENE VANCE
(KIA) on 19 May 2002
In the vicinity of Shkin, Afghanistan

REMEMBERING FALLEN SOLDIERS

The Special Forces Memorial Statue, "Bronze Bruce," stands watch over the USASOC Memorial Plaza outside the command's headquarters building at Fort Bragg. Originally built in 1969, the statue was moved to the plaza from the John F. Kennedy Special Warfare Center and School in 1994. He faces the USASOC Memorial Wall, which displays the names of more than a thousand Army SOF heroes killed in action since the Vietnam War.

In addition to public memorials, fallen soldiers are honored with services and plaques at bases around the world.

Above: 7th Special Forces Green Berets pray over the memorial of a fallen comrade.

Below: plaque in honor of fallen crew members from Operation Enduring Freedom

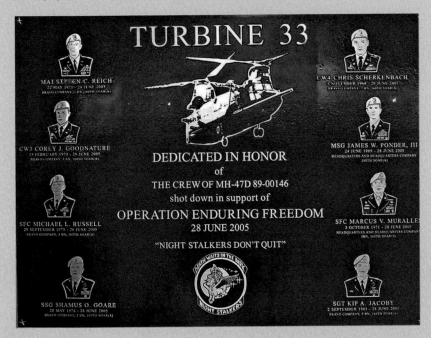

TURBINE 33

MAJ STEPHEN C. REICH
22 MAY 1971 - 28 JUNE 2005
BRAVO COMPANY, 3 BN, 160TH SOAR(A)

CW4 CHRIS SCHERKENBACH
5 NOVEMBER 1964 - 28 JUNE 2005
BRAVO COMPANY, 3 BN, 160TH SOAR(A)

CW3 COREY J. GOODNATURE
13 FEBRUARY 1970 - 28 JUNE 2005
BRAVO COMPANY, 3 BN, 160TH SOAR(A)

MSG JAMES W. PONDER, III
24 JUNE 1969 - 28 JUNE 2005
HEADQUARTERS AND HEADQUARTERS COMPANY
160TH SOAR(A)

SFC MICHAEL L. RUSSELL
29 SEPTEMBER 1973 - 28 JUNE 2005
BRAVO COMPANY, 3 BN, 160TH SOAR(A)

DEDICATED IN HONOR
of
THE CREW OF MH-47D 89-00146
shot down in support of
OPERATION ENDURING FREEDOM
28 JUNE 2005

"NIGHT STALKERS DON'T QUIT"

SFC MARCUS V. MURALLES
5 OCTOBER 1971 - 28 JUNE 2005
HEADQUARTERS AND HEADQUARTERS COMPANY
3 BN, 160TH SOAR(A)

SSG SHAMUS O. GOARE
29 MAY 1976 - 28 JUNE 2005
BRAVO COMPANY, 3 BN, 160TH SOAR(A)

SGT KIP A. JACOBY
2 SEPTEMBER 1983 - 28 JUNE 2005
BRAVO COMPANY, 3 BN, 160TH SOAR(A)

My Trident is a symbol of honor and heritage. Bestowed upon me by the heroes that have gone before, it embodies the trust of those I have sworn to protect. By wearing the Trident I accept the responsibility of my chosen profession and way of life. It is a privilege that I must earn every day.

My loyalty to Country and Team is beyond reproach. I humbly serve as a guardian to my fellow Americans always ready to defend those who are unable to defend themselves. I do not advertise the nature of my work, nor seek recognition for my actions. I voluntarily accept the inherent hazards of my profession, placing the welfare and security of others before my own.

I serve with honor on and off the battlefield. The ability to control my emotions and my actions, regardless of circumstance, sets me apart from other men.

Uncompromising integrity is my standard. My character and honor are steadfast. My word is my bond.

We expect to lead and be led. In the absence of orders I will take charge, lead my teammates and accomplish the mission. I lead by example in all situations.

U.S. NAVY SEAL CREED

In times of war or uncertainty there is a special breed of warrior ready to answer our nation's call. A common man with uncommon desire to succeed.

Forged by adversity, he stands alongside America's finest special operations forces to serve his country, the American people, and protect their way of life.

I am that man.

I will never quit. I persevere and thrive on adversity. My nation expects me to be physically harder and mentally stronger than my enemies. If knocked down, I will get back up, every time. I will draw on every remaining ounce of strength to protect my teammates and to accomplish our mission. I am never out of the fight.

We demand discipline. We expect innovation. The lives of my teammates and the success of our mission depend on me—my technical skill, tactical proficiency, and attention to detail. My training is never complete.

We train for war and fight to win. I stand ready to bring the full spectrum of combat power to bear in order to achieve my mission and the goals established by my country. The execution of my duties will be swift and violent when required yet guided by the very principles that I serve to defend.

Brave men have fought and died building the proud tradition and feared reputation that I am bound to uphold. In the worst of conditions, the legacy of my teammates steadies my resolve and silently guides my every deed.

I will not fail.

SPECIAL WARFARE COMBATANT-CRAFT CREWMEN

When it comes to Naval Special Operators, the SEALS normally get most of the press. But there's another, lesser known component of the Naval Special Warfare Command—a much smaller group of men who are known as SWCCCs, or "Swicks."

Special Warfare Combatant-craft Crewmen follow a selection and training pipeline similar to the SEALs but with a few important specialties. They learn to operate high-tech, state-of-the-art small boats in environments that are too restrictive for large naval vessels. This includes rivers, lakes, and places where even crocodiles fear to tread.

Thirty weeks of initial training at Coronado, California, augmented by the full gamut of Special

Operations schools makes these men masters at riverine warfare, covert insertion, extraction, and reconnaissance. They have participated in every major military conflict since the Vietnam War and can often be found fighting alongside their SEAL brethren today in places like the Philippines and even Colombia, where in 1996, six SWCCC's took on a force of about 150 FARC rebels in a three-day gun battle—and won. After it was all over, the boat team had killed more than forty rebels and sustained only one friendly casualty.

Some people call them the Navy's best kept secret, because they are rarely mentioned in the media. But the men of SWCCC like it that way, because in their business, being unseen and unheard is the mark of a true professional.

Special Warfare Combatant-craft Crewmen assigned to Special Boat Team 22 (SBT-22) conduct live-fire immediate action drills at the riverine training range at Fort Knox. SBT-22 operates the Special Operations craft-riverine and is the only U.S. Special Operations Command dedicated to operating in the riverine environment.

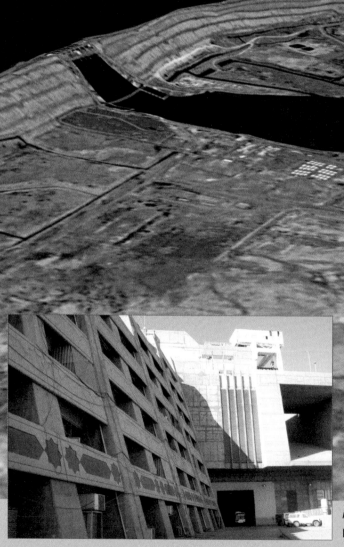

2003

©2010 Goog

Above: Aerial view of Haditha Dam
Inset: Western side of Haditha Dam

THE NEW ENEMY: SADDAM HUSSEIN

By the time Operation Mountain Lion commenced in the mountains of Afghanistan, SOCOM was already preparing contingency plans for operations in Iraq. Reports from U.S. and European intelligence services indicated that despite United Nations sanctions, Saddam Hussein was buying or building nuclear, chemical, and perhaps even biological weapons of mass destruction (WMD).

Well before any U.S. forces were issued warning orders for deployment, military and intelligence planners began identifying possible WMD laboratories and key infrastructure inside Iraq. The final list of "must protect" sites included power plants, oil facilities, airfields, and bridges that would have to be seized intact before Saddam could destroy them. Among the strategic locations assigned to SOCOM planners: the Ramadi Highway Bridge and the Haditha Dam—both on the Euphrates River.

The Haditha Dam was especially important. The road atop the concrete structure was designed to carry armored vehicles and the massive turbines inside generated almost a third of Iraq's electrical power. Even more important, the dam was holding back more than eight cubic kilometers of water—enough to inundate the Euphrates Valley with a flood of biblical proportions.

Turbine room at Haditha Dam

SOCOM planners estimated Saddam had positioned at least six thousand Iraq troops—including heavy armor, artillery, and anti-aircraft batteries—within twenty miles of the dam. Mobile surface-to-air missiles (MSNPADs) deployed around the site rendered a parachute assault by airborne troops suicidal. The objective—more than two hundred miles from the Jordanian border—was deemed "too far from friendlies" for an assault by helicopter.

29 MAR 03

THE BATTLE FOR RAMADI
BRIDGE AND HADITHA DAM
WESTERN IRAQI AIRBASE

Operation Iraqi Freedom began on 19 March with twenty-four hours of nonstop air and missile strikes against Saddam's air defenses and command and control facilities.

Even before U.S. armored and mechanized units began pushing northward from Kuwait toward Baghdad, Special Operations units were already on the ground.

From a secret base on the Jordanian border, Combined Joint Special Operations Task Force-West (CJSOTF-W) launched teams to capture key airfields in Al Anbar Province and take out ballistic missile sites capable of launching attacks against Kuwait, Jordan, and Saudi Arabia. CJSOTF-W was comprised of U.S., British, and Australian Special Operations units, the largest of which was the 3rd Battalion of the elite 75th Ranger Regiment.

By 29 March the Rangers had already made two combat parachute jumps to seize Iraqi airfields designated as H1 and H2 and conducted several helo-borne raids on suspected WMD sites. The seizure of H1 provided their commander, Colonel John Mulholland, with a staging base within range of the Ramadi Bridge and Haditha Dam.

Lt Gen John Mulholland, now commander of USASOC

Bravo Company of the 3rd Ranger Battalion had already seen its share of combat. Only a month after the attacks on the World Trade Center and Pentagon in 2001, they deployed to Afghanistan. They came home in January 2002 and went right back the following June for a second four-month combat tour. The lessons they learned under fire in Afghanistan were already proving valuable in the fight to liberate Iraq.

Captain David Doyle had been the Battalion Air Operations Officer before assuming command of B 3/75 just prior to its second deployment to Afghanistan. Before daylight on March 29, he pushed his company out to a small dirt airstrip near H1.

Rangers work in darkness whenever possible, taking full advantage of sophisticated thermal and infrared night-vision systems to give them an edge over the enemy. During the day they would often "hole up," covering their specially modified "Ground Mobility Vehicles," beneath camouflage to rest, refit, and prepare before their next operation. When B 3/75 departed H1, their orders were to hold at the dirt airstrip and be prepared to support another SOF unit. In accord with established procedures, they carried ammunition and supplies for seventy-two hours.

But war is never predictable. They would not see H1 again for almost two weeks.

Shortly after they arrived at the airstrip, Captain Doyle received a coded data Flag Order from then LTC Mulholland alerting him to a change in the mission. B 3/75 was now directed to seize the Haditha Dam complex, about thirty kilometers from his current location. Doyle's company was reinforced with a platoon from C Co 3/75, two sniper teams, and a small contingent of headquarters personnel including a Physician's Assistant and an Air Force Combat Controller, to call in air support. The FRAGO ended with the words: "hold until relieved."

The Ranger Captain had to immediately devise how to seize one of the most heavily guarded targets in Iraq and hold it against a force that conceivably outnumbered his 154 Rangers by more than thirty-to-one. Four hours after receiving the FRAGO from Mulholland, Doyle had a plan, albeit a very simple one.

The dam was code named "Objective Lynx." Approaching from the west, Doyle's small force would simply drive straight up the access road and seize control of it before the Iraqis could muster their defenses. The most challenging part was the sheer size of the objective. Nearly two hundred feet tall and over six miles long, the dam's structure included a nine-story administration building, miles of tunnels inside the dam, a huge power plant, and dozens of other concrete buildings scattered around the site.

Just after dark the company mounted its GMVs and moved out toward the objective. Along the way one of the vehicles broke a steering box, but by borrowing parts from three other vehicles they had it back on the road in less than half an hour.

Ground Mobility Vehicle

Ranger sniper

The only obstacle they encountered when they reached the dam was a high chain-link fence, which was easily breached by the lead GMV. Once inside the perimeter, the platoons split up and raced to strategic points throughout the dam complex. Charlie Company's 3rd Platoon followed the road to the power plant at the bottom of the dam while 2nd Platoon drove across the top of the structure to set up a position on the far side. 1st Platoon and the command element would take and hold the southwest portion.

Initially there was no resistance. The Rangers captured several guards and civilian employees working at the structure without a shot being fired. The men from Charlie Company were first to take contact from a few Iraqis holed up inside a building near the foot of the dam. The Rangers engaged with .50 caliber machine guns mounted on their GMVs, quickly eliminating the threat.

Across the dam, 1st Lieutenant Graham White, a twenty-three-year-old West Point graduate, had one of the toughest parts of the mission. His Bravo Co. 2nd Platoon had to seize and secure the far side of the dam and clear the massive nine-story administration building of any opposition.

View from a guard shack at Haditha Dam

Leaving half his platoon with SFC Jeffrey Duncan, White entered the administration building with fewer than two dozen Rangers. Using night-vision goggles and weapon-mounted lights as they began to clear the dark corridors. Every door was locked, so they began by attaching breaching charges to them and blowing each door while a squad of men stood back, ready to enter with weapons high once the charge blew. Most of the rooms were unoccupied but there were hundreds of rooms and the team quickly ran out of breaching charges. They used shotguns to blow the locks off the doors until that ammo too was exhausted.

Forced to improvise, some of the Rangers claim they succeeded by tossing one another against the doors like battering rams. "That's appropriate," said one Ranger veteran. "Our motto is 'Sua Sponte,' Latin for 'of our own accord.' We do what it takes to get to the job done."

The task took hours and when they finished, all of them were exhausted. They had, however, captured twenty-five civilian engineers and workers who were corralled for their own safety.

SFC Duncan, meanwhile, directed his two squads to take up blocking positions on top of the dam. They were soon engaged by an Iraqi Army unit and began receiving small arms and RPG fire from the river bank. Duncan directed one of his sniper teams to engage the enemy. The Ranger's first round went through the RPG gunner and hit a propane tank, which exploded, killing two more enemy soldiers. Three kills with one shot.

Duncan was then ordered to push his team northwest to the far side of the dam. As they mounted up, they were joined by the Battalion Command Sergeant Major, Alfred Birch. Birch was a living legend in the Regiment, having participated in every major combat operation since he joined the military in 1977, which was before most of the Rangers he oversaw were born.

Just minutes after the section moved out, driving across the causeway to the northwest, they encountered a truckload of armed Iraqi soldiers. A firefight broke out, lasting almost an hour and resulting in a truckload of dead and wounded Iraqis but no American casualties.

During the duel, three Iraqi soldiers fell over the side of the dam and down a steep embankment. CSM Birch joined Duncan in scaling down, under fire, to rescue two of the wounded Iraqis. Though one of the enemy soldiers rescued by the CSM and Duncan expired of his wounds, Ranger medics saved the other's life—and provided a vivid example of how quickly well-trained Americans can shift from lethal action to compassion in the midst of battle.

Ranger training is tough and realistic, because it has to be.

Down at the power plant, code named "Objective Cobalt," 3rd Platoon of Charlie Company fared slightly worse. Upon approaching the cluster of buildings at the base of the dam, they began taking fire and the platoon leader ordered them to pull back so they could put a support element in place before commencing an assault. In the process, one GMV with four Rangers took a wrong turn and drove up to a building full of Iraqi soldiers, who proceeded to open fire. The GMV driver punched the accelerator and raced out of the killing zone. Rangers watching the engagement from the top of the dam were certain there had to be several dead and wounded Americans inside the lightly armored vehicle.

As it turned out, the GMV was the only serious casualty. It was riddled with bullets and its block ruined. The driver was hit in the foot by a ricochet, and the Ranger manning the gun took several rounds in the ceramic plate on his body armor. He was

sore afterward, but otherwise unharmed. The other two men inside miraculously escaped injury. With the vehicle bleeding out oil and engine coolant, the Rangers moved it into an over-watch position before it quit so they could make use of its top-mounted weapon system.

The buildings the GMV mistakenly approached turned out to be the command-and-control center for Iraqi forces in the area. Inside was a large armory with stockpiles of weapons, ammunition, and communications gear. The Iraqis occupying the buildings refused to surrender and the U.S. force was too small to root them out so the Rangers called in air strikes to eliminate the threat the position posed to their mission.

In front of the dam was a stretch of wide-open desert initially appeared to be devoid of any threat. But at dawn the Rangers discovered the area was crisscrossed with trench lines and bunkers, from which the Iraqis staged multiple attacks in the coming days.

On the morning of 1 April, 1st and 2nd Platoons were in the process

Rangers firing the M3 Carl Gustav recoiless rifle

of fortifying their positions on the southwest end of the dam when Iraqi machine guns began raking the front of the dam. Mortar rounds and RPGs soon followed, raining down among the Rangers as they dove into their fighting positions and returned fire.

The Iraqis followed up with human wave attacks against C Company at the base of the dam. Fifteen to twenty Iraqi soldiers at a time would charge their positions, only to be cut down by accurate rifle fire, 120-mm mortars and Army attack helicopters. These gunfights went on for the entire day, leaving the weary Rangers no time for rest.

During one of these engagements, a Ranger observed a puff of smoke from an island too far out in Lake Haditha to engage with small arms. Concluding that he had discovered an Iraqi mortar position, he alerted his squad leader who brought up a Javelin anti-tank missile. The gunner crouched down atop the dam, lined up the island in his sights and fired. The missile exited the tube, ignited, and detonated on the target with a muffled explosion. To make sure the position wouldn't be reoccupied, the Rangers hit the island with multiple air strikes.

The Ranger in the foreground is armed with an MK-48 Mod belt-fed machine gun.

Though enemy attacks continued throughout the day accompanied by intensified artillery and mortar bombardments, Captain Doyle was able to evacuate his casualties and Iraqi detainees. The helicopters also brought in ammunition, water, food, and more medical supplies—but no replacements or reinforcements.

When his Rangers noticed a man in a kayak near the dam they were ordered to try and capture the individual. Two well-aimed shots from a .50 caliber sent the kayak to the bottom and the man, unhurt, was apprehended by a Ranger fire team. He was found to be carrying drawings of the dam and the Ranger positions on and around it.

It was becoming very apparent the enemy was preparing a major counter-offensive to retake the dam complex. The Rangers would soon be pressed to the limits of their endurance.

The real fight began on 2 April. Hundreds of artillery rounds began to fall all around and inside their perimeter. Huge explosions rocked the dam as Iraqi 155-mm artillery unloaded on them from multiple positions. Human wave attacks continued sporadically, but most of the Rangers had nothing to shoot at, and the feeling of helplessness intensified as indirect fire screamed in and exploded around them. It continued day and night for the next seventy-two hours. They had already been on the move and in combat nearly nonstop for two straight weeks. Now, a steady rain of exploding steel meant these men who had already gone without rest for more than thirty hours would be unable to do so until the bombardment stopped.

Warfare of this sort is horrific. Hunkered down, unable to shoot back, every man begins to wonder where the next incoming high explosive round is going to detonate.

For three days straight the Rangers endured the barrage, forcing themselves to stay alert for the enemy and wishing for a way to fight back. Their only recourse, air strikes called in by their USAF JTAC on enemy gun positions were often too far away to observe their effect.

Incredibly there were few American casualties inflicted by the bombardment. Several Rangers were wounded by shrapnel, but none were killed. One Ranger who was there said, "We really gauged the passing of time by the consumption of our ammunition." In the end only four of them had to be evacuated due to wounds or injury. The remaining 150 men held their ground for ten days and nights against everything the Iraqi army threw at them. During the operation, they, and the air strikes they call in are credited with killing nearly three hundred enemy soldiers and destroying two dozen mortar positions, thirty tanks, twenty-eight artillery pieces, and almost as many anti-aircraft sites.

The only American KIAs during the operation came at a blocking point several miles from the dam. The circumstances of how they were killed indicate the nature of the enemy American troops faced in Iraq.

Captain Russell Rippetoe, a Ranger Forward Air Controller, and his team were tasked with setting up a blocking position on a highway south of the Haditha Dam. The twenty-seven-year-old Colorado native, and son of a two-tour Ranger veteran of Vietnam, Rippetoe knew from his training and earlier experience in Afghanistan exactly how to call in air strikes on any approaching Iraqi units.

Captain Russell Rippetoe (wearing ball cap)

With him at the blocking position were SSG Nino Livaudais, the father of two, with a pregnant wife at home; SPC Chad Thibodeau, also with a pregnant wife at home; and SPC Ryan Long—a fourth-generation soldier from Delaware. All of them were combat-hardened by two previous deployments to Afghanistan.

Charged with the responsibility of interdicting an attack from the south against the Rangers at the dam, they prepared fighting positions beside the road and began stopping vehicles, searching for weapons and enemy fighters.

COURAGE: A COMMON VIRTUE

The battle for Haditha Dam saw so much Ranger gallantry, the entire unit was given a Valorous Unit Award. Though the Ranger Regiment is notoriously stingy in handing out personal decorations, four of those who took part in the mission were awarded the Silver Star, twenty-seven others received the Bronze Star for valor, and seventy-one Rangers were presented with Army Commendation Medals, for their actions over ten days of intense combat.

For their courage and sacrifice, Captain Rippetoe, Specialist Livaudais, and Specialist Long were posthumously awarded Bronze Stars with "V" device for valor.

Initially, all went as planned. But on 3 April, an SUV carrying several people, including two women approached their position. One of the women, apparently pregnant and obviously in distress, got out of the vehicle. All five Rangers at the checkpoint started to go to her aid, but Captain Rippetoe ordered them back and approached her himself.

He had almost reached the vehicle when it detonated. Packed with explosives, the SUV erupted in a cloud of fire and flying steel, instantly killing Rippetoe, Livaudais, and Long. Chad Thibodeau was knocked unconscious and suffered multiple shrapnel wounds.

Around his neck Captain Rippetoe wore a small medallion called a "shield of strength" next to his dog tags. On it was inscribed a verse from the book of Joshua 1:9: "I will be strong and courageous. I will not be terrified, or discouraged, for the Lord my God is with me wherever I go." Tags like it have been worn throughout the war zone by tens of thousands of American Soldiers, Sailors, Airmen, Guardsmen, and Marines.

A week later Captain Russell Rippetoe was interred beside other American heroes at Arlington National Cemetery, becoming the first casualty of the Iraq War to be buried there. At his funeral, many spoke of the bigger-than-life warrior with an even bigger heart.

His father, Lt Col Joe Rippetoe, is convinced it was his son's big heart that got him killed. But he also believes that a big heart is something of which to be very proud.

THE RANGERS CREED

Recognizing that I volunteered as a Ranger, fully knowing the hazards of my chosen profession, I will always endeavor to uphold the prestige, honor, and high esprit de corps of the Rangers.

Acknowledging the fact that a Ranger is a more elite soldier who arrives at the cutting edge of battle by land, sea, or air, I accept the fact that as a Ranger my country expects me to move further, faster, and fight harder than any other soldier.

Never shall I fail my comrades. I will always keep myself mentally alert, physically strong, and morally straight, and I will shoulder more than my share of the task whatever it may be, one hundred percent and then some.

Gallantly will I show the world that I am a specially selected and well-trained soldier. My courtesy to superior officers, neatness of dress and care of equipment shall set the example for others to follow.

Energetically will I meet the enemies of my country. I shall defeat them on the field of battle for I am better trained and will fight with all my might. Surrender is not a Ranger word. I will never leave a fallen comrade to fall into the hands of the enemy and under no circumstances will I ever embarrass my country.

Readily will I display the intestinal fortitude required to fight on to the Ranger objective and complete the mission though I be the lone survivor.

Rangers Lead the Way!

RANGER SCHOOL

Duration: Sixty-one days

Course Type: Leadership

Mission/Objective: Conduct Ranger, Reconnaissance, and Surveillance leader courses to further develop the combat arms related functional skills of officer and enlisted volunteers who are eligible for assignment to units whose primary mission is to engage in the close combat, direct fire battle. Rangers.

Two months carrying a forty-pound rucksack with very little to eat, even less sleep, being graded on everything. That's Ranger school in a nutshell.

Named for the Army's fabled experts in small unit infantry tactics, Ranger school is not a Special Operations course, per se. It is the Army's premiere leadership course, open to combat arms volunteers from both the officer and enlisted corps. Only forty percent of those who enter will pin the Ranger tab on their shoulder two months later.

Located at Fort Benning, Georgia, the 4th Ranger Training Battalion exists to train Ranger students to lead small unit operations in close combat. The Benning or "Crawl" phase of Ranger School is twenty-one days long. It is designed to develop the military skills, physical and mental endurance, and the confidence a soldier must possess in order to successfully motivate men in the heat of battle. This is accomplished through a process of stress inoculation meant to simulate the strain of

combat, but since they can't actually shoot at the students, pressure is applied by forcing them to operate under field conditions where there is never enough food, sleep, or time to get the job done. Ranger students are given a variety of challenges in the initial phase of training designed to weed out those whose physical or mental conditioning are lacking. These include physical testing, hours of training in the hand-to-hand pit, a swim test, land navigation, and the obstacle course.

The mountain phase is also twenty-one days long and is overseen by the 5th Ranger Training Battalion, Dahlonega, Georgia. During this phase students learn knot tying, rope bridges, and assault climbing skills. They also perform nightly patrols through the north Georgia mountains on reconnaissance, ambush missions, and raids.

Combat patrol missions are directed against a conventionally equipped threat force in a low intensity conflict scenario. These patrol missions are conducted both day and night over a four-day squad field training exercise (FTX) and a platoon five-day FTX that includes long distance patrols through rugged mountain terrain, vehicle ambushes, river crossings, and raids on simulated mortar or communications sites. During these missions the Ranger student may be selected to lead tired, hungry, physically expended students to accomplish yet another combat patrol mission at any time. All patrols are student-led and must be accomplished under the watchful

eyes of their Ranger instructors. Most students will also participate in a parachute jump.

At the conclusion of the mountain phase, the students move by bus or parachute assault into the final (Florida) phase of Ranger training, conducted at Camp Rudder, near Eglin Air Force Base, Florida.

The swamp phase is seventeen days long. Each

student trains an average of eighteen to twenty hours each day, with more patrolling, as well as small boat tactics, river crossings, and road marches, all while under the threat of enemy attack by soldiers of the 6th Ranger Training Battalion.

The Florida Phase ramps up the stress with progressive, realistic operations that stretch each student more than he ever thought possible. The ten-day FTX is a fast paced, extremely challenging exercise in which the students are required to prove their ability to apply small unit tactics they have learned throughout the course.

At the end of the course, those who have successfully completed all three phases return to Fort Benning to stand in front of Victory pond and have their loved ones pin the coveted Ranger tab on their shoulders. It is always a proud moment, as fewer than one percent of all soldiers ever earn the right to join the brotherhood who call themselves "Ranger."

25 OCT 03

HUNTING PARTIES

SHKIN, AFGHANISTAN

The border region along Pakistan's Federally Administrated Tribal Areas has long been one of the most dangerous places in the world. By Autumn 2003, the Operating Base at Shkin was similiar to the closest target at a carnival shooting gallery—everyone liked shooting at it. Foreign fighters aligned with al-Qaeda and Taliban supporters hiding just across the border in Pakistan frequently slipped across into Afghanistan at night to attack the nearest American outpost.

The base, manned by U.S. Special Operations Forces, an Afghan commando force, and a contingent of the 10th Mountain Division, also included members of the CIA's super-secret Special Activities Division. One of them, William "Chief" Carlson, had done just about everything a Special Operator could do. A member of the Montana Blackfoot Nation, he began his Army career as an enlisted soldier in the 75th Ranger regiment and went on to become a Green Beret. From there he was selected for Delta Force, where he served out the remainder of his twenty-year Army career. Retirement didn't suit him, so Carlson signed on as a contractor with the CIA, where his dark complexion and résumé guaranteed he would be deployed to Afghanistan almost immediately.

William "Chief" Carlson

Though Chief Carlson had a reputation as "one of the toughest of the tough," all who knew him well admired his steadfast loyalty and sincere friendship. His wife, Cherri, in Fayetteville, North Carolina, cared for and raised their two sons during Chief's long absences.

Another operator on the team at Shkin, Christopher Glenn Mueller, followed a different path into the ranks of the CIA. Overcoming asthma and a learning disability in high school prepared him for the challenges after graduation, when he enlisted in the Navy. Because of injuries in training, it took him three tries to make it

Chris Mueller

Chris Mueller in Iraq

through the rigorous SEAL selection process. Normally, a man is washed out of the program after being "recycled" twice. But Mueller's instructors admired his tenacity and he finally became a SEAL.

He spent four years with SEAL Team Five, deploying around the world for training and real-world missions. Enticed to apply for a position with the CIA's Special Activities Division, Mueller left the Navy to attend UC San Diego to get the required college degree. Sheepskin and glowing transcript in hand, he joined the CIA as a paramilitary officer. His first overseas deployment was in support of operations in Iraq, where he spent nearly a year. After that he was sent to Afghanistan, where he linked up with Chief Carlson.

Both CIA operators were friends with Mark Donald, a highly trained SEAL medical officer and a key member of the small team at Shkin. Dark haired and intense, the wiry Latino's career path was also unique. Mark grew up in New Mexico, where he excelled in athletics but struggled with academics. Though his mother hailed from Matamoros, Mexico, his parents were fiercely American—a trait that rubbed off on their sons. During his senior year, Mark was impressed by the Marine recruiters who visited his high school. Deciding he wanted their self-confidence and bearing, Mark enlisted after graduation, though not yet eighteen. In the Marine Corps, he found the self-discipline he sought—and he put it to work in the area he was weakest—academics.

After long hours of study, he applied for an inter-service transfer to become a Navy Corpsman and was immediately recruited into SEAL training. After nearly a decade as a SEAL he received a commission in the Navy Medical Corps as a Physician's Assistant.

The small group of operators at the Shkin Base was close-knit and team members would often stay up late into the night debating politics, history, or the likelihood that they would succeed in their primary mission: tracking down Osama bin Laden, target #1 on the Americans' "kill or capture" list.

All those in this very selective, highly secret unit had faced danger before. So when they were handed the mission of heading out of the base to follow up on some new intelligence, they went loaded for bear. They all knew they were about to kick a hornet's nest.

Accompanied by a detachment of Afghan commandos mounted in Humvees, trucks, SUVs, and Toyota Hilux pickups, the team drove out the gates of the base before sunup. To call the route they took into the hills a road is a gross overstatement. This part of Afghanistan doesn't have roads. The dusty track they followed was better suited for, and well used by, the local goat herds.

On mission before daylight

As the convoy bumped and wound its way into the mountains, rocky peaks loomed on either side and stone outcroppings closed in tight. Tactically they were sitting ducks and though nobody liked it, neither could they do much about it. Just behind the lead vehicle—a Toyota Hilux carrying Afghan soldiers—Chief piloted a soft-sided Humvee with "Doc" Donald riding shotgun.

Three hours after leaving the base, the mountain path literally exploded around them.

An RPG streaking from above detonated just inches from the second vehicle occupied by Chief Carlson, Doc Donald, and two of their teammates. A direct hit would have killed all inside but the near miss was enough to throw the Humvee upward and spray shrapnel into the vehicle, filling the cab with smoke and all but disabling it.

A heavy machine gun opened up from a ridgeline off to the left. Through the cracked windshield, it appeared another RPG turned the Hilux truck full of Afghan soldiers ahead of them into a smoldering wreck.

Ignoring the blistering fire, Chief quickly turned hard to shield Mark and the others inside from the worst of it, putting them as close as possible to a ditch running beside the path and up against a hill that would provide cover.

Ground assault convoy

Mark Donald looked over at his teammate. "Bailout, Chief?"

Carlson nodded and shouted over the din, "The vehicle's down. Go. Go!"

They were the last words Mark would hear Chief say.

By positioning the vehicle to provide as much cover as possible for his teammates, the rugged former Delta operator fully exposed himself to the enemy fire. Mark and the others rolled out and tried to engage the enemy, but even with the rear of the vehicle affording some protection, rounds were impacting all around them. As a bullet tore gear from Mark's harness, he could see others around him still fighting, though blood was soaking through their uniforms where bullets and shrapnel found flesh.

In the seconds it took for Chief to maneuver the vehicle to the side of the path, the enemy above found their range and zeroed in on Carlson with a deadly volley. He was cut down before he could exit the vehicle.

For the surviving team members, there wasn't time to grieve. With the volume of fire still increasing all around them, they tried to escape the kill zone by laying down a base of fire while screaming at their Afghan counterparts to do the same.

Though already wounded in his right arm, Doc Donald was still able to move thanks to copious amounts of adrenaline coursing through his veins. In the chaos he realized they would have to break out of the ambush and link up with the rest of the column, from which they were now separated by a wall of flying lead and shrapnel. To rescue the wounded still trapped in the kill zone, they would have to get the Afghan soldiers still able to fight to lay down a base of covering fire long enough for him to drag the wounded to safety.

Danger close

Shouts and vigorous arm gestures finally got the Afghan commandos on the same sheet of music. Braving the rounds aimed at him, Mark dashed to the nearest wounded, grabbed the man's harness and dragged him back to the shelter of some rocks. Then he did it a second time, moving as swiftly as his own wounds and heavy gear would allow.

Twice more he ran from cover up to the lead vehicle to treat wounded Afghan commandos and coordinate with others still able to pull a trigger, directing the fight as best he could. More than once he had to dive for cover to avoid a blast of gunfire directed his way, pressing himself into a depression less than a foot deep and feeling somewhat amazed at how small a man can get when properly motivated.

Incoming fire increased and became more accurate as the al-Qaeda fighters above maneuvered to close in on them. Though he concluded they would soon have to retreat or be overrun, Mark conferred with his teammates and they decided abandoning Chief's body and several other gravely wounded men was not an option. They would stand and fight together, and if need be, die together.

Then suddenly the hail of incoming fire stopped. Unbeknownst to Mark Donald and the others trapped in the kill zone, the rest of the troops further back in the column dismounted and moved uphill on the enemy flank. Well-aimed volleys of fire visited swift retribution on the closest of the al-Qaeda attackers.

While the desperate battle raged on the mountain east of the Shkin Base, Chris Mueller was briefing a 10th Mountain Division quick reaction force (QRF). He reluctantly agreed to stay behind for just such a mission if the need arose. As the soldiers sprinted to their vehicles, shrugging on body armor while they ran, Mueller estimated it would take at least half an hour to reach his embattled mates.

Back at the ambush site, Doc Donald searched the terrain for a suitable casualty collection point. There were still people shooting at them, but it seemed the enemy was a little less enthusiastic after seeing their first string wiped out. Still, he estimated the al-Qaeda or Taliban or both, would soon have reinforcements en route.

Aware that their current location was too exposed and certain their reprieve would likely be short-lived, Doc Donald organized some of the Afghan soldiers to lay down a barrage of suppressive fire. Then, on his signal, they piled themselves and the wounded into two, still operational Toyota trucks.

Mark sprinted to the driver's door of the lead vehicle, jerked it open, and threw himself inside. He started the engine, popped the clutch and the truck took off like a rodeo pony, heading for a bend in the path that would put them in defilade from direct enemy fire.

Afghan commando

Somehow, they made it without further casualties and for a short time, it seemed the battle might be over. For the next half hour or so, Doc Donald hustled from one group of men to another, distributing ammunition and water, feeling more tired than ever before in his life as the adrenaline subsided and blood from his own wounds continued to seep into his clothing. Focused on treating those with the most serious injuries, he made a grim discovery: nearly every man was hit by either bullets or shrapnel.

The arrival of Chris Mueller and the QRF provided a brief respite for Doc Donald as 10th Mountain Division medics pitched in to help treat the wounded. While the U.S. soldiers took up positions along the shallow perimeter, Mark briefed Chris and the infantry platoon commander on what happened and what he expected. Though the enemy fire finally ceased, Donald told them to anticipate a running gun battle as they headed back to the base at Shkin.

As he told Chris of Chief Carlson's heroism and how he died, Mark could tell Mueller was deeply troubled by the loss of their friend. Chris and Doc Donald talked alone for a few minutes and then Mueller departed to join a team of his Afghan commandos whom would serve as a point element for the 10th Mountain Div troops scouting the road ahead.

They were barely out of sight beyond the next wadi when the sound of gunfire echoed through the canyon again. As he raced to a vantage point, Doc Donald's heart sank. Chris and his advance team were taking fire from hidden snipers as another band of al-Qaeda fighters moved in to press the attack.

Casualty evacuation

Now it was time for the rescued to become the rescuer.

With his reserves of adrenaline all but spent, the SEAL Doc wearily picked up his rifle and headed toward the gunfight. Just as he did, he saw Chris dash from a covered position to help a wounded Afghan commando. Suddenly, an unseen enemy opened

fire from Chris's right rear and Mark saw him fall—hard—then roll and try to keep fighting. Mark and a group of American and Afghan soldiers moved as quickly as possible, but by the time he made it to Mueller's side, it was obvious there was nothing he could do. Chris Mueller, like Chief Carlson just hours before, lost their lives trying to save the lives of others. Doc Donald lost two of his brothers in one fight and no amount of medical expertise was going to change that.

What followed next were periods of intense fire interrupted by brief moments of silence as air support arrived overhead. Al-Qaeda fighters, drawn by the sound of battle tried to close in for the kill. Attack helicopters and A-10 Thunderbolts, directed by radio rolled in with rocket pods and nose-mounted cannons blazing. Despite heavy losses from the aerial firepower, the enemy pressed so close that several times the pilots were reluctant to fire—fearful of hitting "friendlies."

When the sun began dropping toward the horizon, American helicopters swooped in to evacuate the most urgent casualties. As al-Qaeda fire slackened, the battered CIA team, Afghan commandos, and the 10th Mountain QRF seized the opportunity to break out. They made it safely back to the base under the cover of close air support.

At the end of the battle, only one man on the team was unscathed and two were dead. Everyone else, including Doc Donald, was wounded. The bullet and shrapnel holes in his body armor and equipment told the story: It simply wasn't his day to die.

Today, in a quiet spot at the CIA Headquarters in Langley, Virginia, a wall of honor bears a star for every CIA employee who lost his or her life in the service to our country. There, among so many other heroes, are stars bearing the names of Chris Mueller and Chief Carlson.

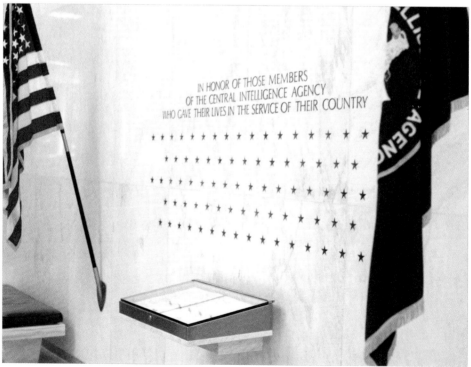

CIA Memorial wall

In relation to what they gave, a simple star seems far too little, but according to those who knew them best and whose lives have been touched by their sacrifice, those understated stars are fitting, since both were the kind of men who said, "It's not about me."

Doc Mark Donald, eventually retired, feeling compelled to serve in a different capacity. Today he is an advocate for wounded veterans around the country. With Mark's help, one of Chief's two sons, Shayne Carlson, embarked on an expedition to skateboard across the United States to raise awareness for wounded warriors.

AGENCY SEAL MEDALLION: CHRISTOPHER G. MUELLER

Christopher G. Mueller is posthumously awarded the AGENCY SEAL MEDALLION in recognition of his outstanding performance and courage in the face of hazardous and unpredictable conditions, personal courage under enemy fire, and making the ultimate sacrifice for his nation on 25 October 2003. Mr. Mueller displayed great valor in the face of the enemy, exposing himself to render aid to a wounded comrade. His selfless

action under fire was undertaken knowing that it could cost him his life. Mr. Mueller's service and contributions in the war against terrorism were instrumental in defeating al-Qaeda forces and achieving America's goals of peace, justice, and stability. His actions and his performance were in the finest traditions of the Agency. Mr. Mueller's contributions to the national security and, in particular, to the mission of this organization reflect credit upon him, his institution, and the Federal service.

Chris Mueller's last free-fall jump

NAVY CROSS: LIEUTENANT MARK L. DONALD

The President of the United States of America takes pleasure in presenting the Navy Cross to Lieutenant Mark L. Donald, United States Navy, for extraordinary heroism as Medical Officer assigned to a Joint Operational Unit conducting combat operations against al-Qaeda and Taliban enemy forces in support of Operation Enduring Freedom, in October 2003. Lieutenant Donald was part of a multi-vehicle mounted patrol ambushed by extremely heavy fire from rocket-propelled grenades and small arms. When two rocket-propelled grenades exploded immediately in front of his vehicle, Lieutenant Donald exited the vehicle and began returning fire. While under heavy and continuous machine gun fire he pulled the wounded Afghan commander to relative safety behind the vehicle's engine block. He left his position, completely exposing himself to the small arms fire, and pulled a wounded American trapped behind the steering wheel to cover behind the vehicle. He covered the wounded with his own body while returning fire and providing care. In the process, multiple bullets passed through his clothing and equipment. Identifying wounded Afghan personnel in the two lead vehicles, Lieutenant Donald moved to their aid under heavy fire and began medical treatment. After treating the wounded, he took charge of an Afghan squad in disarray, deployed

them to break the ambush, and continued to treat numerous critically injured personnel, while arranging for their prompt medical evacuation. That afternoon, while sweeping an area of earlier action, a U.S./Afghan element was ambushed by a platoon-sized enemy force near Lieutenant Donald's position. Knowing personnel were gravely wounded, Lieutenant Donald without hesitation and with complete disregard for his own safety ran two hundred meters between opposing forces exposing him to withering and continuous heavy machine gun and small arms fire to render medical treatment to two wounded personnel, one Afghan and one American. He placed himself between the casualties and the extremely heavy enemy fire now directed at him and began emergency medical treatment. Still under intense enemy fire, wounded by shrapnel, and knowingly within dangerously close range of attacking U.S. Army AH-64 Apache helicopter rockets, he organized the surviving Afghan soldiers and led a two-hundred-meter fighting withdrawal to friendly positions. Lieutenant Donald coordinated the medical evacuation of wounded soldiers and withdrew overland back to base before treating his own wounds. By his heroic display of decisive and tenacious leadership, unyielding courage in the face of constant enemy fire, and utmost devotion to duty, Lieutenant Donald reflected great credit upon himself and upheld the highest traditions of the United States Naval Service.

2004

Soldiers walk the streets of Fallujah during Operation Vigilant Resolve.

26 APR 04

© 2010 ORION-ME
Image © 2010 DigitalGlobe
© 2010 Europa Technologies

©2009 Google

OPERATION VIGILANT RESOLVE

FALLUJAH, AL ANBAR PROVINCE, IRAQ

In the spring of 2004 Al Anbar Province, Iraq, was the most dangerous place on planet Earth. The cities of Fallujah and Ramadi, the provincial capital, were the heart of the insurgency in the "Sunni Triangle."

Abu Musab Al-Zarqawi, the Jordanian terrorist who headed al-Qaeda in Iraq, established his headquarters in Fallujah. The urban area was firmly under the control of insurgent factions, all of whom defied coalition attempts to establish Iraqi government control over the city of four hundred thousand. Entering Fallujah's warren of narrow streets and tight packed, multi-story buildings was a virtual suicide mission.

On 31 March 2004, a convoy of trucks delivering supplies to U.S. and Iraqi forces was ambushed by insurgents. Four Blackwater security guards meeting the vehicles

Lt Gen James Conway

were killed and their mutilated bodies were hung from a bridge over the Euphrates. Images of dead Americans being desecrated brought a firestorm of indignation across America, prompting the Interim Iraqi Government to declare they would—with U.S. support—send in new Iraqi Army troops to "pacify" the city. The operation was code named "Vigilant Resolve."

The task of cordoning the city so the insurgents couldn't be reinforced while the Iraqi Army prepared for the fight fell to the 1st Marine Expeditionary Force, led by Lieutenant General James Conway. On the night of 4 April 2004, the Marines surrounded the city, blocking off all roads and bridges leading in or out and called on peaceful citizens to evacuate. Many did. But intelligence officers warned that perhaps four thousand insurgents remained and were fortifying whole city blocks against an expected attack.

Urban warfare is the worst kind of combat, especially when the enemy has had time to prepare defenses and use hapless civilians as shields. While Iraqi government leaders debated how and when their forces would fight, the Marines used every play in the handbook—from leaflet drops to blaring heavy metal music over loudspeakers. The insurgents made it clear they weren't going anywhere—firing back with RPGs, mortars, and machine guns. They also managed to infiltrate the city with reporters from Arab media outlets who did their best to turn American and Iraqi public opinion against the operation.

While the interim government in Baghdad vacillated, U.S. commanders on the ground continued to probe insurgent defenses. On 26 April, a platoon of Marines was tasked with "dropping" a seven-man Special Operations unit in the northeast section of the city. If all went as planned, the Marines and Special Operators would move together on a patrol to the designated site and the Green Berets would establish a covert observation post to call in fire on the enemy after the Marines returned to the perimeter. Like many things in war, it didn't work out as planned.

The leader of the Spec-Ops team, Master Sergeant Donald R. Hollenbaugh, was a twenty-year veteran of the Special Operations community—a member of the super-secret 1st Special Forces Operational Detachment—Delta, or "Delta Force" for eight years. The tough, wiry Master Sergeant from Prescott, Washington, had already seen more combat than most men alive, including the "Black Hawk Down" incident in Mogadishu, Somalia, in 1993.

He and his fellow Delta Operators, accompanied by thirty Marines, departed friendly lines in the dark of night. Before dawn they occupied two abandoned buildings

Capt Doug Zembiec, the commanding officer of Company E, 2nd Battalion, 1st Marine Regiment, 1st Marine Division, gives orders to his men over a radio prior to leaving their secured compound for a short patrol in Fallujah, Iraq, 8 April 2004. The company entered Fallujah 6 April to begin the effort of destroying enemy holding up in the city.

several city blocks forward of the nearest American positions. Hollenbaugh, along with a squad of Marines and a Delta Force medic, Staff Sergeant Daniel Briggs, occupied the rooftop of the southern-most building where they had a good vantage point over possible routes of enemy attack. Several hours passed without any sign of movement around their position.

Fallujah is known across Iraq as the "city of mosques," and as the Marines set about fortifying the observation posts, the Muslim call to prayer echoed across the city. Hollenbaugh listened for a moment to the wavering tones, then turned to Briggs and said, "Oh boy, this is not going to be a good day," he shook his head and continued. "This is how Somalia started. This could get ugly quick."

The sun was barely above the horizon when the first rocket propelled grenade swooshed in and exploded against the side of the building.

On the flat roof of the structure, Hollenbaugh crouched low and moving fast, moved among the Marines, encouraging them and telling them to get ready for action. As he did, machine gun fire began peppering the front of the building, and when the Delta Master Sergeant stood up to try and pinpoint the shooter's location, another RPG came straight toward him. He ducked and felt the heat of the round as it missed him by just inches. It impacted against the wall on the far edge of the roof, nearly blowing his eardrums out.

It quickly became evident that a well-armed group of insurgents were occupying the buildings around them and now had every intention of overrunning the two mutually supporting but tenuous U.S. outposts. One of the black-clad fighters stepped out of a doorway right next to the northern building where half the Marine platoon was positioned. Before anyone could react, he lobbed a grenade onto the roof of the northern building, directly into the center of a Marine fire team. To make matters worse, the insurgent grenade bounced into a case of U.S. grenades the Marines prepared for their defense and when it went off, the entire case detonated along with it. The effect was like a direct hit from heavy artillery—shrapnel flew in all directions, grievously wounding everyone on the rooftop.

The grizzled Delta Master Sergeant turned to Briggs, his "Eighteen Delta" medic. Before he could say anything, Staff Sergeant Briggs picked up his aid bag and weapon and sprinted down the stairs. Hollenbaugh shouted to the rest of

Soldiers from the 1st Infantry Divisions 3rd Brigade Reconnaissance Troop clear houses in Fallujah on 12 November during Operation Al-Fajr.

A Marine of the 1st Marine Division shouts instructions to soldiers of the Iraqi Civil Defense Corps during a firefight while on a joint patrol in Nasir Waal Salaam, Iraq, on 5 June 2004. The 1st Marine Division is deployed in support of Operation Iraqi Freedom and is engaged in Security and Stabilization Operations in the Al Anbar province of Iraq.

his men, "Cover him!" They opened up with everything they had on the insurgents as Briggs emerged from the south building below, dodging withering fire as he raced toward the injured Marines atop the north building. Somehow, the fearless Staff Sergeant zig-zagged through exploding grenades and mortar rounds and made it unharmed. The men he treated couldn't have hoped for better care under the circumstances. Delta medics are among the most highly trained combat medical personnel on the planet.

Hollenbaugh and his group in the southern building stayed busy as insurgents began firing from nearly every door and window around their position. It was like a deadly game of Whack-a-Mole, only these moles whacked back. The noise was deafening as enemy grenades, rockets, mortars, and machine gun fire began tearing apart the brick and stone buildings. On the street level, Marines inside held down the triggers on their weapons until their barrels glowed red in a desperate attempt to stem the tide of suicidal enemy fighters.

On the roof, MSG Hollenbaugh carefully picked his shots, watching insurgents fall almost every time he pulled the trigger. But less than an hour into the fight, he caught sight of something several blocks down the street that did nothing to boost his morale. Buses. He saw buses and trucks pulling up, filled to overflowing with enemy fighters, disgorging what looked like ten reinforcements for every one the Americans killed. Then it hit him: the terrorists had to believe this tiny element of Marines and Delta operators was the main assault on Fallujah and they were rushing every fighter they could into this fight. He knew then, this was going to be a very long day.

With accurate, heavy fire they succeeded in driving the enemy back and for about an hour the men in the two buildings endured only sporadic enemy incoming. But the insurgents were only pausing to mass their forces, intent on delivering a crushing final blow on the besieged Marines and Green Berets.

When the attack came, it felt like a tornado of flying lead suddenly descended from the cloudless sky over Fallujah. Dozens of enemy automatic weapons and machine guns opened up simultaneously and rocket propelled grenades filled the air, blasting holes in the masonry walls of the buildings where the Americans were holed up. Before long, more Marines were wounded and Hollenbaugh could hear the urgent radio calls for medevac.

There were simply too many enemy fighters to shoot them all. They came like

ants, scrambling across rooftops, running through alleyways, firing from windows on every side. The Americans kept killing them but the insurgents still managed to advance on the two increasingly vulnerable positions. It was like the Iraqi Alamo and Hollenbaugh knew how that story ended.

More than once, groups of terrorists charged their buildings, attempting to enter and overrun the Marines holding the ground floors. As the insurgents tried to batter down the barricaded doors, Hollenbaugh and the men on the roof dropped grenades against the outside walls of the building to discourage them. And through it all, the calls for "Corpsman up!" were coming more and more often. They had already lost one Marine, Lance Corporal Aaron Austin, killed by machine gun fire while throwing a grenade. Hollenbaugh was firing and Briggs was busy patching up the wounded as several Humvees raced forward from the nearest Marine position, braving a hail of gunfire to reach their buildings and evacuate several severely wounded troops.

Temporarily out of patients, Briggs reappeared next to Hollenbaugh on the rooftop, calmly firing at enemy fighters, as he filled his team leader in on their deteriorating situation. If something didn't change soon, they would surely be overwhelmed.

"Grenade!"

Hollenbaugh didn't wait to see who yelled it. Instead, he

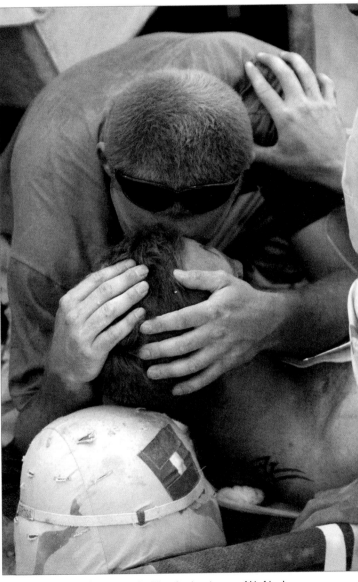

A combat medic consoles an injured soldier after learning one of his friends didn't survive the attack they had emerged from. The soldiers were part of an assault launched on Fallujah by the Marines and elements from the Army's 1st Calvary Division.

dove into the stairwell and put his head down. A second later, the detonation created a lethal cloud of shrapnel, dust, and smoke on the rooftop and he felt like a mule kicked him in the head. When he emerged from the stairwell once again, he heard one of the Marine's cry out, "I'm hit!"

Stumbling where two wounded Marines lay, blood soaking through their uniforms from multiple fragment wounds, Hollenbaugh knelt beside the first one and felt for the man's first aid pouch on his harness. He was hastily treating the two Marines when he heard his medic say in a calm, matter-of-fact voice, "Hey Don, they got me."

He turned to see that Briggs' sleeve was covered in blood, with more pulsing out of a ghastly wound behind the medic's ear. Hollenbaugh took a closer look. "You better let me put something on that, Doc."

In an instant, Hollenbaugh had three urgent surgical casualties to treat and his "doc" was now a patient.

He bandaged them up as best he could, then helped them one by one down the stairs where several wounded Marines were also waiting for a medevac. But he couldn't stay—they would be overrun unless someone held the rooftop and stopped the enemy advance. So the weary Master Sergeant pounded back upstairs to the roof and resumed picking off insurgents, now all alone.

From his vantage point, Hollenbaugh could see machine gun rounds pouring from an alleyway at the Humvees coming to evacuate the wounded. Though the Master Sergeant could not see the gun, he could tell where it was by the effects of its fire. Realizing he couldn't hit the enemy machine gun with direct fire and certain it was too far away to throw a grenade, he came up with a novel course of action that's not in any training manual.

He grabbed an M-249 Squad Automatic Weapon dropped by one of the wounded Marines and gauged the distance between the spot on the roof and the alleyway where he suspected the enemy machine gun was set up. The buildings were brick, like the one he was in, and though he couldn't make bullets fly around the corner, perhaps he could get enemy gunners with a ricochet. He gave it a little "Kentucky windage" and pulled the trigger. The weapon chattered as he "walked" its rounds so they were bouncing off the masonry wall above the machine gun position.

The enemy machine gun went silent. It worked! Hollenbaugh decided he'd have to keep his new technique in mind to teach others—if he succeeded in getting out of this fight alive.

It didn't look entirely likely. Enemy fighters kept coming, swarming up the alleyways any time he stopped to reload. Concerned the insurgents might realize he was the only one shooting from the rooftop, the Delta operator began running from one firing position to another, loosing a burst of gunfire here and there to keep the enemy thinking they were up against more than one man. At one point he intentionally

stepped up and showed himself at one position to draw the fire of a gun team, then ducked and ran to another position from which he could eliminate them while they waited for him to reappear. Periodically, he used an M-203 grenade launcher to send the enemy a few dozen high-explosive reasons to keep their heads down.

Knowing the Marines in the building below were counting on him to hold the rooftop, he was determined not to let them down. This went on for almost two hours, with dozens of mortar rounds, grenades, and rockets tearing the building to bits all around him.

LAST MAN STANDING

Don Hollenbaugh

He was so busy trying to stay alive, he didn't notice how quiet the two buildings had become. Suddenly, a Marine officer appeared in the stairway. "Don!" he shouted. "Come on, we're out of here!" With a few parting shots at the enemy, Don Hollenbaugh followed the Marine downstairs, only to make a stunning realization.

Everyone else was gone.

For nearly two hours, Don Hollenbaugh singlehandedly slugged it out with hundreds of determined enemy fighters and held them off. While the Marines and his fellow Green Berets were being evacuated, he fought off scores of suicidal insurgents by himself. The Marines suffered one killed and twenty-four wounded, 80 percent casualties. Hollenbaugh was the only Green Beret not injured in the engagement.

Later, the Master Sergeant said he was most thankful for the Marine officer who, upon taking a head count back inside friendly lines, realized Hollenbaugh was missing and came back for him. If it weren't for that, the tough Delta operator might have been overrun, captured, or killed, and treated like the Blackwater security guards who were mutilated and hung from the bridge.

For his extraordinary feats, Hollenbaugh became a legend in the Special-Ops community. The Army honored him with a Distinguished Service Cross, just the second awarded since 9/11/01. Staff Sergeant Dan Briggs received the same award for repeatedly braving enemy fire to save wounded Green Berets and Marines.

A Green Beret fires a M4A1 carbine at a range in Iraq.

DISTINGUISHED SERVICE CROSS:
DONALD R. HOLLENBAUGH

The President of the United States takes pleasure in presenting the Distinguished Service Cross to Donald R. Hollenbaugh, Master Sergeant, U.S. Army, for services as set forth in the following Citation:

For extraordinary heroism in action on 26 April 2004, during combat operations against an armed Iraqi insurgent force while supporting United States Marine Corps operations in Fallujah, Iraq. Master Sergeant Hollenbaugh demonstrated the highest degree of courage and excellent leadership through his distinguished performance as Team Leader while engaged in Urban Combat Operations. His heroic actions throughout one of the most intensive firefights of the Operation Iraqi Freedom campaign were directly responsible for preventing enemy insurgent forces from overrunning the United States Force. Master Sergeant Hollenbaugh personally eliminated multiple enemy-controlled weapon positions, essential in turning the tide of the enemy's ground-force assault upon a United States Marine Corps Platoon. His actions under fire as a Leader were performed with marked distinction and bravery. Master Sergeant Hollenbaugh's distinctive accomplishments are in keeping with the finest traditions of military service and reflect great credit upon himself, this Command, and the United States Army.

Vice President Richard B. Cheney participates in the Heroism Awards Ceremony at MacDill Air Force Base, Florida, 10 June. Pictured, from left, are: Navy Chief Petty Officer Donald B. Stokes, Army Chief Warrant Officer David B. Smith, Air Force Maj Matthew R. Glover, Army Sgt 1st Class Stephan Johns, and Army Master Sgt Donald R. Hollenbaugh.

DISTINGUISHED SERVICE CROSS: DANIEL A. BRIGGS

The President of the United States takes pleasure in presenting the Distinguished Service Cross to Daniel A. Briggs, Staff Sergeant, U.S. Army for services as set forth in the following Citation:

For extraordinary heroism in action on 26 April 2004, during combat operations against an armed Iraqi Insurgent force while supporting United States Marine Corps operations in Fallujah, Iraq. Staff Sergeant Briggs repeatedly subjected himself to intense and unrelenting enemy fire in order to provide critical medical attention to severely injured Marines and organized defensive operations. He set the highest example of personal bravery through his demonstrated valor and calmness under fire. Staff Sergeant Briggs' valiant actions prevented enemy insurgent forces from overrunning the United States Force's position and were directly responsible for prevention of additional United States military casualties or Prisoners of War by the enemy. His actions under fire as a combat medic were performed with marked distinction and bravery. Staff Sergeant Briggs' distinctive accomplishments are in keeping with the finest traditions of the military service and reflect great credit upon himself, this command, and the United States Army.

The Combat Medic Memorial at Fort Sam Houston, Texas.

COMBAT MEDICS IN AFGHANISTAN:

Right: A combat medic treats an Afghani man suffering from back problems as U.S. Marines from the 2nd MEB, 2nd Battalion, 3rd Marines visit people in the village of Khwaja Jamal in Afghanistan's Helmand province.

Below: A combat medic examines an infant girl during a dismounted patrol to a village in the Deh Chopan district of Afghanistan's Zabul province.

2005

U.S. Army Soldiers assigned to the 20th Special Forces Group, ODA 342 and Afghanistan Military Forces Soldiers patrol through the mountains near Orgun, located in the Paktika Province of Afghanistan. The purpose of the patrol is to establish an observation point while denying ease of movement to Taliban and al-Qaeda forces.

2 MAR 05

SARUN SAR

PAKTIKA PROVINCE, AFGHANISTAN

★　★　★　★　★　★　★　★　★　★　★　★

The two Black Hawk helicopters wheeling through the dark rocky mountain passes were flying with their doors closed to avoid freezing their passengers: the warriors of Operational Detachment (ODA) 732. Though spring wouldn't arrive at this altitude for another two months, intelligence reports indicated the bitterly cold, snow-covered terrain below was a haven for enemy fighters—members of the Taliban, al-Qaeda, even opium smugglers.

All aboard the two aircraft knew flying low and fast in the night—just a few meters about the rough, rocky slopes was their best protection from anti-aircraft fire—but no guarantee that enemy outposts in the tiny compounds flashing by beneath them wouldn't be alerted. The unmistakable sound of rotor blades cutting through the thin air was impossible to muffle.

The small villages on the valley floor and those cut into the terraced hillsides were almost all the same: a dozen or so mud brick and dry-stack stone structures with the nearest flat ground cultivated for wheat or corn. Nearly all had at least one small field for Afghanistan's only cash crop: opium poppy.

The ODA Team Sergeant, a five-foot-two powerhouse with an oriental accent named Sarun Sar peered out the plexiglass window as the snow-covered terrain flashed by beneath them, the rotors whipping up the smoke from cooking and warming fires from the mud-walled houses below. From long experience Master Sergeant Sar knew the gauzy mist blanketing the valley floor was a pungent haze created by the resident's most plentiful fuel: dried goat dung.

Master Sergeant Sar's introduction to lethal combat came long before he became a U.S. military special operator. Sarun grew up in Cambodia, the son of a school teacher and rice farmer. It was an idyllic life until the North Vietnamese conquered America's abandoned ally in neighboring Saigon and promptly installed a brutal communist regime in Cambodia.

ODA Team Sergeant Sarun Sar

His father was arrested and sent to a "reeducation camp," where he was tortured, worked, and starved to death. His brother was executed without trial for "anti-socialist activities." His mother and sister, forced from their land and home, fled into the jungle when they both died of malnutrition and disease. Sar was recruited by an anti-communist resistance unit and for a time fought against the Khmer Rouge communist regime—a child soldier with nowhere else to go. Barely a teenager, he went to live in a refugee camp. Almost a year later, in 1980, a church in Rockville, Maryland, heard about his plight and sponsored him to come to the United States as a refugee.

Sar flourished in his new surroundings, learning English quickly and getting involved in sports. After high school he joined the U.S. Army and adapted to a life of discipline and purpose. A year after enlisting he became a U.S. citizen. When he tried out for Special Forces and was accepted, he knew he'd found a home. The camaraderie of the close-knit Special Forces A team gave him a sense of belonging he'd never had before.

Sarun Sar with ODA 732

As the Black Hawk approached the team's objective, the helicopter crew chief shoved an index finger in front of Sar's face and shouted "One minute!" He immediately flashed the signal to his men and they commenced their final check before touch down on what could well be a "hot LZ."

Before launching on the mission, they pored over intelligence reports indicating the mountain valley was a stopover point on a major Taliban "ratline" for moving men and materiel in and out of Pakistan. They identified several of the cliff-clinging compounds to search and knew any enemy fighters they found would likely be well armed and willing to put up a fight.

The landing at first light was uneventful and as soon as the helicopter lifted off, MSG Sar and his men moved out to their first objective. It turned out to be a dry hole.

These kinds of missions were always delicate balancing acts between diplomacy and destruction. They were, after all, supposed to be winning the hearts and minds of the people here—the key component in defeating any insurgency. That of course worked best when the "locals" weren't trying to kill every American they saw. MSG Sar and his men saw both sides of this fight. They won the support of a good number of fiercely tribal Afghans—and weathered numerous attacks since arriving at the remote special forces camp where they were based.

The A-Team aggressively pursued both facets of their job with equal vigor—humanitarian activities to improve the lives of the people and operational missions

Master Sgt Sarun Sar takes a break while conducting combat operations in eastern Afghanistan. Sar and his team frequently conducted patrols along the snow-covered mountains in Afghanistan.

to root out the enemy. Though few Americans are even aware that Special Operations units conduct medical support and civil-affairs missions in combat zones, Sar and his men knew they were effective. Attacks had decreased over the previous several weeks. Nevertheless, the team didn't go anywhere without plenty of ammo. Just in case.

The choppers lifted the team to their next objective—a tiny cluster of stone houses clinging to a promontory of rock about a hundred meters above the valley floor. Tactically, it's always best to advance against a known or suspected enemy position from the high ground, but here, the only place to land a helicopter was on the valley floor. So the choppers split up. Sar's turned into the draw on one side of the village while the other flared hard, to land on the other side of the hillside compound.

The helos hadn't even touched down when Taliban insurgents opened fire from the slopes above.

From the door of his Black Hawk, MSG Sar could see armed fighters scurrying out of the village, taking up firing positions on the ridge. Already they were engaging the other half of his team, now obscured from his view by a finger of rocks separating the two LZs. There were a half dozen fighters visible and from the volume of fire, he knew there were many more he couldn't see.

Determined to get on the ground and help his teammates, Sar yanked open the door of the H-60 and looked down. The pilot was hovering about six feet up, looking for a solid place to land. But Sar couldn't wait. He turned to his comrades, shouted, "Follow me!" and jumped.

He landed in two feet of wet snow and began wading as fast as he could toward the enemy, sighting down the barrel of his M4 rifle as he ran and firing each time an enemy appeared in his sights. One Taliban fighter dropped, then another, as Sar raced toward them, determined to make every shot count.

The Taliban on the slope above turned and began shooting at him and he could hear their rounds snap past him as he ran. But the insurgents never went to the rifle range and he did. Another shot. Another enemy down.

Their ranks rapidly depleted by the charging Master Sergeant, the remaining insurgents decided discretion was the better part of valor. A half dozen of them jumped up and ran for a tree line near the compound. One turned and dashed through a small doorway into one of the stone houses. Another simply dropped his weapon and raised his hands in surrender.

Sar was almost to the huts. He waved his hand in a downward motion at the surrendering fighter. "Get down!" he yelled, realizing the man probably didn't speak English. Or Spanish. Or Cambodian. Hand signals would have to suffice.

In the end, it didn't matter anyway. The man changed his mind, snatched up his AK-47 and ran for the woodline. Two carefully-aimed shots from Sar's M4 ended the drama. Nice try, buddy.

Sar ran to the structure he saw the insurgent enter and crouched near the doorway, preparing to clean house. But that's when he realized he had a serious problem.

He was completely alone.

Looking back toward the landing zone, he saw the rest of his men fully engaged with the Taliban in the woodline. Only the team medic was moving toward his position. Sar waved at the man and shouted, "Get up here! I need a hand!"

Sarun Sar with recovered cache of munitions.

The medic arrived moments later, out of breath from the hundred-meter uphill sprint from the LZ. Now that he had someone covering his back, Sar quickly determined to press on and keep momentum instead of waiting for the rest of his team to close up. He flicked on the SureFire light on the end of his weapon and said, "I'm going in."

He chould have thrown a fragmentation grenade into the house before he entered. Tactically, he knew it was the right thing to do. But he didn't know if there were any women or children inside. Sar decided to put the safety of potential noncombatants ahead of his own.

It nearly cost him his life.

He pointed his weapon in the doorway of the dark, musty hut, quickly scanning the room starting in the nearest corner—like cutting off slices of a pie. The light swept across the room, then stopped on the face of the Taliban fighter crouched in the corner. In an instant, Sar took in the man's malevolent look, and the AK-47 pointed directly at his head. Before he could react, the man fired. Sar saw the muzzle flash light up the room just before the bullet snapped his head back with the force of a sledge-hammer. He fell back out the door and cried "I'm hit!"

The medic pulled him away from the doorway and checked him over. Sar's Kevlar helmet was on the ground nearby, its chinstrap broken. "I don't see any blood," the medic replied. "It looks like he hit you in the helmet. You're okay."

Okay was a relative term, but considering what just happened, Sar could have fared much worse. The stocky Team Sergeant scrambled to his feet, adrenaline pumping, resolved that the man who shot him was about to have his day end very badly. Still unwilling to risk killing anyone who didn't deserve to die, he reached for a flash-bang grenade instead of a frag. Pulling the pin, he tossed the stun grenade through the door, waited for the explosion, then charged into the smoke-filled space and fired twice, killing the insurgent. There was no one else in the room.

Before Sar's ears stopped ringing, the rest of his team had killed and driven off the remaining Taliban fighters. In a matter of minutes they cleared the remaining structures, uncovering a large cache of insurgent weapons, ammunition, rockets, explosives, and communication equipment.

Months later the unit returned to their home base in Hawaii, and Master Sergeant Sarun Sar was awarded the Silver Star for his actions that snowy day in March 2005. True to the nature of most Special Operators, he was uncomfortable with all the attention. In his mind he wasn't doing anything particularly heroic, only protecting his men. They are, after all, his family.

Sarun Sar with Afghanistan children

SILVER STAR:
MASTER SGT SARUN SAR

The President of the United States of America, authorized by Act of Congress July 9, 1918 (amended by an act of July 25, 1963), takes pleasure in presenting the Silver Star to Master Sergeant Sarun Sar, United States Army, for conspicuous gallantry and intrepidity in action while serving as Operations Sergeant of Special Forces Operational Detachment Alpha 732 (ODA 732), during combat operations in support of Operation ENDURING FREEDOM, in Afghanistan, on 2 March 2005.

Master Sergeant Sar was part of an Aerial Reconnaissance Force mission that landed to examine a suspicious collection of buildings. His actions under overwhelming direct enemy fire, even after receiving a head wound, were instrumental in securing the objective area and in the survival of his fellow Soldiers. Master Sergeant Sar's actions are in keeping with the finest traditions of military service and reflect great credit upon himself, the Combined Joint Task Force Afghanistan, and the United States Army.

Sarun Sar with his wife at awards ceremony

SPECIAL FORCES OPERATIONAL DETACHMENT ALPHA

The Special Forces "A-team," more commonly called an "ODA" was the primary unit used to take down the Taliban. It is a highly trained force of a dozen Green Berets, each with a particular specialty, but cross trained in the jobs of all the others. All are language trained and have received specialized military training such as military free-fall parachuting, scuba, or sniper training, among others. The unit is normally led by a captain and a warrant officer. There is a team sergeant whose job is to oversee all operations and manage enlisted personnel.

The rest of the team is composed of two each of weapons specialists, medics, engineers, communications specialists, and ops/Intel specialists. One or two Air Force Tactical Air Controllers are usually attached to the team.

This tried-and-true configuration gives the ODA incredible flexibility to be able to further split the team into various elements based on the mission at hand and enables the unit to bring the full spectrum of U.S. military combat power to bear against the enemy.

ODA in Afghanistan traveling by all terrain vehicle

In each of the following photos of ODA teams, at least one team member has been killed since the photo was taken. These men have all paid a huge cost in the war on terror.

ODA 531 in Iraq

ODA 7326 in Zerikoh, Afghanistan

ODA 7315 in dive training in Florida

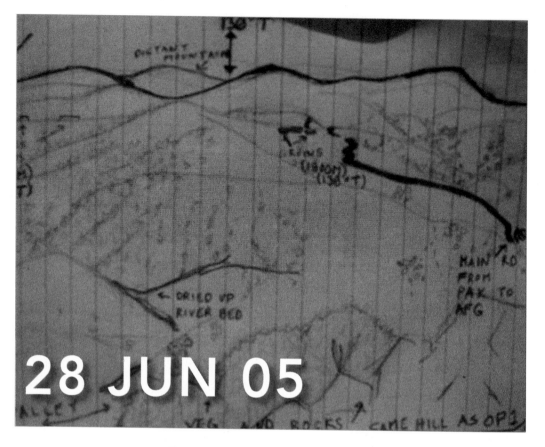

28 JUN 05

OPERATION REDWING

EAST OF ASADABAD

★ ★ ★ ★ ★ ★ ★ ★ ★ ★ ★ ★

Night high in the Hindu Kush. In the dark, near-freezing rain pelted four, almost invisible figures crouched in the tall grass of a pasture terraced into the rocky mountainside. The faint greenish glow of their night vision goggles was the only potential giveaway, but without them the men would have fallen off the mountain during their arduous trek from where they fast-roped into a tiny clearing hours earlier. They dared not stop for long; both hypothermia and the approaching dawn pursued them.

The operators were members of SEAL Team 10, on an armed reconnaissance mission deep in hostile territory near the Af-Pak border. This was a hunting trip and their prey was a terrorist named Ahmad Shah, leader of a vicious band of thugs called the "mountain tigers."

The heavy rain was deathly cold, but for these four seasoned warriors, that was a good thing. The storm reduced their chances of being compromised because nobody in their right mind would be outside on a night like this. Nobody except U.S. Navy SEALs. These were exactly the conditions and misery their training prepared them to endure.

Twenty-nine year old Lieutenant Michael Murphy commanded the mission. An athlete and former lifeguard from Patchogue, New York, he graduated with honors from Penn State and turned down offers to attend law school to earn the SEAL trident. Known affectionately by his men as "Murph," the energetic officer made multiple deployments around the globe in support of the Global War on Terror.

Above: Lieutenant Michael Murphy

Right: Petty Officer First Class Marcus Luttrell

One of two snipers on the team, Petty Officer First Class Marcus Luttrell was determined to become a SEAL since he was a teenager in rural Texas. He prepared for missions like this nearly all his life—hunting with his twin brother, taking long runs with an older mentor who drove him to get in shape, and swimming every summer at the lake near his home. Though incredibly fit, the altitude was taking its toll as he and his mates struggled up one slippery draw and down another. The biggest member of the team, Luttrell doubled as the unit's medic—carrying a standard load of weapons, grenades, ammunition, and field equipment—plus a full field trauma kit. He was the only member of the team who wasn't married or engaged.

Fellow sniper, Sonar Technician 2nd Class Matt Axelson was a mountain goat by comparison. The wiry native of Cupertino, California, was pensive and quiet, but well respected for his keen intellect and easygoing manner. Axe never lost his cool. He was also an expert mountaineer, having grown up climbing in the the Sierra Nevadas.

Luttrell's spotter, Petty Officer Danny Dietz also grew up in the mountains—the Rockies around Littleton, Colorado. A superb athlete and martial arts expert, Dietz was also a devoted husband, a devout Roman Catholic, and served as the communications specialist on this mission.

Snow still covered the jagged peaks above ten thousand feet. The four-man team found precious little cover as they slowly picked their way upward among loose shale and stubbly trees. Before dawn that day the team moved, unseen, into a position where they could observe the tiny mountain village believed to be the home of Ahmad Shah.

The SEALs spent the early morning hours concealed behind jagged rock outcroppings, putting their binoculars on the village below them anytime it wasn't obscured by clouds that periodically enveloped them. Hours passed and as the sun rose, its rays dried their soaked bodies and equipment. Soon however, the temperature shot up and the men began to envy Danny, who occupied the only spot of shade.

Sonar Technician 2nd Class Matt Axelson

Petty Officer Danny Dietz

Villages cling to the mountainsides in the harsh terrain of Afghanistan.

Marcus Luttrell was wedged beneath a log, carefully noting patterns of life in the village through his binoculars when he heard approaching footsteps. He rolled over just in time to see a turbaned Afghan wielding an ax standing over his position. He snapped his rifle up and pointed it at the man, whose eyes went wide, clearly terrified at encountering a heavily armed American. He dropped the ax.

The team had no time to discuss the sudden turn of events before a herd of goats trotted up behind the frightened shepherd, surrounding the equally startled SEALs. With them were two more goat herders.

The Special Operators quickly rounded up the three men and sat them down on a log. A nightmarish question lay before them. What to do with the three herdsmen? If they let them go, there was a good chance the local men would immediately alert the Taliban of their position. The other option—killing three unarmed civilians—wasn't part of their "win hearts and minds" plan.

The unarmed Afghan herders were in the wrong place at the wrong time and posed a serious risk. But no matter how they are portrayed by Hollywood or the media, American warriors aren't cold blooded killers. The ethical dilemma of what to do about the three unarmed noncombatants was very real and the team wrestled with it for some time. Petty Officer Dietz tried repeatedly to raise higher headquarters on the radio, to no avail. They were on their own, faced with a life-or-death decision.

In the end, they put it to a vote. When the tally was taken, each man weighed in with his opinion and in the battle between sound tactics and compassion, compassion won out.

They let the three men go. In this case, their compassion turned out to be more a greater sacrifice than any of them could anticipate.

Their cover blown, Lieutenant Murphy made the decision to move. They shouldered their packs and began picking their way higher on the mountain, looking for an easily defensible site where they could lay low until headquarters could be contacted. The four SEALs picked their way higher up the rocky slope for over an hour and then stopped to rest and observe the village below. Though the cluster of mud-brick and stone structures appeared quiet, each man had a gut sense they had been betrayed by the herders they set free. By mid-afternoon the sun was beating down on them with the intensity of a blowtorch. They sat perfectly still, each in his own hiding spot and tried to get some rest.

"Ssssst!" It was Matt Axelson. The other men looked over to see him rigidly aiming his rifle up the slope behind them. The men followed his gaze and saw that their worst nightmare had just become reality.

Nearly one hundred Taliban fighters were arrayed along the ridge above them, each armed with either an AK-47 or RPG. The SEALs could see the men moving to flank them on both sides. They were all but surrounded.

Above and on opposite page: Taliban fighters

Matt Axelson with a silenced SOPMOD M4 rifle.

Seconds later the whole mountainside erupted in a hellstorm of bullets and explosions. Taking advantage of all available cover and concealment, the SEALs returned fire with everything they had, picking off insurgents with each shot in a "target-rich" environment. But every time they cut down the lead rank of advancing fighters, another dozen replaced them. RPGs impacting around the SEALs reduced boulders to showers of rock shards with the same effect as shrapnel.

It soon became apparent they would be overwhelmed if they stayed where they were. So Lieutenant Murphy gave the order. "Fall back!"

There was only one way to go—down. The problem was, they had no idea just how far down it was, not being able to see over the edge of the precipice where they stood. At that moment, however, it was certain death on three sides and probable death below. They opted for probable.

One by one the men crawled out of their covered positions and let the laws of physics do the rest. They slid down the incredibly steep slope on their backs, out of control and praying for a miracle.

Luttrell and Murphy hit the bottom first, like a couple of bags of wet cement. They were still trying to determine if all of their limbs were functioning when a fusillade of bullets, RPGs, and hand grenades sent them diving for the cover of some downed trees. That was when Luttrell noticed Lieutenant Murphy was wounded. But having lost all their medical equipment in the fall and with grenades still showering them with shrapnel, rocks, and dirt, there was nothing they could do but face uphill and fight back.

Both SEALs continued picking off advancing Taliban fighters coming toward them down the mountainside. As the two men fired repeatedly, covering each other, Axelson arrived much the same way they had and joined them in dropping the seemingly endless supply of enemy fighters. Then the limp figure of Danny Dietz came rolling down the mountain and stopped, apparently lifeless in front of their covered position.

Despite his own wounds, Murphy joined Luttrell in braving enemy fire to drag their unconscious teammate back to the downed trees. A moment later, Dan came to, and though he was gravely injured and obviously in great pain, he gritted his teeth and began killing Taliban.

They held as long as they could, but the sheer number of enemy fighters finally forced the SEALs to head downhill once again. As they tried to make their escape, Dietz took an AK round in the back and then another in the neck—either one should have put him out of the fight for good. But in an incredible display of sheer willpower, he continued firing.

The beleaguered special operators fell back once more and continued whittling away at the enemy. But then Dietz was hit twice more—and the last round finally tore the life from the devout family man. Moments later, Matt Axelson was hit in the chest and then both he and Murphy were shot yet again.

Navy SEALs operating in Afghanistan in support of Operation Enduring Freedom. From left to right, Sonar Technician (Surface) 2nd Class Matthew G. Axelson, Senior Chief Information Systems Technician Daniel R. Healy of Exeter, Quartermaster 2nd Class James Suh, Hospital Corpsman 2nd Class Marcus Luttrell, Machinist's Mate 2nd Class Eric S. Patton, and Lt Michael P. Murphy.

CH-47 Chinook Helicopter

As scores of Taliban fighters closed in on them, Lieutenant Michael Murphy got up and by sheer will, crawled out into the only open spot where he might be able to establish communications—directly in the line of enemy fire. In his hand was a phone—their last hope for calling in a rescue force. He sat down in an exposed position and placed a call to headquarters. As he was speaking, he was shot again in the back and dropped the phone. Somehow, with bullets striking all around him, he managed to retrieve it, finished his call for help, and staggered back to the others to continue the fight. Shortly afterwards both Murphy and Axleson succumbed to their many wounds, leaving Marcus Luttrell as the only survivor. He continued fighting until he was blown over a cliff by a rocket-propelled grenade and knocked unconscious.

Lieutenant Murphy's call for help succeeded. Before he died, a QRF—Quick Reaction Force—was rushing to the scene—eight more SEALs and eight crewmen in a Night Stalker MH-47, hoping against hope they would arrive in time to rescue their teammates.

Unfortunately, the rescue operation quickly went all wrong. As the Chinook descended to a hover, preparing to fast-rope the SEALs to the ground, a Taliban fighter stood and fired an RPG right through the open ramp, instantly transforming the helicopter into a blazing inferno, and the mission into the largest disaster in SEAL history. The chopper crashed to the mountainside and rolled, flaming, several hundred yards down the mountain. There were no survivors.

Marcus Luttrell regained consciousness in a hole, bleeding, and covered with dirt. Now alone, he tucked himself into a crevasse and sat, unmoving as he listened to scores of enemy fighters scouring the mountain, looking for him. As darkness fell,

Marcus knew he was on his own in hostile territory. His superiors back at base had only a vague idea of his whereabouts. He still had his weapon and some ammo, but little else. Even his trousers had been torn from his body.

It would have been easy for Luttrell, wounded, alone, and still hunted on that mountain, to stay hidden in hopes that another rescue party would be dispatched to come and find him. If the Taliban discovered him first, he could have gone down fighting, taking as many Taliban as possible with him. That would have been the easy way out. But Marcus Luttrell now had a new mission. He had to make it out of there alive, not for himself, but so the extraordinary heroic deeds of Michael Murphy, Matt Axelson, and Danny Dietz could be told to the world. When his friends went down on that godforsaken mountain, he wanted nothing more than to die alongside them. Now, he understood he'd been spared for a reason—and he resolved to do everything in his power to make it back.

Escape became its own incredible ordeal. He dragged himself along in incredible pain, crawling at times, desperately thirsty. Along the way he cried out to God, begging for help. Instead, he got a bullet in the thigh. Spotted by a Taliban sniper, Marcus felt the round rip through the flesh of his left leg. This sent him crashing down the mountain again, as more enemy chased him with a fusillade of AK fire. He crawled into a concealed position badly wounded, exhausted, and dehydrated—but he was still a SEAL, and prayer was answered when he got the drop on a group of three Taliban—killing them before they did the same to him.

He resumed his search for water, and by the time he found it, he was passing in and out of consciousness.

He was plunging his entire head into the rippling brook, sucking down mouthfuls of the sweetest water he'd ever tasted when he saw them looking at him. Three men. Two of them armed.

If he had been able, he would have shot them where they stood. But he was completely spent. He had nothing left. And that fact, saved his life.

Afghan shepherd

The men were from a tribal village opposed to the Taliban. They gently picked him up and took him to the home of a village elder, who treated his wounds. The villagers protected him day and night, even when the Taliban came and demanded that he be turned over to them. There he remained, weak and in pain for several days, unsure of his fate.

In the meantime, the military was mounting one of the largest combat search and rescue operations ever conducted, in a massive effort to find the missing SEAL team. Eventually, a man from the village where Luttrell was being sheltered, made his way to a nearby Marine base with a handwritten note informing them of his whereabouts. A short time later, a force of U.S. Army Rangers found Luttrell as he was being moved to another village.

Danny Dietz, Matt Axelson, and Marcus Luttrell received the Navy Cross for their heroic actions on 28 June 2005. Their team leader, Lieutenant Michael Murphy, was awarded the Medal of Honor.

Two years later Ahmad Shah, the man Murphy's team was sent to find, was killed in a shoot-out with a Pakistani Army unit in the Federally Administered Tribal Area near the Af-Pak border.

Matt Axelson, James Suh, Michael Russell, and Michael Murphy, all killed in Operation Redwing

MEDAL OF HONOR: LIEUTENANT MICHAEL P. MURPHY

For service as set forth in the following citation:

For conspicuous gallantry and intrepidity at the risk of his life above and beyond the call of duty as the leader of a Special Reconnaissance Element with Naval Special Warfare Task Unit Afghanistan on 27 and 28 June 2005. While leading a mission to locate a high-level anti-coalition militia leader, Lieutenant Murphy demonstrated extraordinary heroism in the face of grave danger in the vicinity of Asadabad, Konar Province, Afghanistan. On 28 June 2005, operating in an extremely rugged enemy-controlled area, Lieutenant Murphy's team was discovered by anti-coalition militia sympathizers, who revealed their position to Taliban fighters. As a result, between thirty and forty enemy fighters besieged his four-member team. Demonstrating exceptional resolve, Lieutenant Murphy valiantly led his men in engaging the large enemy force. The ensuring fierce firefight resulted in numerous enemy casualties, as well as the wounding of all four members of the team. Ignoring his own wounds and demonstrating exceptional composure, Lieutenant Murphy continued to lead and encourage his men. When the primary communicator fell mortally wounded, Lieutenant Murphy repeatedly attempted to call for assistance for his beleaguered teammates. Realizing the impossibility of communicating in the extreme terrain, and in the face of almost certain death, he fought his way into open terrain to gain a better position to transmit a call. This deliberate, heroic act deprived him of cover, exposing him to direct enemy fire. Finally achieving contact with his headquarters, Lieutenant Murphy maintained his exposed position while he provided his location and requested immediate support for his team. In his final act of bravery, he continued to engage the enemy until he was mortally wounded, gallantly giving his life for his country and for the cause of freedom. By his selfless leadership, courageous actions, and extraordinary devotion to duty, Lieutenant Murphy reflected great credit upon himself and upheld the highest traditions of the United States Naval Service.

Signed, George W. Bush

A portrait of Lt Michael P. Murphy is unveiled at a ceremony in his honor.

2006

F-16 Fighting Falcon Jet Fighters

22 JUN 06

OPERATION KAIKA

KANDAHAR PROVINCE, AFGHANISTAN

In early 2006, the government in Islamabad, Pakistan, enforced an edict to close Afghan refugee camps in their territory. At the time, nearly 2.5 million Afghans, many of them supporters of the deposed Taliban regime, were sequestered in Pakistan.

Taliban leaders like Mullah Omar in Quetta used the measure to launch a resurgent movement in their homeland. Taliban cadre, rearmed and trained by radical Islamists in the Pakistani Inter-Services Intelligence (ISI) Directorate, were infiltrated across the border—with the mission of building armed resistance to the democratically elected Karzai government in Kabul. The Taliban's immediate objective: re-establish

Aerial view of an Afghan village

their authority and impose Sharia Law in Kandahar and Helmand Provinces—their traditional heartland in southern Afghanistan.

To counter the Taliban moves, the NATO-led Coalition committed more than eleven thousand U.S., British, Canadian, and Afghan soldiers to Operation Mountain Thrust. With the mission of securing key population centers and going directly after insurgent leaders, it was the largest operation mounted in the war that had simmered in the shadows of the Hindu Kush for five long years.

One portion of Operation Mountain Thrust was a Special Forces mission dubbed Operation Kaika. *Kaika* means "tick"—the blood-sucking insect in Pashto—the "official" dialect in Afghanistan.

The Kaika operation plan called for ODA 765 of the 7th Special Forces Group to accompany a unit of forth-eight Afghan soldiers on a capture-kill mission in the village of Pashmul, about twelve miles southwest of Kandahar. Human and communications intelligence indicated that a wanted Taliban commander was there.

Capt Sheffield Ford

The seventeen Americans, nine Green Berets, four Special Operations communication specialists, two Embedded Training Team Members, (National Guard NCOs), the Air Force Special Operations Joint Tactical Air Controller (JTAC), and the Army MP, K-9 handler, (and "Billy" an explosives-sniffing dog) all had extensive combat experience. Captain Sheffield Ford, a California native, commanded the mission. He spent nearly ten years as a Special Forces Engineer and served in the 1st Special Forces Group on a Dive Detachment before receiving a commission through Officer Candidate School.

The Detachment Team Sergeant was Master Sergeant Thomas D. Maholic, a seventeen-year SF veteran from Pennsylvania who commenced his career as a Special Forces Medic. He went on to become a Special Forces Diver, Dive Supervisor, and Dive Medical Supervisor. Like many of his mates, Maholic also served on a Special Forces mountain team and had a reputation for exceptional physical fitness.

The team medic was one of the rarest soldiers in the Army—forty-six-year-old Sergeant First Class Brendan O'Connor. The fifth of six children, O'Connor was born at the United States Military Academy at West Point while his father was stationed there. Seven years later, his father, then a Lieutenant Colonel, deployed to the Vietnam War. He was killed in action while leading his battalion during a battle in Bin Duong province.

Sgt First Class Brendan O'Connor

Brendan, determined to follow his father's footsteps, was commissioned in 1980 and spent the next fourteen years as an Army Reserve Special Forces Officer. Then, in an act that surprised and confounded his peers, he resigned his commission in 1994, enlisted in the regular Army, and qualified as a Special Forces medic. It's not uncommon for a soldier to start out enlisted and later become an officer, but to go the opposite direction said a lot about what was important to Brendan O'Connor.

A typical Afghan home

The Kaika mission was slated to last up to six days. The team moved into the village in the last hours of the evening on the 22 of June to find most of it abandoned. This wasn't particularly alarming to the men of ODA 765. They knew villagers often fled to avoid Taliban brutality when the insurgents moved into an area.

The ODA and their Afghan counterparts set up a patrol base in an abandoned compound. It was the typical Afghan home—a mini-fortress where the home, animal pens, out-buildings, and the high, surrounding courtyard wall were all constructed of sun-baked mud bricks. Usually a foot thick or more, walls like these will withstand machine gun fire, rockets, and even missiles fired from an attack helicopter.

Throughout the day the ODA searched the area around the compound, cleaned weapons, and alternated through periods of standing security and rest. All was quiet as dusk fell. But immediately after dark, in the words of Captain Ford, "All hell broke loose."

Undetected, a large force of Taliban fighters had been hiding on the outskirts of the village, waiting to attack. Even with their Afghan counterparts, engaged in the fight, Ford could tell by the volume of incoming machine gun and rocket fire they were outnumbered, outgunned, and surrounded.

The team took cover and fought back. But the foe was well-disciplined and organized, something that surprised the Green Berets. This was unlike any of their previous engagements. Usually enemy fire was sporadic, from insurgents who fired wildly in a "hit-and-run" contact. Few Taliban units wanted head-to-head confrontations with coalition forces. Rarely did they ever initiate action other than indirect fire attacks with rockets or mortars at night.

This time everything was different. Throughout the night and well into the next day, Taliban fighters steadily advanced on their position, employing the same small-unit tactics the Americans were teaching the Afghan soldiers. These insurgents weren't just trying to kill a few Americans and then slink away. They clearly intended to wipe out the entire patrol.

Mortar rounds began dropping nearby, marching closer with each teeth-rattling explosion. Neither the Americans nor their Afghan counterparts were accustomed to Taliban fighters who were actually trained on how to use indirect fire weapons effectively.

The men of the ODA spent the entire day at their fighting positions around the perimeter—interspersed among the Afghan soldiers, pouring fire back at the enemy. Through the din of battle, Captain Ford moved from man to man encouraging them, paying special attention to the Afghan soldiers, some of whom were clearly terrified and on the verge of breaking.

At one point the Taliban actually broke into their perimeter, but were pushed back by a deafening volley of fire. The situation looked bleak until several fixed-wing aircraft arrived overhead. Directed by the ODA JTAC, the allied jets broke the Taliban attack with a rain of bombs and rocket fire. By dark, the insurgents had melted back into the hills around the village.

Throughout the night, Captain Ford had the American and Afghan soldiers adjust their defenses to confound a renewed Taliban attack. Shortly before dawn, an Afghan Army listening post alerted the perimeter to an insurgent force moving into position for another assault. An ODA sniper team engaged the Taliban, temporarily disrupting their strike while the JTAC summoned Air Force jets and then attack helicopters to support the defenders. The early morning attack dissipated under the defensive fires.

A U.S. soldier from 1st Infantry Division prepares an RQ-11 Raven miniature unmanned aerial vehicle (UAV).

Convinced the best defense would be a good offense, Ford sent out combat patrols in several directions. He also deployed the team's small man-portable, RQ-11 Raven unmanned aerial vehicle (UAV). The tiny UAV looks, for all intents and purposes, like a remote controlled model Cessna, but carries color video and night-vision cameras, from which it streams live video to the ODA operator.

From the RQ-11 imagery, the Americans identified a compound that appeared to be the place from which the Taliban commander was directing the battle. It was near the village cemetery, about a third of a mile west of the SF team.

Master Sergeant Thomas D. Maholic, the detachment's senior NCO, now armed with the UAV data, devised a plan to disrupt the Taliban attack by taking down the enemy command and control site. Maholic quickly assembled a patrol and led them on the double through a network of irrigation ditches toward the objective.

Maholic, a tri-athlete, was renowned for his physical fitness and was legendary for finding unique ways to stay fit. When the ODA was operating from Firebase Gheko—near the "hometown" of Taliban chieftain Mullah Omar—he led endurance runs in full combat kit up and down the rock promontory protruding nine hundred feet about their base.

Now, despite their heavy gear and the heat, the Master Sergeant set a blistering pace, hoping to surprise the enemy. As they approached their objective, he emplaced a fire-support element in a position where they could bring their automatic weapons to bear, then led the assault element of his patrol to envelop the Taliban compound through an orchard. It was a good plan. But it didn't work.

Taliban machine guns, invisible on the RQ-11 imagery, opened up from the left, hitting one of the medics, Staff Sergeant Matthew Binney in the head, fracturing his skull. Thought the wound was not fatal, it rendered Binney unable to hear and he was seeing double. Nevertheless, he got back up and continued to fight. While leading a grenade assault upon one of the Taliban machine gun positions, he was hit a second time, a heavy round smashing into his shoulder, nearly severing his arm.

An enemy fighter stood up and fired a rocket-propelled grenade at him. The fifteen-pound warhead crossed the length of a football field in less than a second and hit his partner, Staff Sergeant Joe Fuerst II in the leg. Though the round failed to detonate, the blunt force trauma all but severed his leg and he began to bleed profusely. He struggled to place a tourniquet on it with help from Jacob, their interpreter, but soon passed out from loss of blood. The only man left uninjured at their position was the twenty-one-year-old Afghan translator. He began firing his rifle, doing his best to hold off the advancing enemy and even shielding his wounded comrades with his own body.

An Iraqi policeman has a rocket-propelled grenade launcher, which can penetrate a wall if needed.

The Taliban were now advancing through the orchard, getting close enough to taunt Jacob—telling him they would let him go if he laid down his weapon and allowed them to capture the Americans alive. In reply, Jacob goaded the enemy fighters to approach and then opened fire. Well aware of what the Taliban would do to his friends if they were captured, Jacob used an undamaged radio to call Captain Ford, informing him that he was prepared to kill the two wounded Americans and then himself to save them from the horrors the enemy would doubtless visit upon them.

"Negative! Negative!" Ford shouted into the radio. "We have people coming to get you. Just hold on!"

But Ford's rescue resources were extremely limited. His ODA and their Afghan allies were now separated into three groups, each surrounded by heavily-armed enemy fighters whose supply of ammunition seemed limitless. And after more than eight hours of fighting, he was beginning to wonder how much longer his Afghan soldiers would hold out.

Tara and Joe Fuerst

Back at the base in Kandahar, Sergeant Tara Fuerst was hard at work in her office. The wife of SSG Joe Fuerst, the two deployed together to Afghanistan nearly a year earlier, just months after their wedding. She was an intelligence analyst at the airbase in Kandahar. Joe, of course, spent nearly all his deployment on remote bases in the field. Though their "in-country" reunions were infrequent and brief, they had recently decided to voluntarily extend their tours of duty in Afghanistan to save money for the house they were building back home.

As she sat working at her computer, she saw a notice scroll across the screen that a team from 7th group was engaged in a "TIC"—meaning Troops In Contact. She called Joe's cell phone but got no answer. Then, more information on the engagement came in—including the battle roster numbers of the wounded. Among them was that of her husband and the knowledge turned her insides to ice.

Afghan police

A squad of Afghan police, dispatched from Kandahar City arrived at the village and attempted to break through to the beleaguered team. They were beaten back with such ferocity that five of them were killed outright and several more wounded. Estimates put the number of enemy fighters arrayed against ODA 765 and their handful of Afghan allies at more than two hundred.

Though he had nobody to spare, rescuing the two gravely wounded Green Berets was already Captain Ford's top priority. He decided to launch a Quick Reaction Force (QRF) led by SFC Brendan O'Connor. The officer-turned-medic gathered eight-men; including SFC Sean Mishra, a former regular Army Green Beret, now serving with the Oregon National Guard as a mentor for the Afghan Army unit they were advising. O'Connor and Mishra consulted the RQ-11 imagery and pinpointed on the map the probable location of their surrounded fire support element.

But as the QRF departed the patrol base they immediately took fire from Taliban machine guns. They had to fire and maneuver just to get to the position where Thom Maholic and SFC Abram Hernandez were busy protecting Binney's beleaguered fire-support element with well aimed carbine fire, while working the radios to keep air strikes on the Taliban surrounding them.

O'Connor and the QRF fought their way to Maholic and Hernandez without casualties, but they still had to get to the wounded Binney, Fuerst, and Jacob, the interpreter. That meant they would have to traverse an open field which was swept by Taliban machine gun fire.

O'Connor knew that no matter how fast he ran, he wouldn't make it across the field alive. So he started crawling instead.

Orchard outside an Afghan village

His first attempt, face down, inching along, wearing his helmet, body armor, and ammunition pouches nearly got him killed. The armor and ammunition pouches beneath him pushed his profile too high in the thin vegetation, so he crawled back in the cover of an irrigation ditch, removed his armored vest, slung his magazines over his shoulder and began again.

With nothing now shielding him from enemy fire, O'Connor pressed his body into the earth, willing himself to get smaller as he crawled out into the no-man's land. He moved carefully, pushing his weapon in front of him as Taliban machine gun bursts raked the air above him, some so close they seemed to mow the grass through which he moved.

The rest of the team rallied to pin down the Taliban who were trying to get to Binney and Fuerst. Team Sergeant Maholic took up an exposed position on the roof of a building and loosed volley after volley of well-placed fire. SFC Abram Hernandez had to fire with one hand while he used his other to brace himself on a rickety ladder perched against the mud wall of the compound.

Their covering fire proved invaluable to O'Connor. The vegetation he used for concealment while crawling across the field ended twenty yards short of the vineyard wall where Jacob was protecting Binney and Fuerst. With no other choice, he bolted from his prone position, sprinted to the wall, and vaulted over it before the surprised Taliban gunners could adjust their fire.

Protected by the low wall, O'Connor, crouched low, began picking his way through the rows of grapevines searching for Jacob, Joe, and Matt. When he found them, he immediately began treating their injuries only stopping to exchange fire with the Taliban fighters still intent on overwhelming the beleaguered team. With the help of Jacob and a coordinated barrage of fire by the other members of the team, O'Connor pulled the wounded men to the shelter of a nearby compound and began first aid in earnest. SSG Binney might have died from loss of blood were it not for O'Connor's daring maneuver. For Joe Fuerst, it was too late. Despite his own and Jacob's efforts to stop the flow of blood from his shattered leg, he succumbed to his wounds shortly after O'Connor reached him.

While O'Connor turned his full attention to Binney, one hundred fifty yards away things were going from bad to worse. Thom Maholic took a Taliban bullet in the head and went down. Abram Hernandez jumped down from his ladder and ran to his side, but there was nothing he could do. He cradled the tough-as-nails team Sergeant in his arms as he died.

With night falling once again, the surviving Green Berets took stock of their situation. Ammunition was running low; two of their teammates were dead, and a third badly wounded. Three of their Afghan soldiers were also killed. Every man wondered how much longer they could hold. Even the bombs and missiles being dropped on the enemy by orbiting helicopters and fighter jets didn't seem to slow the Taliban onslaught.

Captain Ford, determined to extricate his men from their perilous position under cover of darkness, found a place where helicopters could land approximately six hundred meters from their patrol base. Getting there would mean running the same gauntlet O'Connor braved to rescue SSG Binney and Fuerst. But this time, it was dark. They were all equipped with night vision goggles and there were two Apache Attack helicopters overhead with an arsenal of heavy weaponry.

Ford coordinated with the Apache pilots to have the aircraft "paint" a lane with their nose-mounted infrared lasers that would stretch from their current position to the landing zone. The team then moved out along that lane—visible only with their night-vision goggles— and the Apaches engaged anything that moved outside of that illuminated pathway. The plan worked. Before dawn, the Americans and their Afghan counterparts safely boarded rescue helicopters for the flight to Kandahar.

Apache helicopter

When they arrived, Tara Fuerst was waiting on the flight line for her husband. Two of the medics who knew her walked where she was standing and with tears in their eyes, simply shook their heads and embraced her. No words were necessary. Tara knew. She collapsed into their arms, sobbing.

The next day, the surviving members of ODA 765 gathered inside a giant C-17 cargo transport on the airfield in Kandahar and saluted as the flag-draped metal transfer cases containing the bodies of Thom Maholic and Joe Fuerst were boarded. In a brief, tearful ceremony, the team honored their fallen comrades, wrapped their arms around each other's shoulders, and prayed over the men they lost.

Two days later, Tara Fuerst returned to the United States. Another ceremony followed months later when ODA 765 returned home to Fort Bragg. MSG Maholic was posthumously awarded the Silver Star as were Binney, Ford, and Hernandez. In addition, Five Bronze Star Medals and Three Army Commendation Medals with V-device for valor were awarded for Operation Kaika. Master Sergeant Brendan W. O'Connor was subsequently awarded the Distinguished Service Cross.

Tara Fuerst struggled for more than a year with the loss of her husband. In the depths of her grief, she became aware of an organization devoted to young war widows called The American Widow Project. The camaraderie she found there helped her cope with her grief and she now devotes her time to helping others through the organization.

Taryn Davis, right, supported by military wife, Shannon Williford, center, and Davis's mother, Tobi Guerrero, at the memorial service for Davis's husband, Cpl Michael Davis, in San Marcos, Texas. Davis created "The American Widow Project" (AWP) in late 2007.

DISTINGUISHED SERVICE CROSS:
BRENDAN W. O'CONNOR

The President of the United States of America, authorized by Act of Congress, July 9, 1918 (amended by act of July 25, 1963), takes pleasure in presenting the Distinguished Service Cross to Master Sergeant Brendan W. O'Connor, United States Army, for extraordinary heroism in combat as the Senior Medical Sergeant for Special Forces Operational Detachment Alpha 765 (ODA 765), Company A, 2d Battalion, 7th Special Forces Group (Airborne), in support of Operation Enduring Freedom, in Panjawal District, Kandahar Province, Afghanistan. On 24 June 2006, while conducting Operation KAIKA, Sergeant O'Connor led a quick-reaction force to reinforce a surrounded patrol and rescue two wounded comrades. He maneuvered his force through Taliban positions and crawled alone and unprotected, under enemy machine gun fire to reach the wounded soldiers. He provided medical care while exposed to heavy volumes of Taliban fire, then carried one of the wounded 150 meters across open ground to an area of temporary cover. Sergeant First Class O'Connor then climbed over a wall three times, in plain view of the enemy, to assist the wounded soldiers in seeking cover while bullets pounded the structure around them. Sergeant First Class O'Connor assumed duties as the detachment operations sergeant and led the consolidation of three friendly elements, each surrounded, isolated, and receiving fire from all directions. Sergeant First Class O'Connor's distinctive accomplishments and dedication to his comrades are in keeping with the finest traditions of military service and reflect great credit upon himself, the Special Operations Command Central, and the United States Army.

Maj Sheffield Ford and Master Sgt Brendan O'Connor listen to a question during an interview with Lara Logan, a CBS news reporter, at the John F. Kennedy Special Warfare Museum in Fort Bragg, North Carolina, for a *60 Minutes* story on Operation Kaika, the 2006 operation in Afghanistan that resulted in the most decorated Special Forces Operational Detachment-Alpha in the war on terror.

SILVER STAR MEDAL: SHEFFIELD F. FORD III

Citation: The President of the United States takes pleasure in presenting the Silver Star Medal to Sheffield F. Ford, III, Captain (Infantry), U.S. Army, for conspicuous gallantry and intrepidity in action while serving as the Detachment Commander, Operational Detachment Alpha 765 (ODA 765), Company A,

2nd Battalion, 7th Special Forces Group (Airborne), during combat operations in support of Operation Enduring Freedom, on 24 June 2006, at Pashmul, Kandahar, Afghanistan. Captain Ford's heroic actions and courageous leadership were the decisive factors in the defeat of a determined and numerically superior enemy force. His actions are in keeping with the highest traditions of military heroism and reflect distinct credit upon himself, the Combined Special Operations Task Force-Afghanistan, Special Operations Command-Central, and the United States Army.

SILVER STAR MEDAL: THOMAS D. MAHOLIC (KIA)

Citation: The President of the United States takes pride in presenting the Silver Star Medal (Posthumously) to Thomas D. Maholic, Master Sergeant, U.S. Army, for conspicuous gallantry and intrepidity in action while serving as the Detachment Operations Sergeant for Operational Detachment Alpha 765 (ODA 765), Company A, 2nd Battalion, 7th Special Forces Group (Airborne), during combat operations in support of Operation Enduring Freedom, on 24 June 2006, at Pashmul, Kandahar, Afghanistan. Master Sergeant Maholic's heroic actions defeated a Taliban attack, saved the lives of his comrades, and prevented the destruction of his team. His actions are in keeping with the highest traditions of military heroism and reflect distinct credit upon himself, the Combined Joint Special Operations Task Force-Afghanistan, Special Operations Command Central, and the United States Army.

SILVER STAR MEDAL: MATTHEW BINNEY

Citation: The President of the United States takes pleasure in presenting the Silver Star Medal to Matthew Binney, Staff Sergeant, U.S. Army, for conspicuous gallantry and intrepidity in action while serving as the Medical Sergeant for Special Forces Operational Detachment Alpha 765 (ODA 765), Company A, 2nd Battalion, 7th Special Forces Group (Airborne), during combat operations in support of Operation Enduring Freedom, at Pashmul, Kandahar, Afghanistan, on 24 June 2006.

Sergeant Binney's heroic actions, despite two serious wounds, defeated a Taliban attack, saved the lives of his comrades, and prevented the destruction of his team. His actions are in keeping with the highest traditions of military heroism and reflect distinct credit upon himself, the Combined Special Operations Task Force-Afghanistan, Special Operations Command Central, and the United States Army.

SILVER STAR MEDAL: ABRAM HERNANDEZ

Citation: The President of the United States takes pleasure in presenting the Silver Star Medal to Abram Hernandez, Sergeant First Class, U.S. Army, for conspicuous gallantry and intrepidity in action while serving as the Engineer Sergeant for Operational Detachment Alpha 765 (ODA 765), Company A, 2nd Battalion, 7th Special Forces Group (Airborne), during combat operations in support of Operation Enduring Freedom, on 24 June 2006, at Pashmul, Kandahar, Afghanistan. Sergeant

Hernandez's heroic actions and dedication to duty defeated an enemy attack, saved the lives of his comrades, and prevented the destruction of his team. His actions are in keeping with the highest traditions of military heroism and reflect distinct credit upon himself, the Combined Special Operations Task Force-Afghanistan, Special Operations Command Central, and the United States Army.

"The bravest are surely those who have the clearest vision of what is before them, glory and danger alike, and yet notwithstanding, go out to meet it."—THUCYDIDES

29 SEPT 06

OPERATION KENTUCKY JUMPER

RAMADI, IRAQ

By 2006, the city of Ramadi, capital of al-Anbar, Iraq's largest Province, was the hands-down winner for the most violent place on earth. With no functional government, Iraqi and foreign insurgents allied with al-Qaeda visited brutal terror on the city's four hundred thousand residents and made it clear they intended to drive out Coalition forces with brazen attacks on a daily basis.

From 2005 onward, every U.S. Army Combat Brigade, reinforced U.S. Marine Battalion Landing Team, and U.S. Special Operations unit deployed to the city operated with the same goal: find local Sunni leaders who would help secure the city. But recruiting local sheiks and tribal elders to joint this cause, while keeping terrorists at bay, was no simple task. It often required, as one of the Ramadi commanders put it, "a velvet glove, a lot of tea—and the selective application of precise, deadly force." One of those most expert at applying the necessary precision and force was U.S. Navy SEAL, Mike Monsoor.

Growing up in Long Beach, California, Mike as a typical all-American kid: he played football in high school, rode motorcycles, loved to spend time at the beach, and enlisted in the Navy a few months before September 11, 2001. The terror attacks that terrible day changed him forever.

After a tour in Italy as a Navy Quartermaster, Monsoor tried out for the SEALs in 2004, but a broken heel kept him from earning the SEAL trident. Undaunted, Mike recovered and went back to BUDS again in 2005, this time graduating at the top of his class. A year later, as a member of the SEAL Team 3, he deployed to Iraq as a heavy weapons machine gunner.

The team threw itself into the Ramadi mission. They mentored Iraqi military units, conducted nighttime operations into insurgent strongholds to capture or kill high value targets (HVTs), spent endless days and nights in covert observation posts and countless hours in sniper "hides." In more than three dozen combat missions, nearly three out of four resulted in enemy contact.

U.S. Navy SEAL Mike Monsoor

On several operations, Monsoor had to fire so many rounds through his MK-48 machine gun, the barrel had to be replaced. During their deployment to Ramadi, Mike's team killed dozens of enemy combatants and captured dozens more.

On one nighttime mission into the heart of the city, the SEALs were ambushed and one of them went down in the middle of the street, shot though the thigh. Monsoor immediately charged in to save his wounded comrade, holding down the trigger on his MK-48 with one hand while dragging the wounded operator to safety with the other. He continued fighting while the team medic worked to stop the bleeding, then helped load his buddy onto a Humvee before rushing back into the fight. For his actions that day he was awarded the Silver Star.

His mates say the recognition didn't change him a bit and he continued as before, serving as both machine gunner and communications specialist. This meant he often would end up carrying well over one hundred pounds of ammunition and communications gear, all day in temperatures well above one hundred ten degrees. Nobody ever heard him complain.

It isn't uncommon for seasoned warriors to reflect on the things most important to them before they go into battle. After all, those who face death on a daily basis ought to make a person more spiritual than others engaged in a more sedate line of work.

Mike Monsoor was no different. An ardent Catholic, he made a habit of attending mass before each mission. On the morning of 29 September 2006 that's where he was, praying alongside the chaplain, Father Paul Halladay, shortly before the SEALs headed out on a mission code named Kentucky Jumper.

A large combined-force operation involving the U.S. Army Combat Brigade, the Marine Battalion, the SEALs, and Iraqi Army units, the goal was to establish new security posts in the heart of insurgent-controlled territory and neutralize any pockets of resistance.

The SEALs were given the mission of protecting the most endangered flank of the U.S. and Iraqi ground forces as they entered the heart of the city. Twelve men—four SEALs and eight hand-picked Iraqi soldiers were to covertly take up a position on a rooftop inside one of Ramadi's worst neighborhoods and ensure

the heavy U.S. and Iraqi column moving into the city wouldn't be hit by a surprise counter-attack from the west.

Under cover of darkness, the SEALs and their Iraqi counterparts moved quickly and quietly to occupy the designated rooftop. As anticipated, the location afforded good visibility over routes the enemy might use as the operation went forward. As soon as the sun came up, the SEALs on the exposed rooftop quickly became hot—but their vantage point was too good to vacate seeking shade.

As the main column slowly approached the heart of the city up "Route Michigan"—the main road through the center of Ramadi—the SEALs spotted four insurgents carrying AK-47s. They appeared to be scouting the American-Iraqi advance. The SEAL snipers engaged, killing one, and wounding another but the two remaining fighters managed to escape—and the SEALs knew they had announced their presence in a very unfriendly neighborhood.

The word spread quickly. In a matter of minutes, they could see people out blocking off streets and alleys leading to their position. Their escape routes soon closed. Then came the eerie sound of a loudspeaker in a nearby mosque, calling all fighters to repel the Coalition forces.

With the eight Iraqi soldiers guarding the street-level doors and windows below them, the four SEALs knew they would be in for a very lopsided fight if the insurgents decided to obey the local imam. All of them hoped the approaching U.S. forces—and the sniper "hits" would be enough to discourage an attack on their position.

Their hopes were dashed when a carload of armed thugs came speeding toward their building, already firing at them from open windows. Monsoor and the others on the roof opened up on it with everything they had. Then, a rocket-propelled grenade came streaking toward them from one of the barricades down the street. The SEALs and their Iraqi counterparts were stunned as the missile impact shook the building. Before the dust cleared, the SEALs resumed firing, breaking the attack.

The team commander was running out of options. Their position was now completely compromised and they would continue to be targets as long as they stayed. But their escape routes now appeared to be sealed. And abandoning their position would put the left flank of the advancing column of U.S. and Iraqi troops at greater risk. So despite the danger, the team decided to stand and fight.

Monsoor and two SEAL snipers positioned themselves at a rooftop corner to gain a better vantage over the most likely avenue of approach. Behind them as they faced outward, there was a doorway leading downstairs from the rooftop. Monsoor was surveying the street below with a tactical periscope when an insurgent somewhere below hurled a grenade onto the rooftop. It struck Monsoor in the chest and dropped down in the midst of his fellow SEALS. Since he was standing only a few feet from the doorway leading off the rooftop, he could have easily dived through it and saved himself from the blast.

But that wasn't Michael Monsoor.

Instead, the young SEAL shouted "Grenade!" and dropped on top of the device just as it detonated. The explosion threw up a cloud of dust and when it cleared, Monsoor lay mortally wounded, having saved the lives of his teammates. The two snipers were both hit by shrapnel, but they survived because of his heroic sacrifice.

Mike Monsoor was a fighter. Despite his horrific wounds, he stayed alive for half an hour after the blast—long enough to be evacuated to a field hospital and one last visit with Father Halladay, who administered last rites before he died.

Those who served with Mike Monsoor knew his selfless sacrifice was an incredible gift. Every man on the rooftop that day remains convinced they would have died had Monsoor not intentionally jumped on that grenade. But Monsoor's heroism extended

far beyond just those whose lives he saved on that rooftop. Having been in the company of such a hero is itself an amazing privilege—one acknowledged by hundreds of SEALs on the day of his funeral at Fort Rosecrans National Cemetery in San Diego, California. After his mother was given the carefully folded flag that draped his casket, a long line of his SEAL brethren stepped forward to pound their gold tridents into the polished wooden lid. It was a powerful testament—one reflected in the eulogy one of his fellow SEALs offered at the funeral: "Mike Monsoor's service to the band of brothers is a part of our unit history that will never fade. His contribution is as good a part of our history as any of the streamers that hang from our colors."

Mike Monsoor was posthumously awarded the Bronze Star and Purple Heart. Then, in 2008, President George Bush presented the twenty-five-year-old Petty Officer's parents with their son's Medal of Honor—our nation's highest recognition for valor.

Michael A. Monsoor, recipient of the Medal of Honor, the Silver Star, the Bronze Star, the Purple Heart, and a Combat Action Ribbon, is the most highly decorated sailor since the 9/11 attack.

MEDAL OF HONOR: MASTER-AT-ARMS SECOND CLASS (SEA, AIR, AND LAND) MICHAEL A. MONSOOR, UNITED STATES NAVY

For service as set forth in the following Citation: for conspicuous gallantry and intrepidity at the risk of his life above and beyond the call of duty as automatic weapons gunner for Naval Special Warfare Task Group Arabian Peninsula, in support of Operation Iraqi Freedom on 29 September 2006. As a member of a combined SEAL and Iraqi Army sniper over-watch element, tasked with providing early warning and stand-off protection from a rooftop in an insurgent held sector of Ar Ramadi, Iraq, Petty Officer Monsoor distinguished himself by his exceptional bravery in the face of grave danger. In the early morning, insurgents prepared to execute a coordinated attack by reconnoitering the area around the element's position. Element snipers thwarted the enemy's initial attempt by eliminating two insurgents. The enemy continued to assault the element, engaging them with a rocket-propelled grenade and small arms fire. As enemy activity increased, Petty Officer Monsoor took position with his machine gun between two teammates on an outcropping of the roof. While the SEALs vigilantly watched for enemy activity, an insurgent threw a hand grenade from an unseen location, which bounced off Petty Officer Monsoon's chest and landed in front of him. Although only he could have escaped the blast, Petty Officer Monsoor chose instead to protect his teammates. Instantly and without regard for his own safety, he threw himself onto the grenade to absorb the force of the explosion with his body, saving the lives of his two teammates. By his undaunted courage, fighting spirit, and unwavering devotion to duty in the face of certain death, Petty Officer Monsoor gallantly gave his life for country, thereby reflecting great credit upon himself and upholding the highest traditions of the United States Naval Service.

Signed, George W. Bush

27 NOV 06

COOPER'S LITTLE BIRD

TALIL, IRAQ

★ ★ ★ ★ ★ ★ ★ ★ ★ ★ ★ ★

This is it. This is how it ends.

David Cooper knew today was his day to die. Strangely enough, while the thought scared him at first, the fear was replaced by a strange sense of calm and a burning desire to provide those who were trying to kill him their own trip to the afterlife.

The mission should have been simple. As the lead pilot of a flight of six Hughes 500 helicopters, Cooper was supposed to accompany a Special Operators task force into a very bad neighborhood north of Baghdad. The ground troops were to ride to the objective on four modified MH-6s, kick in the door of a wanted "foreign fighter facilitator," take him into custody, and head home. In and out in only a few minutes, while Cooper and his wingmen in their AH-6s bored holes in the sky overhead, each with a full load of fourteen 2.75-inch rockets and two thousand rounds of 7.62-mm for their minigun, just in case.

But they never made it that far. They were en-route to the objective, the two attack helicopters bristling with rockets and miniguns and the four troop-carrying Little Birds following behind. Each of the Little Birds had side pods carrying several men in full combat gear, their legs dangling in the breeze. A Black Hawk helicopter carrying more SOF forces brought up the rear. Twenty operators and fourteen pilots. The day was cool by Baghdad standards, only eighty degrees and a cloudless sky overhead. A perfect day for flying. Then, Cooper's radio crackled to life with the one word no aviator wants to hear.

"Mayday, Mayday, Mayday!" The call was coming from the second AH-6, flying beside him.

"We're hit!" the pilot continued. "RPG!"

An unseen insurgent below loosed a rocket-propelled grenade at the passing formation. With no heat-seeking guidance system, the shooter's chances of actually hitting one of the small, fast-flying helicopters were slim. But this time, he got lucky. And a lucky shot could kill you just as dead as a skillful one.

Chief Warrant Officer 5 David F. Cooper in an AH-6 Little Bird helicopter. Cooper is an AH-6 pilot and the Senior Warrant Officer of the 160th Special Operations Aviation Regiment (Airborne).

Cooper could see the craft next to him was missing its tail rotor. It could still fly without it, as long as it didn't slow down. The problem was, landing a helicopter at seventy miles per hour, while not impossible, certainly isn't ideal. Fortunately, Cooper and his fellow pilots were members of the 160th Special Operations Aviation Regiment, which boasts the best combat pilots in the world, bar none.

They spied a stretch of flat, open ground below. Time for an emergency landing. Though both pilots in the damaged bird sustained minor injuries from the RPG, they skillfully guided their wounded helicopter in for a landing, almost like a small plane would make. It touched down, bounced and skidded several hundred yards to a stop in the middle of the open area, about eight hundred meters from a group of houses. The rest of the choppers landed as well and the ground assault force took up a defensive perimeter around the downed chopper. The two wounded pilots were quickly put aboard the Black Hawk and flown back to base for treatment. The rest of the unit pulled security and waited while arrangements were made for a larger chopper to come and sling-load the broken AH-6 back to base. It would then be sent back to the States for repairs.

Then, somebody spotted approaching trucks. They were civilian pick-ups with large automatic weapons mounted in their beds.

CW5 Cooper could feel his day getting worse by the moment.

He grabbed his copilot and quickly fired up his AH-6. The trucks were still more than a kilometer from the crash site. Cooper intended to fly out to meet the trucks and see if they were friend or foe.

The Little Bird lifted off and flew toward the approaching vehicles. Cooper counted six of them, each mounted with a ZPU-12 anti-aircraft gun. Wonderful. Just great. Seconds later, the trucks opened up directly at him, lobbing what looked like flaming volleyballs in his direction.

The first helicopter Cooper learned to fly was the AH-64 Apache—an armor-plated marvel, bristling with advanced weaponry. A pair of them would have vaporized all six trucks in less time than it takes to write about it.

The Little Bird, on the other hand, was originally designed as an observation helicopter. In the Vietnam war, pilots flew them low and slow above the treetops in an attempt to lure the enemy into firing at them. If that happened, the "Cayuse" as it was called, would flit away and call in a real attack helicopter to destroy the enemy position.

Then someone got the bright idea to hang a few rockets and then a minigun on the little helicopter. Over the years, it got a bigger engine and more advanced electronics. But it still didn't have a targeting reticle. No, for that, the pilot made a small "X" on the windscreen with a grease pencil, and simply pointed the whole helicopter at whatever he wanted to kill.

Cooper was one of the most experienced little bird pilots in the air. High-tech electronics or no, the Iraqi insurgents were shooting at the wrong pilot.

He juked the chopper left and right, up and down, drawing the enemy fire away from the small force on the ground. The sound of large-caliber bullets snapping past his windscreen sounded like popcorn, and he figured it was a matter of time before one of them struck home. But he knew the small ground force was exposed in the open field without cover. If the gun trucks got to them, the results would be catastrophic.

He lined up his Little Bird and made a run at the trucks, loosing off a burst with his 7.62-mm miniguns, which shredded the cab of one of the trucks. That got their attention. Cooper went at them again, this time firing off a couple of 2.75-inch rockets before changing course and eluding their antiaircraft fire once again.

"They're shooting at us! They're shooting at us!" his copilot yelled as they turned over a small group of mud-brick compounds.

"Yeah, I know they're shooting at us, I can see them." Cooper replied tersely.

"No, look down!" The copilot pointed to the houses. "Them! They're shooting at us!"

Cooper looked down and spied at least twenty men running around the courtyard below with AK-47s and RPGs. This just wasn't his day. Things were looking worse for the friendlies on the ground, too, since the fighters at the house below were in range of the crash site.

He made another run at the gun trucks, miniguns blazing. Then he came back and fired a couple of rockets at the house. His copilot unstrapped his rifle from the seat and began firing out the open door as they zoomed past at rooftop level.

The radio crackled to life again. "QRF on it's way." the ground force team sergeant reported.

Rangers deploy on Little Bird helicopters.

Back at base, the black hawks landed and the slightly wounded pilots of the other MH-6 could see the Quick Reaction Force gearing up. They knew their friends were in trouble, so rather than report to the medical aid station to have their wounds treated, they ran back to their compound and hopped in another AH-6 attack helicopter. They were going back into the fight.

But it would take time to get there, and in the meantime David Cooper and his copilot were single-handedly holding off the enemy force. Low on ammo, he set down next to the downed AH-6. The men on the ground were exchanging fire with the insurgents in the house, but David ignored the flying bullets and grabbed a few guys to help him transfer the rockets from the disabled bird over to his own as it idled nearby. Rockets loaded and armed, he jumped back in and took off, continuing the fight.

He continued making gun runs, and on one of them two bullets struck the windscreen only inches from his face. The bullet holes in his windscreen reinforced his feeling he wouldn't survive the day, but in a strange way they also doubled his resolve not to go down without making his death very costly for the enemy. A second time he landed and re-armed his Bird, then shot skyward to continue the fight. There were a pair of F-16 fighter jets overhead, but they were having trouble distinguishing the friendly from enemy forces at high altitude.

F-16's over Iraq

David Cooper didn't have that problem. The enemy forces were the ones still trying to blow him out of the air.

A few more runs at the enemy trucks and his rocket pods were empty and this time he was almost out of fuel as well. Again he landed next to the broken Little Bird inside the perimeter of operators who were ferociously pouring fire on the two dozen insurgents in the house. While one group of operators transferred some minigun ammo over to his chopper, he and some others used a Leatherman tool to remove the downed chopper's auxiliary fuel tank and install it on his craft. Cooper knew what they were doing likely broke several dozen U.S. Army flight regulations and might even be insane to boot. But he also concluded they might even be able to hold the enemy off long enough for the QRF to arrive. And, if he could do that, he and his copilot might just survive long enough to get chewed out by their superiors.

He took off once more and was overjoyed to see two more AH-6s come buzzing out of the distance. They joined up in the air and the trio of Night Stalkers turned on the remaining gun trucks and shredded them with their rockets and miniguns. They watched as the remaining two trucks still working turned and hightailed it away from the battlefield.

As they ran, one of the F-16s above got them in his sights and the pilot, Air Force Major Troy Gilbert, rolled in for a strafing run. His 20-mm Vulcan cannon obliterated one of the trucks. Gilbert tried a high-speed maneuver to get the second truck, but was too low and unable to pull out. The F-16 clipped the ground and disappeared in a ball of flame. Major Gilbert was the only American killed in action during the operation.

His ammunition, fuel, and emotions completely spent, CW5 David Cooper piloted his trusty AH-6 back to base, concluding nearly four hours of intense air-to-ground combat.

CW5 Cooper is one of the most highly decorated soldiers alive and still serving in today's Army. Yet, his disarming, self-deprecating humor and trademark humility give no hint of the highly classified and dangerous operations that have resulted in his receiving the Silver Star, Distinguished Flying Cross, two Bronze Stars, three meritorious service medals, seven air medals, including three for valor, and an Army Commendation medal for valor. For his actions on that day in November 2006 over Talil, Iraq, Cooper was awarded the Distinguished Service Cross, second only to the Medal of Honor. When the medal was pinned on his chest, he was the only recipient in the war on terror not given the award posthumously. CW5 David Cooper was inducted into the Aviation Hall of Fame in early 2010.

At the ceremony Lt General Robert W. Wagner called him "a true hero in every sense of the word." But if you talk to Cooper, he says, "I just happened to be the guy there that day. Any one of the Night Stalkers that's in this formation would have done the same thing I did."

CW5 Cooper at Awards Ceremony

CW5 DAVID COOPER, U.S. ARMY

CW5 David Cooper distinguished himself through conspicuous gallantry in action while serving as an AH-6 Flight Lead Pilot, operating against an enemy force northeast of Baghdad, Iraq. On 27 November 2006, CW5 Cooper launched his AH-6 as part of a daytime Helicopter Assault Force (HAF) in order to kill or capture an Iraqi-based foreign fighter facilitator. During the flight CW5 Cooper's AH-6 wingman sustained significant damage by enemy fire and crash landed. The remainder of the HAF landed in a defensive perimeter around the badly damaged aircraft. Although both pilots were without significant injury, the aircraft could no longer be flown and the Air Mission Commander made the decision to secure the site and await a Downed Aircraft Recovery Team (DART).

Approximately forty minutes after landing, several enemy trucks with heavy weapons moved into position and began engaging the ground force and aircraft with anti-aircraft machine guns, rocket propelled grenades and small arms fire. The entire ground force was outgunned and outnumbered. Without hesitation and while receiving direct enemy fire, CW5 Cooper and his copilot moved to their aircraft and took off to provide much-needed suppression on the enemy forces. Coming under intense enemy fire, CW5 Cooper began to engage the enemy. He made multiple passes, initially destroying several gun trucks and killing at least ten enemy personnel. At this point all enemy weapon systems and personnel were clearly aiming at him, yet he continued to fly multiple gun runs straight into the heavy machine gunfire of the enemy and placed devastating fires upon them.

Out of ammunition and low on fuel, CW5 Cooper landed back at the ground force location and immediately began re-arming his helicopter with rockets and ammunition, and transferring fuel from his wingman's downed aircraft. He then took off again and began to engage enemy vehicles and personnel. As he continued with his engagements, he repeatedly found that some of the rockets removed from the downed AH-6 malfunctioned and did not launch. Very much aware of the possibility that unstable rockets could detonate in his launcher, he continued to engage the enemy and destroyed several more gun trucks and killed nearly ten more personnel.

As a result of CW5 Cooper's devastating fire and aggressive actions, the enemy completely broke contact and began to flee the area. His performance of duty assured the survival of this embattled element and is in keeping with the finest traditions of the Special Operations community. His actions displayed the highest levels of valor and gallantry in combat and reflect great credit upon himself, this Command, and the United States Army.

AH-6M & MH-6M LITTLE BIRD FACT SHEET

The AH-6M Little Bird is a highly modified version of the McDonnell Douglas 530 series commercial helicopter. The light attack aircraft has a single turbine engine and dual flight control. It is primarily employed in close air support of ground troops, target destruction raids, and armed escort of other aircraft. The AH-6M is normally flown by two pilots.

The Little Bird variants can be deployed on any Air Force transport aircraft. Both can be prepared for, transported, and reconfigured for flight in a minimal amount of time.

AH-6M MISSION EQUIPMENT

• Communications equipment capable of secure operations including UHF and VHF modes. SATCOM is installed on some aircraft and available as an option on all aircraft.

• Forward Looking Infrared, or FLIR, is a controllable, infrared surveillance system that provides a TV video-type infrared image of terrain features and ground or airborne objects of interest. The FLIR is a passive system and detects long wavelength radiant IR energy emitted, naturally or artificially, by any object in daylight or darkness.

AH-6M WEAPONS SYSTEMS

• The AH-6M is capable of mounting a variety of weapons systems, including both M-134 miniguns and rocket pods.

MH-6M LITTLE BIRD

The MH-6M Little Bird is a single-engine light utility helicopter that has been modified to externally transport several combat troops and their equipment. It is capable of conducting infiltrations, exfiltrations, and combat assaults over a wide variety of terrain and environmental conditions.

161

Two U.S. Army (USA) AH-6J Little Bird helicopters take off for a mission at a forward deployed location in southern Iraq during Operation Iraqi Freedom.

The MH-6M is also used for reconnaissance missions.

MH-6M MISSION EQUIPMENT

• External Personnel System mounted on each side of the aircraft.

• Rapid configuration for fast rope and short tactical airborne operations.

• Systems to assist the crew in identifying enemy positions.

Soldiers from the 75th Ranger Regiment descend in an MH-6M Little Bird helicopter flown by pilots from the 160th Special Operations Aviation Regiment, into a staged firefight during an exercise demonstrating the range of U.S. Army Special Operations capabilities.

2007

U.S. Army Ranger comes in for a landing during a combat equipment static line jump.

10 SEPT 07

OPERATION CHROMIUM

SAMARRA, IRAQ

The "surge," ordered by President George W. Bush, in late 2006, changed everything about the campaign in Iraq. By the time Operation Chromium was launched in September 2007, combat in the Land Between the Rivers had all but disappeared from America's televisions and dropped off the front pages of our newspapers.

In the months since General David Petraeus took command and thirty thousand more U.S. troops were being dispatched to Iraq, Sheikh Sattar—the chief instigator of the Sunni "Awakening"—was killed—but the movement he helped start was still alive. Average Iraqis in al Anbar province were cooperating with coalition forces. Ramadi, the provincial capital was no longer the most violent place on the planet. The streets once full of improvised explosive devices were being cleaned up. At home, Republicans took a drubbing in the previous November's Congressional elections but the "experts" were

"The Awakening" in Iraq in 2007 gave rise to "neighborhood watch" programs around the country and began to turn the tide of the war.

no longer saying Iraq was descending into an abyss of sectarian conflict.

The masters of the mainstream media who once contended that the campaign in Iraq was "lost" now ignored it. Nobody much recalled the Associated Press, in a piece headlined "Many U.S. Troops in Iraq Oppose Escalation," baldly declaring we were "embroiled in civil warfare between majority Shiite Muslims and Sunni Arabs that no number of American troops can stop." America's newspapers and television screens once full of stories about U.S. and Iraqi casualties and vicious condemnation of "Bush's War" disregarded the success of the surge.

When the first reinforcements arrived in February 2007 U.S. casualties spiked and the potentates of the press proclaimed the additional troops were "too little, too late." Radical Islamic Web sites agreed and predicted the toll of dead and wounded would force the Americans to abandon Iraq just as they quit Vietnam, Beirut, and Somalia. Osama bin Laden declared the "American infidels" were being "driven from Mesopotamia."

The "surge" in combat power—and trainers—has changed everything. Why? Because the additional commitment was the assurance the Iraqi people were looking for. They didn't want to commit to a lost cause but the "surge" meant the U.S. wasn't going to abandon them. They were emboldened to rise up and kick out the criminal elements trying to destroy the new Iraqi government.

Many of those tasked to train and mentor the fledgling Iraqi army were American Special Forces. After all, training foreign militaries is a key mission for which Green Berets are specially trained. Special Forces soldiers usually live alongside their Iraqi army counterparts, providing an example of leadership that goes beyond simple classroom and field instruction. In September 2007 when the time came for one Iraqi unit to mount an important mission to capture or kill a high-ranking insurgent leader, three Green Berets found themselves required to go far "above and beyond" when it came to setting the example for the green Iraqi soldiers in their charge.

The objective was simple: capture or kill the brutal leader of a kidnapping ring with ties to the Islamic State of Iraq (ISI), a terrorist group devoted to the overthrow of the democratically elected Iraqi government. By September 2007, many of the sectarian militias and insurgent groups had been pushed out of central Baghdad and into havens outside the capital. Samarra, a historic city on the Tigris River, eighty miles north of Baghdad became the refuge for a particularly vicious insurgent faction.

ODA 083, a Special Forces A-team from 10th group, out of Fort Carson, Colorado, had been mentoring an Iraqi Special Operations unit for several months when they received orders to capture an insurgent kingpin named Abu Obaeideah—known for brutally killing the families of those found to be associating with the Americans or the new Iraqi government. He financed his operations by kidnapping others for ransom.

Intelligence indicated Obaeideah moved frequently and rarely stayed in one place more than a few days. At that moment he was hiding out in a small farm compound outside Samarra and believed to be protected by a ten to twelve man personal security

Iraqi SWAT

contingent. Because of the time-sensitive nature of the mission, the Green Berets hastily prepared an operations order calling for two helicopters to drop a total of twenty Iraqi troops and several of their American mentors to advise them during the mission. The Iraqi Special Operators would take the lead in clearing the farm compound and apprehending Obaeideah.

Shortly after midnight on 19 September 2007 the combined U.S.-Iraqi force boarded two Black Hawk helicopters and lifted off for Samarra. There was almost no lunar illumination, so the three Green Berets on the first Bird, Staff Sgt Jarion Halbisengibbs, Sgt 1st Class Michael Lindsay, and Capt Matthew Chaney wore their night-vision goggles right from the start of the mission.

The flight to the target area was quick and uneventful. But when the Birds descended toward their planned insertion zone, the field they planned to land in was unexpectedly flooded with water. The pilots pulled up and made a quick decision to land in an alternate LZ, much closer to the objective. Unfortunately, the site they chose was a bit too close—only thirty meters from the primary objective. As the unit jumped off the helicopters into a blinding cloud of swirling dust, enemy machine guns opened fire.

The best strategy in an assault is to maintain momentum through quick, violent action to keep the enemy off guard. With this in mind, the three Green Berets jumped

Staff Sgt Jarion Halbisengibbs

up and rushed the objective, reaching the first building as more enemy fighters began to respond with fire from each of the three buildings the mission called for the Iraqis to clear. But as they stacked up on the first doorway, Halbisengibbs, Lindsay, and Chaney made a horrifying discovery—the second helicopter was forced to land at least three hundred meters away and the Iraqis who landed with them in the first chopper were still back on the landing zone, disoriented and surprised to be taken under fire so quickly. The three Americans were alone.

They quickly concluded that staying where they were, awaiting the rest of the assault force was suicide. Retreat wasn't an option, either. So the three Special Operators chose the only other course of action—they pressed the attack by themselves.

They entered the first building with weapons leading the way. Lindsey saw a man raise a rifle and point it at him. The Green Beret snapped his M4 up and shot the man dead before he could fire. First building clear.

They were moving toward the second building when a machine gun opened up on them from the third structure—the one Intel said was where they would find Obaeideah. With no choice but to deal with the immediate threat and with their Iraqi

Night raid

teammates still on the LZ, the team bypassed the second building and raced toward the third. Two enemy fighters emerged from it, firing machine guns from the hip. Well-aimed shots from the three Green Berets eliminated the threat in seconds.

When they reached the building, Halbisengibbs threw a grenade in the door, killing two of the enemy inside. Immediately after the grenade blast, the three Special Operators charged through the doorway as they practiced many times before, each man cordoning off a sector of the room with his weapon.

The muzzle flash from an AK-47 lit up the room and Halbisengibbs fired back instinctively, killing the shooter even as one of the enemy rounds smashed his night-vision goggles and another pierced his hand. More insurgents fired, striking SSG Lindsey in the throat and Captain Chaney in the pelvis. They all returned fire—and one of their bullets took out an enemy fighter who was, at that moment, pulling the pin on a grenade. The grenade dropped to the floor and exploded three feet from Chaney; hurling him and Lindsey back through the doorway to land in a heap in the courtyard. Halbisengibbs took shrapnel in several places, some of which destroyed his radio. He picked himself up, realized his night-vision goggles were ruined as well, and he was now alone in the building. With no time to wait for reinforcements, he continued to clear the building alone. A man who turned out to be the high value target—Abu Obaeideah—stepped out of a doorway and raised a rifle. The wounded Green Beret Staff Sergeant dropped him with a quick three-round burst.

Meanwhile Chaney and Lindsey, wounded and stunned, were still in the courtyard. As they struggled to rise, Chaney discovered he was temporarily paralyzed from the waist down. At that instant, an enemy fighter started shooting at him from another doorway in the building. The wounded Captain crawled to the body of a dead terrorist and using it for cover, returned fire, taking out the shooter trying to kill him. He adjusted his night-vision and looked over at Lindsey, who was badly wounded, bleeding and vomiting after taking shrapnel in the abdomen. Too weak to lift his rifle, the injured Staff Sergeant pulled out his pistol and fired in the direction of the second doorway.

Once he cleared the inside of the building, Halbisengibbs went back outside to check on his teammates. As soon as he stepped out the door, another insurgent appeared in the second doorway and shot him at a range of about ten feet. The bullet hit Halbisengibbs in the stomach, just below his body armor. Still standing, the

Special forces foot patrol

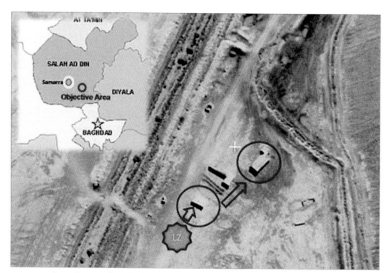

Drone images show the layout of the farming compound where wanted terrorist Abu Obaideah was hiding.

twice-wounded Green Beret killed his attacker and began shouting instructions at the Iraqi assault force, which was finally arriving at the objective from the LZ.

In all, the Americans killed eleven enemy fighters, six of them attributed to Halbisengibbs. A kidnap victim was found bound and gagged in one of the buildings and returned to his family—a great public relations coup for the fledgling Iraqi security forces. Of greater benefit, the green Iraqi Special Operators received a powerful lesson in the courage and tenacity from their American mentors—one that would be profoundly important in the months ahead as they assumed increasing responsibility for their nation's future.

At the end of December 2007, as we were completing our ninth FOX News embed covering U.S. troops in Iraq, the story of what Staff Sgt. Jarion Halbisengibbs, Sgt 1st Class Michael Lindsay, and Capt Matthew Chaney did in September was hardly known to the American people. We were preparing to return home for the holidays. They were recuperating from the terrible wounds they received during Operation Chromium.

Our FOX News crew traversed the length and breadth of Iraq, interviewing hundreds of Americans and Iraqis, both civilian and military. In our travels, we documented stunning progress in bringing security and civil law and order to the country. While we were there, Basra province reverted to full Iraqi control, as British troops completed their withdrawal from Iraq's southernmost prefecture.

In Baghdad, we accompanied another U.S. trained and supported Iraqi Special Operations unit on a nighttime raid to apprehend a member of the Mahdi Army—a feat that would have been impossible one year earlier. In Fallujah, the former al-Qaeda stronghold, Iraqi police in blue uniforms watched as we stood on a residential street, rebuilt from the rubble of urban combat in November 2004. In Ramadi, where we previously dodged gunfire on multiple occasions, we dined with Sheikh Mohammad al Heiss, the new leader of the Sunni reconciliation movement and then went to the "souk" to buy Christmas presents for my grandchildren. On a street where terrorists tried to kill us twelve months previously, we walked without flak jackets or helmets—something that would have been unthinkable even a few months before we arrived.

It was nearly Christmas. We were going home, but very few of the young Americans we met on this deployment would enjoy the holidays with their families. For many, it was their third Nativity season away from home since Operation Iraqi Freedom began in 2003.

As I thought about it, I realized the best Christmas gift I could give my grandchildren was to tell them the stories of these American heroes. Their example of heroism and devotion to duty is the kind of thing all people, young and old, need to be reminded of—the uplifting example of these warriors deployed in harm's way and protecting the rest of us from those who are dying to kill us all.

Sgt 1st Class Jarion Halbisengibbs, recipient of the Distinguished Service Cross, Capt Matthew Chaney and Sgt 1st Class Michael Lindsay, recipients of the Silver Star, received their awards during a ceremony at the Special Events Center, Fort Carson, Colorado.

DISTINGUISHED SERVICE CROSS: STAFF SERGEANT JARION HALBISENGIBBS

The President of the United States of America, authorized by Act of Congress, July 9, 1918 (amended by act of July 25, 1963), takes pleasure in presenting the Distinguished Service Cross to Staff Sergeant Jarion Halbisengibbs, United States Army, for extraordinary heroism in action on 10 September 2007 in combat operations in support of Operation Iraqi Freedom. As the detachment weapon sergeant, Operational Detachment Alpha 083 (ODA 083), 10th Special Forces Group (Airborne), Staff Sergeant Halbisengibbs displayed extraordinary courage under fire while combat-advising a combined assault element of the Iraqi National Police during Operation Chromium, a raid to capture al Qaeda in Iraq's Minister of Defense for Ad Din Province in Samarra. Through his fearless actions, Staff Sergeant Halbisengibbs directly saved the lives of two of his fellow soldiers, personally killed six of the eleven enemies killed in action, enabled the rescue of one hostage, and ensured the elimination of a terrorist responsible for kidnappings and murders throughout the Samarra region. His unparalleled courage under fire, decisive leadership, and personal sacrifice were directly responsible for the operations success and ensured the province of Ad Din did not fall into insurgent hands. Staff Sergeant Jarion Halbisengibbs's outstanding performance of duty is in keeping with the finest traditions of military service and reflects great credit upon himself, the 10th Special Forces Group (Airborne), and the United States Army.

Sgt 1st Class Jarion Halbisengibbs, 10th Special Forces Group (Airborne) receives the Distinguished Service Cross from Adm. Eric T. Olson, United States Special Operations Command commander.

The wind tunnel at HALO school, Fort Bragg, North Carolina

HALO SCHOOL

Military Free Fall Parachute School is one of the most dangerous, most coveted military Special Ops schools. In it, students are taught the art of High-altitude, Low Opening (HALO) and High-altitude, High Opening (HAHO) parachuting.

This month-long course may be one of the most demanding the military has to offer, but it isn't the drop-and-give-me-fifty kind. In fact, since most of those attending are already seasoned Special Operators who have proven their motivation and skill, instructors at HALO school can focus on giving students the best education possible without having to be all that in-your-face.

Nevertheless, students at this school will be challenged and stretched in ways they never thought possible. After all, exiting an aircraft in the dead of night at twenty thousand feet while wearing one hundred twenty pounds of combat equipment leaves absolutely no room for error. But those who have done it successfully say the difference between flying in a plane at those altitudes and freefalling is like the difference between riding in a ship and swimming, only about one hundred twenty miles-per-hour faster.

The first week of HALO school takes place at Fort Bragg, North Carolina. The students receive classroom instruction, which helps explain the differences between static line parachuting (in which all must already be qualified) and free-fall parachuting. The students also experience the wind tunnel for the first time. This facility has a giant fan blowing air vertically in a tunnel, and with the help of instructors, students spend the first of many hours in the tunnel perfecting their flying skills.

The next three weeks' training is done at Yuma Proving Ground, Arizona, where the climate is almost perfect for year-round skydiving. There the students learn by doing—jumping up to several times a day, five days per week. They learn various exit techniques and how to stay together in the air as a group. They then move up to night operations with combat equipment and high-altitude jumps requiring the use of oxygen. They may also get a couple of high-altitude, high-opening jumps, where they deploy their chutes shortly after exiting the plane and can fly for more than thirty miles, perfect for covert insertion into hostile areas, and in training, it's some of the best fun you can have in the military. Only about five hundred men receive this training each year.

Right: Pararescuemen from the 38th Rescue Squadron and the 58th Rescue Squadron, Nellis Air Force Base, Nevada, jump from a HC-130P/N for a High Altitude Low Opening free fall drop from 12,999 feet in support of Operation Enduring Freedom. PJs use a variety of jumps depending on the mission.

2008

An F-15E Strike Eagle over the mountains and high desert of Afghanistan

25 JAN 08

Ambush Site

Image ©2010 DigitalGlobe
©2010 Cnes/spot Image

©2009 Google

THE BATTLE FOR BARI KOWT

KONAR PROVINCE, AFGHANISTAN

There are few places in Afghanistan that wouldn't qualify as "remote." Flying over the country gives one an education in the meaning of the word. But Bari Kowt is remote even for Afghanistan. Thirty-five miles as the crow flies northeast of Asadabad, this arid mountain landscape is bisected by a fast-running, gravelly river that runs out of Pakistan, only a half mile away. The river is overlooked by ancient hand-terraced hillsides, which are still farmed as they were a hundred and likely a thousand years ago. The strategic value of Bari Kowt to the Taliban lies in its remoteness, which makes it an ideal "rat line" for the insurgent organizations to move men and material across the border from their havens in the lawless tribal areas of Pakistan.

The 3rd Special Forces Group maintains small outposts along the border, and has built a good reputation with the fledgling Afghan Border Police, providing training and support for them as they work at protecting their frontier.

In January 2008, a Special Forces ODA teamed up with a group of Afghan Border Police to do a simple reconnaissance patrol of the valley. Staff Sergeant Robert J. Miller was on his second combat deployment to Afghanistan and loved his job. Coming from a family with eight children in the suburbs of Chicago, Miller stood out as a talented athlete and gymnast and after high school graduation spent a year in college before he enlisted in the military. He signed up specifically to become a Green Beret under a relatively new program that gives new recruits a shot at the Special Forces Assessment and Selection course right out of basic training and Airborne school. That route entailed significant risk, however, because failure at any point in the process meant reassignment "at the needs of the army," which was almost a sure way to end up doing something he didn't want to do for the term of his enlistment. At least 70 percent of those who signed up failed.

Staff Sgt Robert J. Miller

Special Forces Assessment and Selection is the price of admission for those who want to wear the Green Beret.

Miller made it on the first try, but it was a long, arduous process. From the day he started basic training in 2003 to the day he pinned on the coveted Special Forces tab spanned more than two years of nonstop training in weapons, tactics, languages, and more. It was a proud day in 2005 when he reported for duty as a newly minted sergeant at Company A, 3rd Battalion, 3rd Special Forces Group.

A year later he deployed for the first time to Afghanistan. In that seven-month tour, Miller distinguished himself in combat and was awarded two Army Commendation Medals for courage under fire.

During the following seven months back at Fort Bragg, the team kept busy with additional training and then headed right back to Afghanistan. The relationships they'd built during their first deployment were still intact, and they were able to pretty much pick up where they left off.

In Afghanistan there is no "routine" mission. The objective for the operation that began 24 January 2008, was reconnaissance in search of a Taliban leader—a "high-value target"—who was known to be hiding somewhere in the mountains near the border. It was an area known to be crawling with insurgents, so the ODA team, along with fifteen Afghan National Border Patrol (ANBP) troops headed out heavily armed and ready for anything.

The first sign of trouble came in the form of two huge boulders blocking the road. The team brought up their demolitions men—Special Forces engineers. One huge explosion later, the road was again open and the team continued its trek into the mountains, doubly wary now that they were forced to announce their presence.

Attached to the unit was Air Force Staff Sergeant Robert Gutierrez Jr., a stocky Latino from the suburbs of San Diego, California. Everyone on the team liked him for his easy sense of humor and even more for his skill with the radio. As a Combat Controller, Gutierrez was responsible for calling in air support if they got in trouble on the ground. His laid-back demeanor belied the intellect and tactical wisdom Gutierrez possessed in order to make it through the grueling two-year training cycle it took to become a combat controller.

In the early morning hours of 25 January the patrol neared the village of Bari Kowt, which was believed to be where the insurgent leader was hiding. As they cautiously rolled up the dirt road to the village, gunfire rang out from the mountains to their right. Then another machine gun opened up. The ODA immediately countered with controlled bursts from their roof-mounted .50 caliber machine guns and 40-mm Mark 19 grenade launchers. For good measure, Gutierrez quickly called in a pair of F-15E fighter jets to drop bombs on the enemy positions. Another couple of strafing runs by a flight of A-10 warthogs, called down by Gutierrez and the men who had been shooting at them were doing so no longer.

Staff Sgt Robert Gutierrez

183

An eerie quiet settled over the dark valley. All that separated the patrol from the compound they came to search was a bridge—now damaged—which crossed a small wadi.

The decision was made to dismount and check out the village on foot, since the bridge was out. They wondered if the air strikes took care of their high-value target. Miller and a few others jumped out of their vehicles and volunteered to accompany the ODA commander into the village. Gutierrez went along as well, staying close to the commander to act as a liaison between the ODA captain and the U.S. Air Force.

They spread out and ventured across the bridge as the eastern sky began to grow light. Once they reached the other side, things went south in a hurry.

Machine guns spat flame from three directions, especially the mountainside they just bombed. Apparently the enemy wasn't neutralized after all, but biding his time to draw them in. Insurgents were shooting from houses in the village, too.

The nearest fighting position held four men. They opened up with AK-47s, immediately hitting the team Captain in the neck. He dropped to the ground, gravely wounded. The enemy was close enough for Gutierrez to have hit them with a slingshot. But he didn't have one of those, so he killed all four with well-placed shots from his M4. Then he dove for cover as the rest of the bad guys honed in on him, peppering the ground around his feet as he ran.

They were taking fire from three sides and were cut off from the heavy weapons on their Humvees. Judging from the volume of fire, there had to be a hundred of them. But the Captain was still alive, though he wouldn't be for long in his vulnerable position. They had to help.

The team unleashed a fusillade of fire to get the enemy's heads down. Then Rob Miller, Gutierrez, and another man sprinted to the Captain's side, spraying rounds at the enemy. Gutierrez dragged the Captain out of the kill zone while the others drew the enemy's fire away from him.

Then Miller got hit. He took a round in the chest, just above his breastplate and fell hard. Gutierrez was working on the Captain, getting a dressing on his wound. He could hear Miller crying out in the darkness.

"I'm hurt! Hey, I'm hurt real bad!" he screamed. The enemy heard it too. They tore up the earth between Miller and where Gutierrez was crouched, working on the Captain with one hand and calling in the Air Force with the other. It was time for some heavy ordnance.

But they couldn't wait for air support. He and the other operator changed magazines and sprinted from cover to their wounded comrade, firing at anything that moved. The rest of the team poured rounds at enemy positions, too. They made it to where Miller fell, but every time Gutierrez tried to move him to safer ground, the incoming rounds were just too thick. He kept calling for emergency air support while trying to stop the bleeding.

A-10 Thunderbolt

They did their best, but the bullet hit Miller right in the heart. He died within a minute.

The survivors were still in a very bad position. Pinned down in the ambush zone by a numerically superior force. Gutierrez and his teammate tried to move Miller's body out of the kill zone but were driven back by heavy machine-gun fire. They needed a miracle.

Just then one called on the radio. A pair of A-10 Thunderbolts were overhead with a full load of ammunition. The only problem was, the Air Force Controller who would have to clear them hot was right smack in the middle of the guys that needed killing. This was beyond danger close. But they were out of options. Gutierrez called them in, then put his head down and tried to become very small.

The world exploded around him—the A-10s Gatling guns shredding the terrain and everything in it. Incredibly, no friendlies got hit. The insurgents, however, were still coming. Gutierrez called the A-10s in again. And again. A dozen gun runs were all that stood between the cut-off team and being overrun by the enemy. Twice, the man next to Gutierrez got hit in the breastplate by 7.62-mm slugs, then jumped back up to keep fighting. The small group was fighting for their lives. Every chance they got to move Miller's body a little closer to cover, they took. The problem was dawn was starting to break and in their present position, without the cover of darkness, they wouldn't have a chance. They had to find cover.

The call came over the radio that the rest of the team had taken up a defensible position to the rear of where Gutierrez and the other Special Forces Sergeant were positioned. They talked it over briefly and decided it would be okay to leave Miller's body where they could keep eyes on it and fall back temporarily until more air support showed up to suppress the enemy. Together the two men ran about ten yards through withering fire and dropped over the lip of a terrace where it was relatively safe.

Now it was time to dial up some serious retribution. Gutierrez got on the radio and called in everything they would give him. A couple of five-hundred-pound bombs would show the enemy they were serious. The ground shook as two enemy positions vaporized in a cloud of dust. That gave Gutierrez and his partner the break they needed to pull back to rejoin the rest of the group.

He kept the pressure on, directing strafing missions from A-10s and attack helicopters. They destroyed a couple of houses encasing the enemy. They emptied their magazines at a group of Taliban who tried to steal Miller's body.

Gutierrez was reloading when he heard his partner yell "RP . . ." that was as far as he got. He looked up just in time to see two men who had stepped outside a building and were pointing a rocket-propelled grenade launcher at him. Before he could react, the tube puffed and almost simultaneously the RPG detonated a few feet in front of him.

The explosion sent Gutierrez flying. He hit hard, losing whatever breath hadn't already been sucked from his lungs by the blast. He couldn't see anything but smoke and dust and his head felt like the inside of a bass drum.

An A-10 Thunderbolt II pulls up after destroying a ground target with its 30-mm Gatling gun.

Casualty evac training is serious business.

He sat up, everything hurt, but miraculously, everything seemed to still be working. He couldn't believe he wasn't dead. Unwilling to give the Taliban rocket man another shot at it, he clawed his way to his feet and called in another air strike, right on top of the house the guy was hiding in.

Two of the operators near him were wounded by the grenade. As his head cleared, Gutierrez realized his body armor and equipment had absorbed most of the shrapnel. Must not have been his day to die. At least not yet. The battle wasn't over and the A-10s were getting low on gas.

They still needed the beautiful, lethal jets, though. Gutierrez asked them to make another pass up the valley. The sound of their engines alone was enough to keep the Taliban in their holes.

The new team commander decided it was time to collect their dead and wounded and get out of Dodge. That meant going back for Miller's body—another trip into the kill zone.

They worked together. Gutierrez called in another air strike, then they all rushed to where Miller lay and two men grabbed him while the rest peppered enemy positions with their assault rifles. In this way they pulled their fallen comrade from the battlefield.

Never leave a man behind. That's the rule.

For his fearless actions that day, to include calling in at least a couple dozen air strikes and helping to evacuate the wounded—there were seventeen of them, total—the stocky Air Force Staff Sergeant was awarded the Bronze Star with "V" device for valor. But one of the best accolades came from the enemy as they withdrew from the battlefield. Having seen at least half their fighters killed or wounded by the terrifying display of accurate air-to-ground precision strikes orchestrated by one man with a radio, the Afghan police radios picked up "chatter" from the enemy as the ODA pulled out. They were saying, "Don't attack them! If you do, you will die!"

Finally Robert Gutierrez found some common sentiment with his enemy.

A memorial ceremony was given for Robert J. Miller at Bagram Air Force base after he was killed in battle at Bari Kowt, Afghanistan.

6 APR 08

FIGHTING THE HIG

SHOK VALLEY, AFGHANISTAN

The Taliban aren't the only enemies we face in Afghanistan. Another insurgent group is called Hezb-e-Islami Gulbuddin (HIG). Founded in 1977 by Hektamyar Gulbuddin, a warlord living in the mountainous border region of Afghanistan and Pakistan. During the Soviet occupation of Afghanistan, his organization received hundreds of millions of dollars in military aid from Pakistan, Saudi Arabia, and even the United States, despite their hard-line anti-western ideology. Though this militant Muslim group shares its ideology with al-Qaeda and others, it often fought with other factions and was pushed aside when the Taliban came to power in 1994.

When the U.S.-supported Northern Alliance pushed the Taliban out of Kabul in 2001, and NATO troops joined in the coalition, HIG leaders set aside their differences with the Taliban and found new purpose in opposing the coalition. HIG strongholds are still found in remote villages in the area along the Pakistan border. One of them is the Shok Valley.

The Shok Valley has always been dangerous for outsiders—so much so the Soviets never dared venture into it. The deep, narrow mountain cleft has no road leading into it, making the fortress-like village at the valley's head a perfect hideout for the HIG, situated at nearly ten thousand feet above sea level.

Afghan Commandos, however, don't share the Russian's fear.

Trained by teams of U.S. Special Operators, the Afghan Commandos have earned a reputation as tough, capable soldiers who won't back down in battle. In early April 2008, the Afghan Commandos and the men of Special Forces ODA 3336, who trained them decided to take the fight to the HIG in the Shok Valley, knowing coalition forces had never been up there. Intel reports indicated the village held several high-value targets, as well as a sizable force of foreign fighters who were believed to be stockpiling ammunition and weapons for future attacks against the Afghan government.

Aerial view of Shok Valley

Staff Sgt Zachary Rhyner

In the early morning hours of 6 April, two twin-rotor Chinook helicopters carrying ODA 3336 commanded by Captain Kyle M. Walton thundered away from Jalalabad and dropped into the Shok Valley, following its contours at low level. In addition to the Green Berets and Afghans, a few others were along for this mission. Twenty-two-year-old Staff Sergeant Zachary Rhyner was on his first combat deployment as an Air Force Joint Terminal Air Controller, or JTAC. A Wisconsin native, he'd only recently finished the intensive two-year training required to qualify for his job.

Staff Sergeant John Wayne Walding was about as American as a man can get. Born on the fourth of July, his parents named him after the iconic hero of the American western. His early life was full of heroes—men who mentored him in his hometown of Groesbeck, Texas, as well as those he watched on television. As they approached the drop zone, however, it became clear there was already a problem. There wasn't a square foot of level ground upon which the choppers could land, despite their incredibly skilled pilots. Hovering as close as possible to the valley floor, right over a swollen, fast-moving stream, the one hundred Afghan Commandos and two A-teams of Green Berets were forced to jump nearly ten feet to the ground. Some landed in the river—a very bad thing considering temperatures were hovering around freezing.

Once the choppers were gone and the dust settled, the team was able to get a good view of the village and of the challenging climb they would have to reach it. The cluster of stone houses was perched high above, stacked one atop the other and clinging to the steep hillside marked by dozens of stone terraces, each one hand cut by generations of farmers over hundreds of years.

Staff Sgt John Wayne Walding

The people in these villages lived much like their ancestors—scratching a meager existence out of what little crops they could grow or animals they could raise in the harsh mountain environment. They burned the dung of their animals in the winter to stay warm, and the village had no electricity, no running water, and no school. Children born there most likely would never travel much beyond the confines of this valley, and so would likely never see the kinds of things American children take for granted, like television, toilets, or even paved roads.

But they did have too much of one thing—militant Islam. And as the team moved out and began their trek up the mountain, they realized HIG wasn't their only enemy on this mission. The other was gravity. With hearts pounding as they labored upward in the thin air, the men split into three maneuver elements and wondered what kind of reception they would receive once they arrived.

The answer to that question came sooner than anyone hoped. The climb took longer than expected due to the extreme topography and the climb left them much more exposed than anyone would have liked. They were still several hundred meters from the first of the stone houses when one of the men with Walton's group, SSG Luis Morales, saw several insurgents taking up fighting positions with RPG grenade launchers. Morales opened fire, killing both men.

Then in the words of one participant in the fight, "all hell broke loose." Enemy fighters appeared from dug-in positions in almost every direction. The Americans were trapped below, separated on two sides of a narrow wadi, with stone houses on either side. As the firefight erupted, bullets began splattering around the Green Berets like hailstones, raining down from more than a hundred HIG fighters arrayed in an obviously well-planned ambush.

Walton's interpreter, an Afghan who did his job faithfully for more than six years and weathered hundreds of firefights, was killed instantly. Moments later Staff Sergeant Dillon Behr, Captain Walton's radio operator, was struck in the leg and went down. He immediately got back up and kept firing.

ODA 3336 opened up with everything they had, intent on pushing up the hill and taking the village. But the three elements were at that point separated by some distance. The command element, including Captain Walton, Behr, the Combat Controller Zachary Rhyner, and Carter, the combat cameraman, took cover in a small cut in the face of the cliff and began trying to suppress the enemy. Then Behr was hit again, this time in the arm. Morales ran to help him and took a bullet in the leg. He continued to work on Behr until he was hit again in the ankle.

Cpt Walton stepped from his position and unloaded on the enemy, drawing fire away from the two wounded men long enough for the combat cameraman, Michael

Carter, to drag Behr to safety. Then Carter took the Captain's place, laying down supressive fire while Walton rescued Morales. One more volley by Carter and SSG Rhyner allowed Walton to retrieve the body of his interpreter and friend.

Closer to the village, the lead assault element led by Staff Sgt David Sanders was pinned down. They could, however, identify the buildings where the enemy took up fighting positions and relay that information back to the control element. The problem then became that when Behr went down, his radio was left in the open. This made it impossible for Walton to communicate effectively. They had to get that radio.

That's when the young Army combat cameraman, Specialist Carter, volunteered to go get the radio. Walton and Rhyner popped up and gave the insurgents everything they had while Carter sprinted from cover and retrieved the vital communications equipment.

Below them, the Team Sergeant, MSG Scott Ford, was sending 40-mm high-explosive grenades into windows from which insurgents were firing and directing his Afghan counterparts to do the same with their RPGs.

The effect of a five-hundred-pound GBU-38 Joint Direct Attack Munition (JDAM) on a building

SSG Rhyner was able to make contact with a pair of F-15s on station above them. At Walton's command, he immediately began to call them in, specifying to the pilots that their bombs would be impacting "danger close." If the ordnance fell even the slightest bit off target, friendly personnel were sure to be killed or injured. In fact, the enemy was so close even if the bombs landed precisely where they were sent, there was no guarantee SSG Sander's element—closest to the enemy—wasn't going to get hurt. But they had little choice. Walton called Sanders to let him know this and received the terse reply, "Send it anyway."

Rhyner gave the order to drop. A moment later the mountain shook as a load of bombs threw a pall of debris and black smoke in the air, covering the battlefield. Walton called Sanders to see if he was still alive. He could hear gunfire in the background as the Staff Sergeant shouted "Hit 'em again!"

Rhyner complied, calling for air support again and again over the next six and a half hours—directing more than seventy danger-close air attacks, which may well be some sort of record. AH-64 Apache helicopters came hammering up the narrow valley at low level to decimate dozens of enemy fighters on rooftops in the village. A-10 Thunderbolts screamed in for the kill, tearing apart buildings with their powerful

A-10 Thunderbolt on a gun run

Aerial view of Shok Valley

nose-mounted Gatling guns, and the jets overhead took turns dropping load after load of ordnance, which detonated with heart-stopping concussions only a few meters from friendly forces. All this firepower may have saved the struggling force from being overrun, but no matter how many enemy they killed, the supply of HIG fighters—and their ammunition—seemed limitless. From the way the insurgents kept pouring fire down at them, they must have been stockpiling ammunition since sometime just after the invasion of Alexander the Great.

Walton's men and their Afghan brethren were still fighting, methodically killing any enemy fighter crazy enough to show himself, but the insurgents punched firing ports through the stone walls of many of the houses and were nearly impossible to kill without a direct hit from a five-hundred-pound bomb. And the volume of fire only let up for a few seconds whenever a bomb came whooshing in. Captain Walton's biggest fear became the weather. If it moved in and the air support couldn't fly, his team would very likely run out of ammunition by nightfall, and they would never survive the night.

Another Combat Controller, Air Force Staff Sergeant Robert Gutierrez had already seen his share of combat, including a harrowing firefight only three months earlier for which he earned the Silver Star. On this mission Gutierrez was with a part of the force separated across the wadi from the command element. He could see enemy scrambling all over the mountains around them and worked with Rhyner to call in hellfires and attack helicopters to keep them at bay. Twice during the battle Gutierrez was hit in the helmet by AK-47 rounds yet continued to fight. By this time the firefight had been going non-stop for hours.

Rhyner called in another air strike and the fighter jet overhead dropped a two-thousand-pound bomb. It hit right on top of a house crawling with enemy fighters and the jaw-dropping explosion brought the entire operation to a halt as everyone gaped at the sight. SSG Seth Howard, a sniper, used the lull to reposition himself to get a much better view of the remaining enemy trying to kill them. But the respite didn't last long and the enemy reinforced their losses and renewed their attack. From his new vantage point, Howard began lining the enemy up in his sights and knocking them down, one by one.

Nearby Master Sergeant Scott Ford was fighting alongside John Walding as they struggled to reach the command element to help evacuate the wounded. They finally made it and were laying down suppressive fire, hammering away side-by-side when Walding took a round just below his right knee, nearly severing his leg. Ford redoubled his rate of fire, watching his comrade out of the corner of his eye as the tough Staff

ODA 3336 recons the Shok Valley

Video capture of Shok Village

Sergeant put a tourniquet on his own leg, the lower half of which was hanging by a few tendons. He tightened the tourniquet down until the bleeding stopped, then folded the severed member up into his crotch and tied it in place using his boot laces. Ford had never seen anyone so hard core.

Then Walding, grimacing in pain, pulled out a pre-loaded syringe of morphine and tried to self-administer the painkiller. But he had it backwards, and the needle shot into his thumb. He let slip an expletive, then started laughing.

"You gonna be okay, John?" Ford asked.

"Well, my thumb feels pretty great."

Despite the dire circumstances, they all laughed at that one. But then Ford took a round in the chest. His interceptor body armor saved his life, but he was blown off his feet as if he'd been kicked by a giant invisible mule. Winded, but angry, he jumped up and resumed firing. It wasn't funny anymore. It was obvious a sniper had them in his sights. As Ford continued firing, he searched in vain for the man who shot him and his partner.

But the sniper found him first. Another round hit him in the arm, almost amputating it right there on the battlefield. He went down again and Walding crawled over and began to administer first aid.

Walton received word over the radio that aircraft spotted another group of two hundred insurgent fighters coming to reinforce the enemy. It was time to get out of there.

Their biggest problem was it would be impossible for them to descend to the valley floor the same way they went up without being shot to pieces. They would have to find another way for those highest on the mountain to get down. Captain Walton ordered Staff Sergeant Sanders and Specialist Carter to find an alternate route down the mountain.

There were no good options. But after some scouting, the two reported they'd found a way down that offered relatively decent cover. That was the good news. The bad news was the route included several drops that from the top looked almost suicidal. Walton was ready to give anything a try, however, so as Rhyner continued to call down retribution from the sky, the least badly wounded began the arduous process of evacuating those hurt the worst.

It took a long time and there were several spots where they had to literally lower each other down using a length of nylon strap. In other spots they had to just slide over the edge of a wall and drop twenty feet to the terrace below. This maneuver would have been a challenge, even without wounded. But at this point half the team had sustained injuries. John Walding was seen calmly making his way down the mountain, carrying his leg. Captain Walton and SPC Carter risked their necks to gather up the weapons left lying around by the wounded, tossing them down the cliff to keep them from the enemy.

As the team slowly worked their way down, one man stayed behind to cover their withdrawal—the sniper, Seth Howard. At one point, when insurgents were threatening to overrun the command element, he ran into the open and engaged the enemy, driving them back. Soon he was down to only one magazine of ammunition. But he stayed and kept methodically picking off targets, making the HIG fighters think twice about pursuing the team as it withdrew back down the valley. Once everyone got away, Seth left his position and made his own way down all alone.

A Black Hawk medevac helicopter tried to land in the narrow valley to pick up wounded, but received a hail of enemy gunfire, damaging its rotor blades. It hovered just long enough for its flight medic to jump out, then pulled out. A second Black Hawk came in to land and it too took fire. But it maintained a hover over the roiling

SPC Michael D. Carter put the "combat" in Combat Camera.

river and the Green Berets picked up the worst of their wounded and waded out into the ice-cold stream and put them aboard. As they did, the pilot was grazed by a bullet, but managed to hold the helicopter steady so the wounded could get aboard.

By the time everyone made it out, two of their Afghan allies were dead and over half the ODA was wounded, four critically. They fought for nearly seven hours, killing upwards of one hundred fifty of the enemy who ambushed them. Many of those kills were thanks to the skillful handling of air support assets by Zachary Rhyner. He called in nearly five thousand rounds of cannon fire, a dozen five-hundred-pound bombs, nine hellfire missiles, a two-thousand-pounder, and one hundred sixty-two rockets, all while fending off the enemy with his own rifle and dodging near-constant machine gun and sniper fire. For his actions, the young Airman received the Air Force Cross.

In all, ten men of ODA 3336 received Silver Stars for valor that day.

And John Wayne Walding—complete with a new prosthetic leg plans to return to combat duty and continue to take the fight to the enemy alongside his buddies in the 3rd Special Forces Group. And if he ever comes across any HIG fighters again . . .

. . . well, they might wish they had killed him when they had the chance.

ODA 3336 receive their Silver Stars.

TEN SILVER STAR AWARDS

STAFF SGT DILLON BEHR, ROCK ISLAND, IL

Sergeant Behr's suppressive fire allowed wounded U.S. and Afghan soldiers to be evacuated to covered positions. Throughout the duration of the six-and-a-half-hour battle, Sergeant Behr continued to fight and kill the enemy, until he was physically incapable of holding his weapon.

SPC MICHAEL DAVID CARTER, SMITHVILLE, TX

Specialist Carter left his covered position and charged fifteen feet into insurgent fire providing suppressive fire and recovering a critically wounded detachment member. Recovering the critically wounded soldier, Specialist Carter immediately began rendering life saving aid and continued to suppress insurgent positions threatening to overrun their element. Specialist Carter once again exposed himself as he ran across open ground under intense Insurgent fire to recover a Satellite Communications Radio. Upon returning to the ODA Commander's position, he assisted him in operating the radio, while continually providing suppressive fire on numerous insurgent positions. His actions allowed the ODA Commander to re-establish communication with higher headquarters, and aided in directing Close Air Support strikes (CAS) onto insurgent positions attempting to maneuver on their location.

Lt Gen John F. Mullholland awards the Silver Star Medal to Master Sgt Scott Ford of 3rd Battalion, 3rd Special Forces Group (Airborne) for his valor in Afghanistan.

MASTER SGT SCOTT FORD, ATHENS, OH

As Sergeant Ford organized a Commando element to assist in moving casualties, he was shot in the chest plate by sniper fire.

He immediately regained his feet and continued to suppress the enemy until his upper left arm was nearly shot off by a second sniper round.

With a tourniquet on his arm to stop arterial bleeding, Sergeant Ford was able to conduct a courageous climb down the mountain, with the assistance of another teammate, under intense machine gun and sniper fire.

Sergeant Ford never stopped leading his men and continued to organize forces to assist his comrades until he was physically incapable of fighting and had to be evacuated.

STAFF SGT SETH E. HOWARD, KEENE, NH

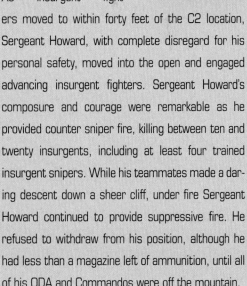

As insurgent fighters moved to within forty feet of the C2 location, Sergeant Howard, with complete disregard for his personal safety, moved into the open and engaged advancing insurgent fighters. Sergeant Howard's composure and courage were remarkable as he provided counter sniper fire, killing between ten and twenty insurgents, including at least four trained insurgent snipers. While his teammates made a daring descent down a sheer cliff, under fire Sergeant Howard continued to provide suppressive fire. He refused to withdraw from his position, although he had less than a magazine left of ammunition, until all of his ODA and Commandos were off the mountain.

STAFF SGT LUIS MORALES, FREDERICKSBURG, VA

As he maneuvered his element into position and began placing a heavy volume of suppressive fire against the elevated insurgent positions, one detachment member in his assault force was critically wounded along with several Afghan Commandos. With total disregard for his own personal safety, Sergeant Morales heroically ran back out into the line of fire to render aid using his body to shield his teammate until he, himself was wounded. Ignoring the severity of his wound, and losing a tremendous amount of blood, he quickly administered self aid and then returned to providing life saving aid to his more severely wounded teammate until he became critically wounded by a second gunshot. After being pulled back to cover, Sergeant Morales assisted in treating three other critically wounded casualties, reassuring both junior soldiers and Commandos. At one point during the six-and-a-half-hour battle, his position was nearly overrun by insurgent fighters, but Sergeant Morales held his ground killing multiple insurgents. During evacuation down a sixty-foot cliff, he again put forth a momentous effort by refusing assistance allowing other detachment members to move more seriously wounded casualties.

STAFF SGT DAVID J. SANDERS, HUNTSVILLE, AL

While organizing casualties for extrication off the mountain, his Team Sergeant was wounded by insurgent fire during movement on the primary route. Sergeant Sanders immediately reconnoitered for and located an alternate but more arduous route down the mountain. Sergeant Sanders ascended and descended the mountain three times in order to move non-ambulatory casualties to the Casualty Collection Point (CCP). During danger CAS strikes he shielded the casualties with his body from falling debris. Once all casualties were consolidated at the CCP Sergeant Sanders reconnoitered and established a Helicopter Landing Zone for extraction.

STAFF SGT RONALD J. SHURER, PULLMAN, WA

Sergeant Shurer courageously exposed himself by running fifteen meters through heavy insurgent fire to render aid to his seriously wounded Team Sergeant. Despite being hit in the helmet and wounded in the arm by Iinsurgent sniper fire, he immediately pulled his Team Sergeant to a covered position, and rendered aid as Insurgent rounds impacted inches

Ten soldiers from the 3rd Special Forces Group (Airborne) are honored at a ceremony in Fort Bragg, North Carolina. They received the Silver Star for their actions in combat during their deployment to Afghanistan. From left are Capt Kyle Walton, Master Sgt Scott Ford, Staff Sgt Dillion Behr, Staff Sgt Seth Howard, Sgt 1st Class Luis Morales, Lt Gen John F. Mullholland, Staff Sgt David Sanders, Staff Sgt John Walding, Staff Sgt Ronald Shurer, Staff Sgt Matthew Williams, Spc Michael D. Carter, Col Gus Benton II, and Command Sgt Maj Terry L. Peters.

from their location. Without hesitation, he moved back through heavy insurgent fire to treat another teammate that suffered a traumatic amputation of his right leg from insurgent sniper fire. Sergeant Shurer rendered life-saving aid to four critically wounded casualties for more than five and a half hours. As the lone medic at the besieged location, and almost overrun by and fighting against nearly two hundred insurgent fighters, Sergeant Shurer's bravery and poise under fire saved the lives of all wounded casualties under his care. He evacuated three critically wounded, non-ambulatory, team-mates down a near vertical sixty-foot cliff, despite being under heavy insurgent fire and falling debris from numerous danger-close air strikes. Sergeant Shurer ingeniously used a six foot length of nylon webbing to lower casualties, and physically shielded them from falling debris to ensure their safety.

STAFF SGT
JOHN W. WALDING,
GROESBECK, TX

Staff Sergeant John W. Walding, United States (U.S.) Army, heroically distinguished himself by exceptionally valorous conduct in the face of the enemy of the U.S., while serving as the Communications Sergeant for Operational Detachment Alpha (ODA) 3336, Special Operations Task Force—33, Combined Joint Special Operations Task Force—Afghanistan, in support of Operation Enduring Freedom.

On 6 April 2008, Sergeant Walding heroically distinguished himself during a combined raid against a high-value target in Shok Valley, Nuristan Province, Afghanistan.

With disregard for his own safety, Sergeant Walding fought his way through intense sniper, machine gun, and RPG fire to reinforce his ODA and Afghan Commandos pinned down by effective insurgent fire.

Sergeant Walding led an assault element from the ODA and Commandos uphill for over an hour to reach the beleaguered force pinned against a near vertical sixty-foot cliff.

Undeterred, knowing they had multiple urgent casualties and in danger of being overrun, Sergeant Walding led a courageous attack five hundred meters up treacherous terrain, braving danger close air strikes to reinforce the most forward position.

After moving forward under insurgent fire for more than an hour and killing multiple insurgents, he finally reached the besieged element and began to organize Commandos to evacuate casualties.

His heroic actions and leadership under the worst of circumstances motivated his Commandos and his team mates to fight on as they faced nearly two hundred well trained insurgents, during the six-and-a-half-hour gun battle.

As Sergeant Walding suppressed iInsurgent positions, in order to protect his fallen comrades, he was shot in the lower right leg by sniper fire, effectively amputating his leg below the knee. Despite receiving a life threatening amputation of his leg, Sergeant Walding continued to suppress insurgent positions in order to defend his comrades.

His heroic actions and determination in the face of extreme pain inspired the entire assault force.

His actions are in keeping with the finest traditions of military heroism and reflect distinct credit upon himself, Special Operations Task Force—33, Combined Joint Special Operations Task Force—Afghanistan, Special Operations Command Central and the United States Army.

Capt Kyle Walton, right, and Master Sgt Scott Ford, left, talk to an interpreter in Eastern Afghanistan.

insurgent forces from overrunning the American and Afghan elements. His audacious decision allowed just enough freedom of maneuver to evacuate all casualties down a sixty-foot cliff in preparation for medical evacuation.

STAFF SGT MATTHEW O. WILLIAMS, CASPER, WY

While under insurgent sniper and machine gun fire, Sergeant Williams descended with his Team Sergeant off a sixty-foot near vertical cliff to the Casualty Collection Point (CCP) and continued providing him first aid. Sergeant Williams observed, shot, and killed two insurgent fighters attempting to maneuver on the CCP. Sergeant Williams then braved a hail of small arms fire and climbed back up to the cliff in order evacuate other injured soldiers, and repair his ODA Commander's radio. After returning to the CCP with three wounded U.S. soldiers, Insurgent fighters began maneuvering to overrun the CCP for the second time. Sergeant Williams and the Afghan Commandos launched a counterattack and gallantly fought for several hours against at least two hundred insurgents. With disregard for his personal safety, he exposed himself to insurgent fire from multiple directions and carried casualties to the Medical Evacuation helicopter, then continued to suppress numerous Insurgent positions and direct Commando fire.

CAPT KYLE M. WALTON, CARMEL, IN

While pulling casualties to cover, the tip of his rifle barrel was shot off. Knowing his weapon was no longer accurate beyond a short distance, Captain Walton courageously continued to identify targets for other soldiers to engage despite being impacted by two rounds to his helmet. As the situation deteriorated and the casualties mounted, Captain Walton came to the realization that his entire element was in danger of being completely overrun by insurgent forces. Captain Walton relayed this information to his headquarters and requested the placement of danger close attack helicopter and fixed wing close air support on all known and suspected insurgent positions. He authorized the use of two-thousand-pound bombs to be dropped almost directly on top of his position in order to prevent

AIR FORCE CROSS:
STAFF SGT
ZACHARY J. RHYNER
AIR FORCE

For service as set forth in the following:

CITATION:

The President of the United States of America, authorized by Title 10, Section 8742, United States Code, takes pleasure in presenting the Air Force Cross to Senior Airman Zachary J. Rhyner, United States Air Force, for extraordinary heroism in military operations against an armed enemy of the United States while serving with the 21st Special Tactics Squadron, at Nuristan Province, Afghanistan on 6 April 2008. On that date, while assigned as Special Tactics Combat Controller, Airman Rhyner executed a day rotary-wing infiltration with his Special Forces team to capture high-value insurgents in a village on the surrounding mountains. While climbing near vertical terrain to reach their objective, the team was attacked in a well-coordinated and deadly ambush. Devastating sniper, machine gun, and rocket-propelled grenade fire poured down on the team from elevated and protected positions on all sides, immediately pinning down the assault force. Without regard for his life, Airman Rhyner placed himself between the most immediate threats and provided suppressive fire with his M-4 rifle against enemy fire while fellow teammates were extracted from the line of fire. Airman Rhyner bravely withstood the hail of enemy fire to control eight United States Air Force fighters and four United States Army attack helicopters. Despite a gunshot wound to the left leg and being trapped on a 60-foot cliff under constant enemy fire, Airman Rhyner controlled more than fifty attack runs and repeatedly repelled the enemy with repeated danger close air strikes, several within one hundred meters of his position. Twice, his actions prevented his element from being overrun during the intense six-and-a-half-hour battle. Through his extraordinary heroism, superb airmanship, and aggressiveness in the face of the enemy, Airman Rhyner reflected the highest credit upon himself and the United States Air Force.

Secretary of the Air Force Michael B. Donley presents Staff Sgt Zachary Rhyner the Air Force Cross.

CITATION TO ACCOMPANY THE AWARD OF THE BRONZE STAR MEDAL (WITH VALOR) TO SSG ROBERT GUTIERREZ JR.

Despite being struck twice by 7.62-mm bullets in the helmet, Sergeant Gutierrez maintained his calm demeanor and continued to prosecute targets. As the fight continued, the insurgents shifted their efforts toward arriving helicopters and engaged them with heavy fire. Sergeant Gutierrez coordinated with the ground force commander to delay friendly force extraction until the enemy positions could be suppressed. Enabled by his systematic control of air power during the fight, all seventeen friendly casualties were safely evacuated and forty enemy fighters were killed.

SSG Robert Gutierrez receiving the Bronze Star and the Purple Heart for action in 2008.

26 APR 08

THE "AWAKENING"

SOMEWHERE IN IRAQ

The pundits were finally pointing to progress in Iraq. The "Awakening" started in al Anbar province as a coalition between tribal sheiks, was bolstered by the added commitment of U.S. troops known as "the surge." By mid-2008, it was beginning to look like the coalition might actually win the war if the Iraqi and American people could be convinced to stay the course.

As the "Awakening" took hold, Special Operations forces were as busy as ever, moving around the country at a frenetic pace, following intelligence leads and hunting down remaining elements of al-Qaeda wherever they could be found.

That is how Specialist Joe Gibson, a Ranger with 2nd Battalion, 75th Ranger Regiment, found himself packed in with a platoon of his comrades on Black Hawk helicopters streaking through the Iraqi night toward the likely hiding place of a band of al-Qaeda holdouts.

Gibson was no stranger to missions like these. In three combat tours of Iraq, he'd participated in dozens of similar missions. It was the kind of thing he'd joined the army to do—go where the action was and do bad things to bad people.

The Black Hawks flared hard and set down in a farmer's field near their objective.

The Rangers piled out and fell into the prone position around the Night Stalker Black Hawks, their weapons loaded and ready to fire.

Seconds later they realized the enemy was similarly prepared. No sooner had the dust from the helos departure begun to settle than AK-47 and RPK machine gun rounds began to crack and zip through the tall grass. The rangers deployed in the tall grass and returned fire, making full use of their sophisticated night vision giving them the edge on the nearly moonless night.

Joe Gibson was returning fire as best he could when he heard a scream that made his blood run cold. It was Jared (pseudonym), a good friend in his platoon. "Joe! I'm hit, man! Help me!" he cried.

Joe thrashed his way through the chest deep grass to reach his wounded comrade. When he reached Jared, there was blood everywhere. Gibson had a medical kit, so he dropped to his knees beside his buddy and started tearing the pouch open, looking for the special hemostatic bandages that would stop the bleeding quickly. Bullets still snapped by him, cutting down stalks of grass, but Joe was totally focused on helping his friend. "I'm here, bro. Hang on. We'll get you fixed up."

A moment later the platoon medic arrived, and the Black Hawks were summoned to take out Jared and another injured man. Due to the ongoing firefight, however, the choppers would have to land several hundred meters away. The wounded Rangers would need to be carried to the extraction zone. Joe volunteered to help.

Rangers train in urban environment.

They put Jared on a skedko litter. Joe and the medic each took one end and began the arduous trek to the pickup zone. Even with the copious amounts of adrenaline flowing through his veins, Joe soon realized carrying the litter was going to be harder than he expected. The night was pitch black and the uneven ground was crisscrossed with deep drainage ditches. Before they'd gone half the distance to the PZ, the young specialist Gibson was more tired than he'd ever been.

In Ranger School, they'd gone for weeks with only a few hours sleep each night and about half as much food as they normally required. They'd patrolled through freezing swamps, up and down steep mountains in southern Appalachia—but nothing was as difficult as this. Concern for his fallen brother simultaneously sapped his strength and spurred him to move faster.

Once they got Jared on the medevac Bird, Gibson felt much better. He knew the hospital back at base offered an incredibly high standard of care and if they could get Jared there quickly, he'd be okay.

Now it was time to go back and find the enemy fighters who shot Jared—if Joe had anything to say about it, those men were going to pay.

He hustled to rejoin his squad. By the time he reached them, the al-Qaeda who had been shooting at them were either dead or melted away into the darkness. The only sound invading the moonless night was the swishing of Gibson's boots as he waded through the tall grass. He picked his feet up as he walked along, placing them carefully to not fall into a ditch or trip over an unseen obstacle. Then he stepped on something soft—like mud, only his foot didn't sink in. At first he thought nothing of it. Iraq hadn't seen regular trash pickup for years, so there was garbage everywhere.

But if it was trash he stepped on, why were there alarm bells going off in his head? If there was anything Gibson learned in three tours in Iraq, it was to listen to those bells.

He turned back to investigate. Before he'd retraced two steps, however, a man materialized out of the ground. That's when Gibson realized there was a ditch there, and the trash he stepped on was actually a man.

The realization came in an instant. But in that instant, the Iraqi raised a rifle and pointed it at him. Gibson was staring down the barrel of an AK-47.

Instinct took over. Gibson swatted the barrel of the AK to the side just as the enemy fighter pulled the trigger. Flame exploded from the barrel—right next to Gibson's face. The muscular Ranger was too close to bring his own weapon to bear, so he simply tackled the guy. The two of them went down in a heap, both men clutching desperately at the rifle. The man screamed like a wounded animal, which Gibson countered by calling for reinforcements. He wrestled the man's rifle away, but the man wouldn't give up that easily. He grabbed Gibson's helmet and pulled so hard it ripped the kevlar right off, nearly taking his head with it. The man then grabbed at Gibson's own M4 assault rifle, but since it was attached to his body armor by a sling, there was no way his assailant was going to be able to shoot him with it, so Joe concentrated on hammering the guy in the face with both fists.

Rangers receive a large amount of instruction in the principles of hand-to-hand combat. It is gruelling, painful, and dangerous even in a training environment, but at the moment, Joe Gibson was glad for every minute of it. Positional control, he'd learned, was paramount in winning such a battle—and he put this into practice by rolling on top of his attacker and bearing down on him, fists still pounding the man's temples. Then, he felt the fighter reaching for something on his waist. At first Gibson assumed the man was going for a knife, but then the man shouted one word in English that made the young Ranger's hopes for surviving the mission diminish rapidly.

"Bomb!"

Joe Gibson was sitting on top of a suicide bomber. The man was attempting to activate his explosives-packed vest.

Gibson reached down and snatched the man's hand away from his belt. He tried to roll himself onto the man's other arm to keep him from reaching the activator with his other hand and killing them both. But this allowed the man to bring his knees up and use them to push Gibson's body armor up into his chin. Lithe and amazingly strong, the man kept increasing the pressure until Gibson thought he might pass out. If that happened, it was all over but the fireworks. Gibson knew he was running out of time.

But one of these dirt bags shot Jared and hurt him bad. Jared had a pregnant wife at home. Come to think of it, Gibson had a wife, too. A fire ignited in his gut. One of them, the Ranger or the terrorist wasn't going home tonight. And Joe Gibson decided that man wasn't going to be him.

With every remaining ounce of strength, Gibson bore down on his opponent and sent his fist crashing into the man's temple. The powerful blow stunned the man and he momentarily went limp. Gibson pushed off of his attacker and swung his M4 around. He pushed the barrel into the terrorist's gut and pulled the trigger. The M4 coughed twice more and the contest was over.

Jared and Joe were both going home to see their wives.

Five months later, to the day, Joe and Jared walked onto the stage in an auditorium on the Army base at Fort Lewis, Washington. Their wives were both there to watch and cheer as Jared received a purple heart for the wounds he suffered that dark

Specialist Joe Gibson

night in Iraq. After that, Specialist Joe Gibbs stood at attention, looking slightly uncomfortable as Admiral Eric Olson, the commander of Special Operations Command, pinned a Silver Star to his chest.

He would gladly have lived without the medal. But the action was just what he joined up for. Not long after that, Gibson reenlisted for another tour with the 3rd Platoon, A Company, 2nd Battalion of the 75th Ranger Regiment.

Rangers practice combatives

26 JUN 08

MARSOC FIREFIGHT

HERAT PROVINCE, AFGHANISTAN

By mid-2008 Coalition intelligence gathering capabilities were improving across Afghanistan. Everything from signals intelligence to human intelligence to unmanned aerial observation platforms blanketed the country, which made it very difficult for Taliban kingpins to move around the country without being spotted.

Spotting big game is only half the battle, though. When a Taliban kingpin is found, someone has to go in and get him. And that job is never easy. Many warlords travel with large security details who will all gladly fight to the death protecting their bosses.

Normally, that's just fine with the warriors of the Marine Special Operations Command, known as MARSOC.

The first MARSOC units were created with veterans of the Marine Force Reconnaissance companies. In 2005 MARSOC became a part of U.S. Special Operations Command. Though new, the organization flourished, taking the same training as and working closely alongside special operators from other services. By 2008, MARSOC teams were colocated with a Special Forces A-teams, training and mentoring Afghan commandos.

In late June 2008, intelligence indicated a Taliban warlord had taken up residence and was stockpiling weapons in a remote canyon north of Herat in western Afghanistan, not far from the Iranian border. Two teams of MARSOC operators were tasked with acting on the crucial, time-sensitive intelligence. They were ordered to capture or kill the Taliban leader before he moved elsewhere.

The MARSOC Marines formed up with a platoon of twenty-four Afghan National Army Commandos on a mission to apprehend the high-value Taliban target. They moved out well before dark in up-armored Ground Mobility Vehicles (GMVs) armed with .50 caliber machine guns and high-tech MK-47 grenade launchers; a machine gun that fires 40-mm grenades instead of bullets. They hoped to arrive on their objective before first light.

The twelve-hour drive across the desert to their target was slow and grueling, as none of the roads in that region are paved, and they avoided most of them anyway, since improvised explosive devices made what roads were passable too dangerous to use. Once they reached the mountains, the danger increased exponentially, as the

Prepping equipment

team was forced to follow existing dirt paths winding through deep, sandy wadis strewn with boulders and hard-to-see washouts.

As they carefully picked their way in the darkness toward the objective, attack helicopters tracked their progress, providing cover from the air. Several kilometers from the objective, they stopped to make sure everything was ready for the final push.

Captain Dan Strelkauskas, the thirty-two-year-old team leader for the mission, had already briefed his men on the complex operation before leaving their Forward Operating Base. Now he carefully checked each of his men to ensure they were ready for action. The cave complex Intel identified as a likely weapons cache was situated in a deep, narrow wadi with only the most rudimentary dirt track leading into it. There was no other way in or out. Once they entered the wadi, even turning the GMVs around was going to be difficult.

They wound their way cautiously up the sandy ravine. Rounding a corner, the team was confronted with two abandoned vehicles in the road—a beat-up white SUV parked to one side and an old red pickup parked directly across from it. One side of the road was a sheer cliff face and the other side was a thirty-foot drop. There was no way around the vehicles. Obviously, someone didn't want people driving any further up the valley. Beyond the vehicles, a cave entrance was visible in the side of the mountain. That was their objective, the likely hideout of the Taliban leader.

The team stopped momentarily and considered whether they should push the pickup out of the road with their powerful GMVs. But the enemy had to know that, too, and the Marines suspected the insurgents may have rigged the abandoned vehicles with explosives. So two of the MARSOC operators, SSgt Eddie Heredia and SSgt Eric Guendner dismounted and cautiously approached the vehicles to see if they were wired.

Heredia was a stocky twenty-eight-year-old gun-team leader, the son of Mexican immigrants, joined the Marines because he wanted to give back to the country that gave his family the opportunity to rise from poverty. Captain Strelkauskas and Staff Sergeant John Mosser, the unit's acting "Gunny"—he was selected but not yet promoted to Gunnery Sergeant—got out with a few others and pulled security while Heredia and Guendner moved up to the vehicles and peered inside and underneath. As they did, several single shots rang out from somewhere overhead. Everyone ducked, but as they scanned the steep and craggy mountainside, nobody could tell from where the firing originated. Quiet returned to the canyon and everyone wondered if their presence might have scared off any insurgents in the area. The presence of attack helicopters often did that.

The vehicles were clean. Captain Strelkauskas received word from the pilots orbiting overhead that they were low on fuel and would have to return to base soon. Their sophisticated thermal optics showed no sign of life in the area. So Strelkauskas bade them farewell and sent them on their way. As the Marines and commandos pressed forward, the sun had yet to rise, but its light was already chasing the shadows into the deepest recesses of the canyon. The men no longer needed their night-vision goggles.

That's when the firestorm began.

Guendner and Heredia were walking back from the disabled vehicles blocking the road. They had almost reached Captain Strelkauskas, Gunny Mosser, and the others in the three lead vehicles when the chatter of machine guns echoed through the canyon from a half-dozen heavily dug-in and well-camouflaged enemy positions somewhere high up the mountainside. Rounds smacked into the ground, coming in from above, ahead, and behind. Within seconds Heredia was hit in the leg, his buddies inside the vehicles watching in horror as he went down in a hail of gunfire. Rounds tore up their vehicles, snapping off antennas and starring the bulletproof-glass windshields. Immediately the turret gunners returned fire, peppering the mountain with grenades and .50 caliber tracer rounds. SSgt Guendner was returning fire when he, too, was hit and went down with a bullet in the leg.

The biggest problem was that the enemy positions were so well camouflaged the Marines couldn't see where the fire was coming from. There was no room to turn around and get out of the kill zone and the disabled vehicles kept them from going forward. The only way to escape the fusillade of fire was for every vehicle in the convoy to back up the road—under fire. One false move, however, would send a vehicle

Taliban fighters hiding out in rocky areas

crashing over the thirty-foot cliff next to the road. Gunny Mosser saw this and diregarding the bullets falling like rain, he broke cover and exposed himself to wave directions at the rest of the convoy to get them to back out of the ambush. His leadership got the convoy moving in the right direction, and several vehicles escaped the worst of the fire. Miraculously Mosser was not hit in the process.

MARSOC Marine

Sgt Carlos Bolaños was driving the second GMV with his partner, Sgt Sam Shoenheit, manning the grenade launcher in the turret. Seeing his two wounded mates still on the ground in the kill zone, Sgt Bolaños jumped out and began laying down suppressive fire with his M240G machine gun while Shoenheit ran through an entire belt of 40-mm grenades, peppering the mountainside. Meanwhile, SSgt Heredia was trying to put a tourniquet on his own leg as bullets slammed into the ground all around him. He needed help.

Bolaños jumped back in the GMV and shouted, "Hold on!" He punched the accelerator and the heavy vehicle shot forward toward their fallen comrade. Standing in the turret, Shoenheit loaded a new belt in his MK-47 and was holding the trigger down, hammering the hillside in front of them with high-explosive shells. Just then, a sniper round smashed into the lip of his helmet, causing his night-vision goggles to practically explode. The bullet ricocheted off the NVG rail and entered his skull. Shoenheit crumpled back into the vehicle, unconscious.

Bolaños dove over the seat to pull his partner out of the line of fire. He was tearing open bandages and trying to stem the flow of blood from Shoenheit's head wound when a Navy medical corpsman ran up to take over the grenade launcher. But before he could mount the vehicle and man the gun, he, too, was hit and fell between the two GMVs. Bolaños jumped out and pulled their injured Doc back to the vehicle behind his own, bandaging his wounds once he got the man inside. Then he ran back to help Shoenheit.

Back in the kill zone, Captain Strelkauskas and his small team took the only cover they could find behind their shot-up GMV. They were completely pinned down. As Strelkauskas returned fire, bullets ricocheted off the GMV's hood, peppering his hands and arms with fragments. When Chief Petty Officer Anthony Shattuck, the senior Corpsman assigned to the mission, was hit, Gunny Mosser stripped off the man's gear and tried to render first aid. Though the bullet hit Shattuck in the torso,

221

he was still conscious and actually diagnosed his own wounds. When he began having trouble breathing, he knew one of his lungs was hit and was filling up with fluid. As Mosser looked on, Shattuck produced a long needle and plunged it between his own ribs to relieve the pressure.

Enemy machine gunners and riflemen zeroed in on their position and even the slightest attempts at movement were met with a hail of deadly accurate gunfire. Knowing the rest of his team would be desperately trying to reach them, Mosser got on his radio and ordered that no one else was to enter the kill zone. "Nobody else comes in. If anybody else comes in, you're going to die. We are pinned and pinned bad."

As he sent the command, Captain Strelkauskas stuck his head up momentarily and could see Heredia about sixty feet away, still fumbling with a tourniquet on his leg. He started to yell at the stocky Latino, but then Heredia was hit again and dropped like a marionette whose strings had just been cut. That was all Strelkauskas could stand. He jumped up and sprinted to Heredia's side, ignoring the bullets snapping by only inches from his body.

The Captain grabbed his wounded Marine and dragged him back to the relative safety of their GMV. As he did, Gunny John Mosser ran out and did the same for the other wounded Marine, Ssgt Guendner. Mosser gave first aid to Guendner while Strelkauskas worked to save Heredia, who was gushing bright-red blood from a hole in his chest, just above his body armor. Despite the Captain's best efforts, Heredia died moments later.

At the rear of the column, another medical Corpsman, Chief Petty Officer Jeremy Torrisi was standing in the bed of a GMV, listening to the chatter on the radio. When he heard all the other medical personnel forward of his position were hit, he stuck his head into the vehicle and yelled at the driver. "Let's go! Get me up there!"

The driver pulled out of the back of the convoy and squeezed past the other vehicles, whose gunners were also probing the mountainside with their heavy weapons, trying to slow the volume of enemy fire. They were still having trouble identifying the well-hidden Taliban positions. Torrisi joined them, firing an M240G machine gun as they swerved around the rest of the vehicles in the convoy. But they were still seventy-five yards short of the three lead vehicles taking all the fire when the road became too narrow to pass, stopping their forward progress. Enemy machine gun fire raked the ground between Torrisi and those he was trying to reach. He closed his eyes for a moment and thought of his family back at home. Then he thought of his friends, wounded and trapped in the kill zone. He picked up his weapon and yelled, "I'm going in."

The gunner in the turret looked back at him and shouted, "Good luck." Torrisi took a deep breath and jumped down out of the back of his vehicle, sprinting across the "beaten zone" where enemy fire was kicking up geysers of dirt. Taliban fighters saw him right away and he could hear incoming rounds snapping by his head as he ran.

He slid in behind the third GMV like a baseball player dodging a throw at home plate. He looked in the open back door and saw a man hit in the arm and shoulder. He'd already been bandaged up and looked like he would survive for a while, so Torrisi pushed off and ran for all he was worth to the second vehicle in the convoy, the one which had been driven by Sgt Bolaños. He found Bolaños cradling Shoenheit, who had a bullet embedded in his skull. Torrisi's eyes went wide when he saw brain matter squeezing out the entry wound. He shouted over the din of battle to Bolaños, "We've gotta get him out of here quick." Schoenheit was conscious, but disoriented and unable to speak. Bolaños jumped into the driver's seat and began backing the vehicle out of the kill zone very slowly while Torrisi put pressure on Schoenheit's wound and tried to reassure him everything was going to be okay.

The enemy was shooting down from such an elevated position that rounds kept coming in through the open gun turret and bouncing around inside the vehicle. Angry now, Torrisi picked up a rifle with an M-203 grenade launcher attached and started sending 40-mm high-explosive grenades up through the hatch back at the enemy. The unorthodox procedure worked and the rain of explosives projectiles landing on the Taliban positions above had the desired effect. The rounds coming in through the hatch stopped.

MARSOC Marine checks out a cave in Afghanistan

When the truck had backed up as far as it could, others came to help with Shoenheit. Torrisi grabbed his aid bag and again sprinted through the kill zone up to the lead vehicle, where he found Captain Strelkauskas, Gunny Mosser, the medic, Anthony Shattuck, SSgt Guendner, and several others, including the body of his friend, Ssgt Heredia. But there wasn't time to grieve.

Though Shattuck was in very bad shape, he was still working on his own wounds. Torrisi took over and immediately patched up the sucking chest wound so his mate could breathe. He also reinserted the needle into his chest cavity to relieve the fluid buildup on that lung.

"Hey!" someone shouted. "I wouldn't stand there if I were you!" Torrisi looked up to see another friend, Army Special Forces medic, Sergeant First Class John Crouse. Crouse, busy putting pressure on a bloody bandage on his own leg, yelled, "Hey, I was standing right where you are when they shot me!" But Torrisi didn't have a lot of options for where to stand—there were seven men huddled behind that GMV and he had to keep working on Shattuck. He'd already jabbed that huge needle between the wounded Corpsman's ribs half a dozen more times to keep him breathing.

Just seconds later Torrisi suddenly realized he should have heeded Crouse's warning, The Taliban bullet felt like he'd been jabbed in the buttocks with a hot poker. But he couldn't let go of Shattuck at that moment to tend to his own wounds.

"Here, I got you covered," shouted one of the Marines, giving Torrisi a chance to shift his body around so another Marine could bandage his backside while he continued to keep pressure on Shattuck's sucking chest wound. Though it was painful, Torrisi figured a bullet in the butt wasn't going to kill him right away. He also knew if they didn't get Shattuck to a hospital quickly, he wasn't going to make it.

Mosser took in the news, then nodded and picked up his handheld GPS unit. "Be right back." He sprinted from cover back into the open where his Global Positioning System could get an unobstructed view of the sky. He stood there, stock-still allowing the little device to lock on to the satellites, while he ignored the enemy fire zipping through the air around him. Once the GPS had a good fix on their position, he ran back to cover. He then called the coordinates in on his radio and ordered an air strike run on the mountainside. When the aircraft checked in overhead, he shouted to the others, "This is gonna be danger close. Keep your heads down."

The bombs shook the mountainside, sending geysers of flame and debris into the air, while Torrisi draped his body over Shattuck, doing his best to shield his friend from debris and shrapnel. As he painfully stood up, he realized the enemy guns had gone silent. He stopped to listen and for the first time in over two hours, nobody was shooting at them.

Gunny Mosser was listening to the chatter over the radio. "Medevac helicopters are inbound. Let's get these guys out of here." Torrisi nodded. Ignoring the pain in his backside, he grabbed Shattuck by the legs. Another Marine got him under the arms, and two others picked up SSgt Guendner in similar fashion. Half expecting the enemy to open up on them again, they hustled the two wounded men out of the kill zone, carrying them all the way to the rear of the convoy where a Black Hawk medevac helicopter found a place to set down.

They wanted Torrisi to get on the helicopter with the rest of the wounded, but since he was the only one of the medical personnel still walking, he refused. Instead, he hobbled back up the road treating other walking wounded—Afghan commandos and American alike.

When they finally got everyone out of the kill zone, Captain Strelkauskas called for more air strikes with two-thousand-pound bombs on the hillside. An after-action battle damage assessment counted forty dead Taliban fighters. Schoenheit had a bullet surgically removed from his brain and was flown back to the states, where he faces years of therapy. Jeremy Torrisi was offered a flight home as well, along with some time off to recover from his gunshot wound. But he refused and stayed in theater another four months.

For his actions during the engagement, John Mosser was awarded the Navy Cross, while Captain Stelkauskas and Doc Torrisi were both presented with the Silver Star. Sergeants Shoenheit and Bolaños each received Bronze Stars with "V" device for valor.

When asked about their awards, they all say the same thing: They didn't do what they did, for an award. They did it for each other.

Sgts Sam Shoenheit and Carlos Bolaños

NAVY CROSS: STAFF SERGEANT JOHN S. MOSSER, UNITED STATES MARINE CORPS

The President of the United States of America takes pleasure in presenting the Navy Cross to Staff Sergeant John S. Mosser, United States Marine Corps, for extraordinary heroism in connection with combat operations against the enemy while serving as Team Sergeant, Marine Special Operations Company H, Second Marine Special Operations Battalion, U.S. Marine Corps Forces, Special Operations Command, in support of Operation Enduring Freedom on 26 June 2008. While maneuvering through restrictive terrain to prosecute a time-sensitive high-value target, dismounted patrol members were engaged with heavy volumes of high-angle automatic and sniper fire. Within seconds, two Marines lay wounded in the kill zone unable to seek cover. With disregard for his own safety, Staff Sergeant Mosser maintained keen situational awareness and calm under fire as he rushed to the aid of the nearest Marines. He single-handedly dragged the wounded Marine over thirty-five feet to a covered position and administered first aid. With the entire patrol desperately pinned down, one Marine killed, and five more severely wounded, Staff Sergeant Mosser devised a plan to break contact and extract his team.

While adjusting close air support, he personally shielded and moved the wounded Marine through the kill zone a second time to safety. He then ordered the extraction of the remaining twenty-two members trapped in the ambush. As he instructed the team to move, Staff Sergeant Mosser exposed himself repeatedly to enemy fire and engaged the enemy until all members were safe. By his courageous actions, bold initiative, and total devotion to duty, Staff Sergeant Mosser reflected great credit upon himself and upheld the highest traditions of the Marine Corps and of the United States Naval Service.

Maj Danny Strelkauskas, commanding officer of Force Company, 1st Reconnaissance Battalion, 1st Marine Division, I Marine Expeditionary Force, pins the Navy Cross on Gunnery Sgt John S. Mosser.

SILVER STAR:
CAPTAIN DANIEL A.
STRELKAUSKAS,
UNITED STATES MARINE CORPS

The President of the United States of America takes pleasure in presenting the Silver Star to Captain Daniel A. Strelkauskas, United States Marine Corps, for conspicuous gallantry and intrepidity in action against the enemy as Mission Commander, Marine Special Operations Company H, Second Marine Special Operations Battalion, U.S. Marine Corps Forces, Special Operations Command, in support of Operation Enduring Freedom, on 26 June 2008.

While conducting a time-sensitive mission, the dismounted patrol Captain Strelkauskas was leading came under heavy machine gun and sniper fire from entrenched positions. He began immediate actions to move his team to cover as the patrol began taking casualties. With complete disregard for his own life, and under heavy fire from more than a dozen positions, Captain Strelkauskas ran deeper into the kill zone to drag a wounded Marine across open terrain to a covered position.

With multiple fragmentation wounds to his hands and rounds ricocheting near his position, and with the enemy machine guns delivering devastating fire and preventing the movement of casualties, he ordered a critical Close Air Support deployment of two-thousand-pound bombs well within danger close parameters. This provided enough suppression of the enemy force to allow the relocation of the wounded to a consolidation point where five friendly Wounded-in-Action and one friendly Killed-in-Action were evacuated.

Upon completion of the evacuation, Captain Strelkauskas coordinated follow on air strikes resulting in an estimated forty enemy killed in action, including several mid-level Taliban leaders. Through his tremendous courage and extraordinary battlefield leadership, he guided his team out of a complex and well-orchestrated ambush executed by an entrenched enemy.

By his bold initiative, undaunted courage, and complete dedication to duty, Captain Strelkauskas reflected great credit upon himself and upheld the highest traditions of the Marine Corps and of the United States Naval Service.

Maj Daniel Strelkauskas, right, shakes the hand of Maj Gen Richard Mills after Mills presented him with the Silver Star for his heroic actions in Afghanistan.

SILVER STAR:
HOSPITAL CORPSMAN FIRST CLASS
JEREMY K. TORRISI
NAVY

For service as set forth in the following Citation: The President of the United States of America takes pleasure in presenting the Silver Star to Hospital Corpsman First Class Jeremy K. Torrisi, United States Navy, for conspicuous gallantry and intrepidity in action against the enemy as Team Corpsman, Marine Special Operations Company H, Second Marine Special Operations Battalion, U.S. Marine Corps Forces, Special Operations Command, in support of Operation Enduring Freedom on 26 June 2008. Petty Officer Torrisi courageously exposed himself to accurate fire numerous times when his company was pinned down in a mountainous draw by withering fire from a concealed enemy position. After several Marines and other medical providers were hit by enemy fire, he ran into the kill zone with total disregard for his own safety to provide desperately needed aid. After stabilizing one Marine and dragging him to cover, he ran back through a hail of bullets to the side of a fellow Corpsman and began to administer lifesaving medical care. Petty Officer Torrisi was subsequently shot in the leg but continued treating casualties for several hours while refusing medical treatment for his own injuries. Under intense fire, while simultaneously directing the evacuation of the wounded Marines and Sailors, he laid down suppressive fire until every team member had evacuated the kill zone. His actions ultimately saved the lives of four of his teammates, and his courage and quick thinking prevented further loss of life. By his relentless resolve, courageous fighting spirit, and unwavering dedication to duty, Petty Officer Torrisi reflected great credit upon himself and upheld the highest traditions of the United States Naval Service.

Maj Gen Paul E. Lefebvre, the commander of U.S. Marine Corps Forces Special Operations Command presents Chief Petty Officer Jeremy K. Torrisi, a hospital corpsman with 2nd Marine Special Operations Battalion, with the Silver Star Medal.

229

"Shura"—a town meeting with local tribal leaders

THE BATTLE FOR AZIZ ABAD

HERAT, AFGHANISTAN

Sometimes the heroes lose, even when they win.

In the war in Afghanistan, the Taliban have consistently bested the Coalition in one very important area: the media battle space. In August 2008 our FOX News combat coverage team was eyewitness to such an event. Though the battle was a spectacular tactical victory, it became a strategic loss because the Taliban did a better job at getting out their side of the story.

A Taliban sentry fired the first shots shortly after 2:30 a.m. as Afghan Commandos and U.S. Special Operations Command troops breached the outer gates of the walled compound at Aziz Abad. Though the Marine Special Operations Team employed a daring deception to achieve surprise, they were engaged by gunfire from AK-47s and machine guns almost immediately after entering the compound.

The target was a Taliban commander named Mullah Siddiq. United States Special Forces and Marine Special Operators had been tracking him for months. Credible information received after a "Shura"—a town meeting with local tribal leaders—revealed the timing and location of a Taliban meeting. The intelligence was confirmed painstakingly and U.S. Special Operations Command officers sat down with their Afghan Commando counterparts to carefully plan a "capture-kill mission" with the goal of taking several key Taliban leaders into custody. Cameraman, Chris Jackson and I accompanied the raid force.

Gunnery Sergeant Joseph Parent, the #2 MARSOC operator on the mission was wounded shortly after they burst into the compound. A Taliban fighter on a rooftop opened up directly above the breach element, hitting the Gunnery Sergeant in the leg. The bullet entered his Achilles tendon and exited the bottom of his foot.

Taliban fighters on the rooftops, concealed from the team on the ground, were clearly visible on the thermal scope aboard a USAF MC-130 Combat Talon aircraft orbiting overhead. The overhead imagery was transmitted via satellite radio to the Joint Tactical Air Controllers with the assault and support elements and they quickly called in a burst from its 20-mm cannons.

At that point the second half of the assault element—members of the 7th Special Forces Group and additional Afghan Commandos arrived on the scene. As they

The heavily-armed AC-130 Hercules is crewed by capable special-operations airmen.

attempted to enter the Taliban compound, they too were engaged by insurgent fighters. Once again the JTAC called in fire from above. For the next 2 1/2 hours, the 207th Afghan Commandos and their U.S. Army and Marine counterparts were in a running gunfight with heavily armed Taliban fighters inside the walled compound. When enemy combatants on rooftops and in narrow alleyways could not be dislodged by fire from U.S. and Afghan troops on the ground, they were hit by supporting fire from manned and unmanned aircraft overhead.

By dawn 22 August, the compound was finally secured. Several dozen noncombatants—women, children, and old men—were segregated and guarded by an Afghan commando security element. Throughout the engagement, Jackson and I watched as noncombatants were humanely treated, provided with medical attention, and quietly questioned about what they knew.

Getting ready for a night op

To those of us who were there, it appeared that the commandos and their American advisers achieved a stunning success. Gunnery Sergeant Parent was the only friendly casualty, a senior Taliban leader and twenty-five of his fighters were dead. One of the houses turned out to contain much more than anticipated—large stockpiles of arms and ammunition, a major cache of IED-making material including explosives and detonators. Because the quantity of contraband was too large to carry off, a representative sample of the material was loaded aboard commando trucks and an engineer placed a small explosive charge on top of the remainder. When the charge detonated it set off a large secondary explosion that literally brought the house down.

The search element also found communications equipment, terrorist training paraphernalia, thousands of dollars in cash, and the biggest shocker—care

packages mailed from the United States and meant for the Special Operators from friends and family members at home. Apparently the Taliban had an agent inside the base who was stealing boxes of cookies before they could be delivered to the intended recipients.

After the compound was secure, we accompanied the ODA team sergeant through the entire objective. We counted about twenty-five bodies, all armed, and apparently all military-age males. The commandos also discovered two wounded females—apparently a mother and her child. They were gently treated by a Special Operations medic and quickly evacuated to a hospital as the commandos withdrew from the objective. As our cameras recorded, the mission was a success due to careful planning and measured application of firepower. It appeared to be a major victory.

Unfortunately the good news quickly turned bad.

While we were en route back to the base from which the raid was launched, the U.S. ground force commander received a report over the radio that pro-Taliban agitators were

Hamid Karzai

already asserting that "the Americans killed thirty civilians." The claims and alleged number of civilian casualties quickly escalated.

Shortly after we arrived back at the Special Operations base, an official in Kabul called the governor of Aziz Abad and assured him the families of any civilian casualties would receive reparations in the amount of $1,000 U.S. per person. Then things really got out of hand. Around noon 22 August, Iranian television reported, "A U.S. air strike south of Herat in western Afghanistan has killed more than fifty innocent civilians, including women and children." This report was soon picked up by news agencies in the U.S., Europe, and the Middle East. The United Nations command in Kabul offered to transport Afghan and foreign reporters to the Special Operations base so they could see the confiscated weapons and other evidence for themselves. It didn't help.

That evening, as we filed our full story with videotape of the raid and an interview with a U.S. Special Forces officer, unnamed "sources" at the Ministry of the Interior in Kabul were telling reporters seventy-six civilians were killed. Little or no attention was paid to the Taliban arms and equipment seized as evidence, the material destroyed at the objective or to the care provided to the wounded woman and child. It was clear families were coming out of the woodwork to claim their $1,000 in reparation money.

By the morning of 23 August, little more than twenty-four hours after the operation, the international press wires and mainstream news outlets were carrying photos of damaged buildings and an Afghan human rights organization was charging that eighty-eight civilians—among them twenty women and fifty children—were killed by U.S. forces. Later in the day, President Hamid Karzai first called for an investigation, then denounced the operation. Though fewer than fifteen new graves were evident in nearby cemeteries—and no local civilians sought medical treatment for wounds, the number of noncombatant casualties allegedly inflicted in the raid continued to rise.

On 24 August, with several investigations under way but not yet complete, the Afghan Commando battalion commander was "suspended." That evening, in a report on FOX News, I noted that neither cameraman Chris Jackson nor I saw any noncombatants killed and that "the Taliban and their supporters are running a very effective propaganda campaign to discredit coalition efforts. Exaggerated claims of damage often result in demands for more money in compensation."

The next day the United Nations Assistance Mission in Afghanistan concluded that ninety civilians were killed during the raid at Aziz Abad. Then, as we were departing for Herat, we were informed the government in Kabul was offering $200,000 to settle the claims and was planning new restrictions on Special Operations Commando missions. In fact, the Special Operations units with which we had been embedded, were ordered to "stand down" and did not perform another mission for more than forty-five days afterward.

The mission accomplished one thing spectacularly well—highlighting the need for the Coalition to do a better job in the media battle space—something that, unfortunately, still has plenty of room for improvement. But for those who participated in the mission, there is no doubt—the raid at Aziz Abad was yet another instance of brave men doing a dangerous and thankless job in the shadows of the Hindu Kush to rid the world of the kind of men who would fly airplanes into buildings full of real, not imaginary, innocent people.

In another sad development that highlights the level of corruption within the Afghan government, the informer who passed the information about the whereabouts of the Taliban safe house was reportedly arrested and sentenced to death by an Afghan court several months later. Proving once again that many times the most dangerous enemies our troops face may not be in the Taliban, but those who reside in the halls of power.

Prisoners of the Taliban liberated by U.S. Special Operations forces

2009

U.S. Army Lt Col Burton Shields, commander of 4th Battalion, 23rd Infantry Regiment, and his interpreter Ali Mohamed discover a pile of dried poppy plants in Badula Qulp, Helmand Province, Afghanistan.

"If not for such men, we would be at the mercy of every demon."—MICHAEL YON

THE HEART OF A HERO

BEN KOPP

Ben Kopp knew what a hero looked like. After all, his great grandfather was an infantryman in World War II and from an early age, he and Ben were buddies. The two were very close and Ben loved to try and pry a war story out of the man who, like most of his generation, preferred not to talk about it.

When his great grandfather passed away in April of 2001, Ben was devastated. A few months later when terrorists attacked America, Ben decided the best way to honor the memory of his hero was to become one himself—at the age of thirteen, the Rosemount, New Mexico, native announced that he planned to become an Army Ranger.

Ben Kopp in Afghanistan

Ben was a scrappy kid—possessed of a kind of frenetic energy that makes parents pull their hair out and wonder how the boy will survive to finish high school. At fourteen he and his buddies decided to play army and soon got into a brutal firefight with each other—using BB guns. At the height of the battle, Ben was sounding the battle cry when he was hit by enemy fire—in the mouth. The small metal pellet miraculously missed his teeth and embedded itself under the skin. He somehow hid the injury from his mother for weeks and when he finally told her about it, the doctor she hired said it wasn't worth taking it out. So from then on he lived with a metal pellet inside his tongue. True to form, he used the anomaly to his advantage with the ladies, claiming it made him a better kisser.

His senior year of high school, Ben kept his oath and joined the Army under the delayed entry program. One month after graduation, he headed for basic training.

There, Ben found the purpose for which he was created. The military fit him—he had a talent for it the way some have an aptitude for baseball or music. He loved the camaraderie, the constant challenge to be better than you were yesterday. Even the discipline it imposed was good for him, though submitting to authority went against his nature.

He sailed through Airborne school and the Ranger indoctrination program. The day he earned his tan beret was one of the proudest moments of his life. It was a hard-won honor he'd wanted for years. After graduation, he reported to the 3rd Battalion, 75th Ranger Regiment at Fort Benning, Georgia.

The Ranger Regiment on a war footing left no room for relationships, however, so Ben chose to stay unencumbered as he fought through two deployments to Iraq. Between deployments he attended the grueling sixty-one-day Ranger school. During the mountain phase of training, he had his first brush with failure and found himself being "recycled," held back one cycle and given a second chance to make it with the following class. It sparked some deep reflection about the kind of man Ben wanted to be. With some time to kill before he could join the next class, a dog-eared book left behind by a previous student caught his eye. The book talked about leadership and the parallels between the life of an elite solider and the life of a Christian. It got him thinking about the things he loved most about the Rangers, being a part of some-thing greater than himself, being a force for good in the world. He realized God's plan for his life was even bigger than the Rangers, bigger than the Army. By the time he successfully graduated Ranger school and pinned on the black and gold Ranger tab, Ben was already on a new mission—one that would continue into eternity.

He grew during his time in Ranger school. He matured physically, emotionally, and spiritually. He made a note in his journal that illustrated his new found purpose. It reads, "God is more concerned with who I am becoming than with what I am doing . . . there is something inherently noble in choosing to put oneself in the line of fire to save a brother." The next line in the notebook indicates he'd found a new hero to emulate: "Christ put himself on the line for the very people who were against him."

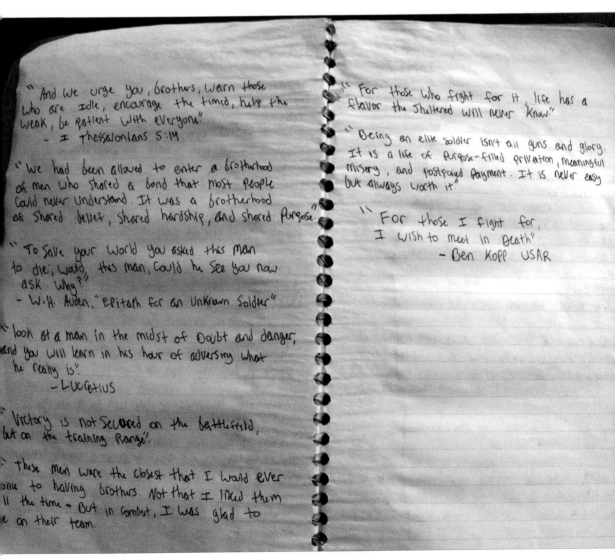

Pages from the journal of Ben Kopp

Ben Kopp in Afghanistan

His next trip to the war zone would provide ample opportunity to put into practice those convictions.

In 2009 Iraq was winding down and the war was heating up in the shadows of the Hindu Kush. Ben's company deployed once again—this time to Afghanistan.

Because of the nature of some of the Tier One units with which the Rangers work, an ongoing need for operational security makes it impossible to release most of the details regarding that deployment. It is known that Ben's unit participated in dozens of important and high-risk missions, in which the newly tabbed Ranger demonstrated the leadership abilities he learned in Ranger school while acting as a gun team leader.

Then two weeks before he was due to return stateside, a call for help came in from a Special Ops reconnaissance team that had been compromised and was taking heavy fire from a large number of Taliban fighters in the southern Helmand province. Ben was part of the Ranger Quick Reaction Force that scrambled to go to the aid of the beleaguered team. They rushed to the sound of the guns and plunged into the firefight, suppressing the enemy so the recon team could make it safely away. Ben was awarded a Bronze Star with Valor for his actions that day. According to the citation, he exposed himself to heavy, close range enemy fire in order to save his comrades. In the process, he took a bullet in the leg.

The Rangers' first-rate medical evacuation system swung into action. Ben was placed aboard a medevac helicopter and flown to a nearby hospital. He was rushed to FOB Dwyer, and doctors there performed two surgeries to try and repair the damage. From there he went to Bagram Airbase, and then Landstuhl, Germany. A day later he was flown to Walter Reed Army Medical Center in Bethesda, Maryland. The doctors kept him in an induced coma and performed more operations to try and save him, but in the end, Ben had simply lost too much blood. A week after he was wounded and with his mother, Jill Stephenson, now by his bedside, the terrible news came that Ben was not going to make it.

But he wasn't done being a hero. Not by a long shot.

Every Ranger fills out a form before each trip to the war zone specifying his wishes in the event he is killed in combat. Ben indicated on his form that he would like his organs donated, if possible. Specifying which organs he would like to donate, he wrote simply, "any that are needed."

Judy Meikle was a fifty-seven-year-old woman from Winnetka, Illinois, who suffered from poor circulation all her adult life. An active lover of the outdoors, she woke up one morning in 2008 and couldn't breathe. A trip to the hospital brought the bad news that her heart was failing. She needed a heart transplant.

A year later, an acceptable match had yet to be found and Judy was running out of time.

One of Judy's friends happened to be a first cousin of Ben's mother and made mention of her need on a post to an Internet guest book set up to honor Ben's memory.

Though she was wracked with grief at the loss of her son, Jill Stephenson saw that post, and in it a chance for Ben to live on in more than memory. On July 20, the day after they turned off the machine that was keeping his body alive, Ben Kopp saved Judy Meikle's life.

Judy Meikle, recipient of Ben Kopp's heart

Now with the heart of a twenty-one-year-old Ranger beating in her chest, Judy's circulation problems are a thing of the past. And while she might not be able to run a six-minute mile—yet—she feels a deep sense of gratitude and responsibility to live her life, like Ben did, according to that tenet of the Ranger creed that states "one-hundred percent, and then some."

Doctors said Ben's other organs and tissues could end up saving as

Jill Stephenson with her son, Ben Kopp

many as seventy lives. He was buried with full military honors at Arlington National Cemetery. His mother made sure Ben received his other last request—a flyover of U.S. Army Black Hawk helicopters at his funeral.

Five months after his death, the wife of one of Ben's Ranger buddies was going through his digital camera and found this photo of Ben, smiling in the back of a Humvee in Afghanistan. Because she had never seen it before, Jill Stephenson likes to imagine the photo came from heaven and Ben sent it to let her know how happy he is there.

Jill Stephenson at Ben's memorial service, holding his journal

20/05/2009

Ben Kopp in the back of a Humvee, taken in Afghanistan

Col North with DEA FAST Alpha

DEA FAST "ALPHA"

KANDAHAR AIRFIELD, AFGHANISTAN

Hulking outlines of four Mi-17 helicopters were all that occupied the "Green Ramp" in front of Kandahar International Airport when we arrived in a convoy of Toyota pickups packed to the gunnels with heavily armed Special Operators. All was dark except for the muted reds and greens of their penlights as they hopped out onto the cool tarmac and began final checks of their gear. They spoke in hushed tones, standing in small groups until the American pilots arrived and fired up auxiliary power units to perform their pre-flight checks.

Most of the Americans wore full, bushy beards, though their athletic bulk would certainly keep the average operator from being mistaken for an Afghan. The dozen or so Afghan Commandos present wore no facial hair. At least a half-dozen different uniforms could be seen: Green Berets who worked as trainers for the commandos wore the same uniforms as their Afghan counterparts, while the American Special Ops unit that made up the bulk of the force, wore Marine MARPAT uniforms. Others wore specially modified multicam and everyone customized their kit to fit their own needs.

For the past two weeks, our FOX News crew wasn't actually embedded with the military. Instead, we'd been following the exploits of what is arguably the most highly specialized group of federal law enforcement officers on the U.S. payroll—agents of the Drug Enforcement Administration's FAST units.

FAST—Foreign-deployed Assistance and Support Team. It sounds innocuous, even harmless. It isn't. All FAST members are experienced DEA special agents who volunteer for the program. FAST teams deploy around the world in support of counter-drug efforts by friendly host nations, with a mission set very similar to that of the Green Berets—a team of ten men advising their host-nation counterparts, gathering intelligence, and assisting with direct action when necessary.

FAST Alpha patch

It's no surprise the DEA is very active in Afghanistan, considering the country produces ninety percent of the world's illegal supply of opium. The Taliban movement, cynically preaching a purer brand of Islam is actually a narco-insurgency, little different from the FARC in Colombia or a Mexican drug cartel. The DEA is in Afghanistan to break the Taliban's opium-money-corruption-terror link.

DEA FAST units of eight agents, a team leader, and an Intel specialist rotate through Afghanistan on one-hundred-twenty-day deployments and bring to the fight their own air wing as well as an intelligence-gathering capability second to none. This makes them very valuable to the Special-Ops community.

We launched on the mission eight years to the day since terrorists trained in Afghanistan killed nearly three thousand innocent people back at home. The thirty-five Special Operators who climbed aboard three Soviet-era Mi-17 helicopters just before first light could think of no better way to mark the anniversary. It was something these men would never forget and if they had anything to say about it, neither would the Taliban.

It was a capture-kill mission on the compound of a Taliban kingpin southwest of Kandahar. Experience told them wherever drugs were present, usually there would be arms and explosives for supporting the insurgency. It was something they called "the nexus" and FAST units have targeted these drug-terror kingpins with good success. Every kilo of heroin they confiscated and destroyed is money out of the Taliban's war chest. And they are getting very good at finding the drugs.

But the Taliban and their supporters are getting smarter, too. The insurgents have learned to plant IEDs and mines around potential landing zones. Lieutenant Dan Cnossen, a Navy SEAL, on his fourth combat deployment stepped on a mine as he disembarked from a helicopter during a night insertion.

The explosion nearly tore him in half, traumatically amputating both his legs. Braving more hidden mines all around, the SEAL corpsmen rushed to his aid and was able to stop the bleeding and save his life. Though every young person going into a fight wants to believe, "that won't happen to me"—the wise warrior knows it can happen to anyone.

We sped down the runway at Kandahar and took off into the first hint of morning and soon the Mi-17 pilots were flying so low and so fast it seemed as though we were driving to the target. Looking out the open rear door of the helicopter, I could see the helo behind us skimming along a field of poppies low enough to harvest it, then pull up to clear the mud wall of the farmer's compound. There could be no question they are incredibly skilled and more than a little crazy.

Poppy fields in Afghanistan where opium is grown

With FAST Alpha team leader Carson Ulrich

Twelve minutes later we got the signal. One minute out. Every man passed it to the man behind him and all began final preparations, checking weapons and adjusting gear one last time. I made sure my camera was on standby and said a quick prayer for the safety of the team.

The helicopters swooped into freshly plowed fields around the target compound, flaring hard and throwing up a curtain of dust and sand. As soon as the wheels touched earth the operators charged out the back, eager to get away from the largest, loudest target on the battlefield. In seconds, everyone was fanned out behind the bird, bracing themselves on one knee, scanning the fading twilight for targets and bracing against forceful gusts of rotor wash as the choppers lifted off again.

When they were gone, we moved quickly to the outer wall of the compound, Holton and I doing our best to stay out of everyone's way and still get the action on "tape." I followed the team leader of FAST Alpha—Carson Ulrich. He was one of the tallest guys on the mission, built like a cross between a swimmer and a pro wrestler. He moved fast, obviously eager to make sure the rest of his team got where they needed to be and didn't get hurt in the process. Carson is the kind of guy whose presence makes any dangerous situation seem a little less so—he looked like he could handle anything.

Two operators breached the outer door of the compound within sixty seconds and then the entire team flowed inside in a practiced ballet of weapons pointing in every direction. They immediately came upon several younger military-age males, who were taken into custody by Afghan Special Police Commandos. There was also a knot of about a dozen women and children, who had been sleeping on a raised dias. Though they were obviously terrified, the Afghan Commandos gently coaxed them into moving to a secure area of the compound where they were sequestered and guarded until the mission was complete.

Old-Vietnam-era UH-1 "Huey" helicopters outfitted with GAU-17 miniguns did racetracks overhead watching for signs of the enemy. Within five minutes the entire compound was secure and a Spec-Ops K-9 dog and handler began searching the various rooms for drugs while the operators took up positions on the rooftop to defend against a possible counterattack from the surrounding orchards and nearby farms. Twice the pilots reported a man with a radio in hand, watching our movements. The helo gunners fired warning shots to discourage him. Taliban insurgents are known to use walkie-talkies to call in mortar fire.

The search of the compound turned up a bag of black tar heroin, a stash of precursor chemicals, and a large bag of glass marbles. I asked the Afghan police captain in charge of the raid why they were important and he pointed out that the enemy has begun using marbles in IEDs because they can't be seen by metal detectors.

These converted Huey Helicopters flew as air cover for missions with the DEA in Afghanistan.

To the west of the target compound, the operators noticed several acres of carefully cultivated, eight-foot-tall hashish producing marijuana plants. The "field of dreams" was so large, the FAST agents didn't even try to destroy it. One of the FAST unit members did take care to burn a large stash of dried poppies stacked against one wall. The marbles, opium, and chemicals were moved a safe distance from the compound into a drainage ditch and wired with several pounds of plastic explosive. Two Afghan Commandos secured several men for questioning and released the rest while everyone else moved toward the pickup zone to wait for the Mi-17s to return. Then the demolitions men called "Fire in the hole!"

We moved two hundred meters outside the compound and I readied my camera, capturing the black cloud of smoke that shot skyward as the contraband heroin, morphine base, and precursor chemicals were destroyed. Moments later the helos swooped in to pick us up and we ran through the dust cloud to the rear ramp and hopped aboard.

The ride home was just as low and fast as the trip out, but the mood was completely different. The men were smiling, joking, and using their personal cameras.

The men of FAST Alpha went on to raid dozens of drug bazaars around southern Afghanistan. Unlike our relatively uneventful 9/11 anniversary mission, they often found themselves involved in pitched battles with hardened terrorists. Then on 26 October, another DEA mission, supported by a U.S. SOCOM Spec-Ops team hit a large drug market in Farah province. They were quickly engaged by several dozen fanatical insurgents, of whom they killed more than thirty. On the objective, they found and destroyed refined opium worth more than a million dollars. The operation was a stunning success,

Dried poppies

Back from a raid with FAST Alpha. Last man on the left is Chad Michael.

but as they were extracting from the site, one of the nightstalker helicopters crashed, killing ten of those inside. Three of those killed were Special Agents—the first DEA casualties in the war on terror. The others were U.S. Army and MARSOC Special Operators with whom we went on numerous ops without losing a man.

It was a devastating blow for all the organizations involved, particularly the tight-knit DEA community. Michelle Leonhart the Acting Administrator, made sure the entire team was brought home to attend all three funerals. For that, FAST commander Carson Ulrich, his men and their families were very grateful, realizing that most warriors aren't afforded that privilege. They arrived back on U.S. soil with only one request— that they be allowed to return to Afghanistan as soon as the memorial services were over to see out the remainder of their tour.

In their minds, it was the only way to properly honor their friends—by picking up the weapons of the fallen and carrying them back into the fight. And that's exactly what happened.

DEA memorial for agents Forrest Leamon, Chad Michael, and Michael Weston

14 SEPT 09

Mi-17 helicopter

DEA DRUG RAID

JALALABAD, AFGHANISTAN

★ ★ ★ ★ ★ ★ ★ ★ ★ ★ ★

We launched well before dawn on three Russian Mi-17 helicopters and while the pilots were American, it was a surreal experience for me. I trained for years in the Marines on how to shoot these down. Now I was riding into combat in one, armed with a camera and covering other young men fighting a different enemy. But most of those in this aircraft were neither Soldiers, Sailors, Airmen, or Marines. This unit was different.

According to colleagues back home, our FOX News team in Afghanistan missed all the excitement. After we left the USA in late August 2009, Washington saw one of the largest peaceful protests in history against a sitting government. A bold congressman rose during a televised joint session of Congress to accuse the president of the United States of prevaricating. The rhetoric in Washington was nearly as hot as the summer sun in Helmand Province. All pretty exciting stuff, I suppose. But as I glanced around the dim interior of the shuddering Mi-17, at steely-eyed warriors riding into battle, I realized I wouldn't trade a single day with the Special Operations raiders with whom we were keeping company for all the hoopla in Washington.

The "raiders" were an extraordinary cross section of talent, tenacity, experience, and courage. But one thing that made them different from many of our previous embeds—most of these Special Operators were not active duty military. In their ranks are U.S. Drug Enforcement Administration special agents, intelligence specialists, linguists, contract pilots, and air crewmen from the Department of Defense and the State Department's Bureau of International Narcotics and Law Enforcement Affairs, contract weapons and tactics experts and some very dedicated, brave, and resourceful Afghan police officers. On this operation we were joined by a team of U.S. and coalition Special Operators.

Throughout 2009 these kinds of "task-organized" units were becoming the nemesis of the Taliban and they did it all beneath the radar of the mainstream media.

Our FOX News team spent nearly a month embedded with them on operations spanning the length and breadth of Afghanistan. By agreement, we would not photograph or videotape most of their faces or identify them by anything but their first names. We were not allowed to broadcast the specific unit to which any of these men belonged. On many of their operations, they flew non-U.S. aircraft and rarely used American military vehicles, in order to confuse the enemy. These measures combined with the DEA's unique ability to collect accurate "full-spectrum intelligence," validate it with human sources, and exploit that information with rapid, direct action account for the raiders' unparalleled effectiveness in taking on the Taliban. The 14 September mission—launched by the DEA—is a dramatic example of how effective these kinds of operations have become.

Afghan narcotics police

The Birds headed southeast from Jalalabad, escorted by Vietnam-era UH-1 "Huey" gunships to the raid objectives, less than ten kilometers from the Afghanistan-Pakistan border in the incredibly mountainous Nangarhar Province. At first light, we touched down—a force of forty-three DEA agents, NATO Special Operators, police officers from Afghanistan's narcotics interdiction and special investigations units, and two confidential informants who were actually residents of the village we were raiding, their heads covered with balaclavas to keep them from being identified and the resulting death sentence.

The informants led the raid force directly to the first target—a way station on an opium ratline into Taliban-controlled territory in Pakistan. I stayed close to Walid, a muscular, bearded senior SIU investigator, as he trudged up the steep hillside to a dry-stack stone hut pointed out by one of the informants. Walid immediately found what he was looking for: precursor chemicals, opium, morphine base, and pure heroin. Some of it was buried in a shallow hole outside the building and the rest was stockpiled inside. As he riffled through a box of morphine base at the site, he looked up at me, smiled and said, "Money from these drugs will never get to the Taliban." He then helped a team of Afghan narcotics police carry the haul to a corner of the courtyard where other Special Operators quickly rigged it with several pounds of plastic explosive.

Moments later, the call "Fire in the hole!" came from the demolitions experts and everyone pulled back a safe distance to watch the explosion. When it went off, so did

Drug lab in Afghanistan making black tar heroin

Taliban drug lab blown up by DEA

all the donkeys in the neighborhood, hee-hawing their displeasure at the thunderclap that echoed up the valley.

Walid was right. Nobody was going to be selling those drugs now.

Then it was back to the landing zone for a quick flight to the second objective—a village much like the first—clinging as it had for centuries to a steep mountainside. This one was the suspected site of a drug-processing lab. The raiders, led by one of the informants, moved rapidly up the hill and set up a cordon, taking advantage of the element of surprise. By the time they made it to the target buildings, however, the occupants had fled—leaving two dirty, malnourished infants behind. The babies lay crying amidst used hypodermic needles and dirty clothes. Apparently the drug processors were also partakers of their poison. Afghan NIU police scooped up the children, trying to console them and find their mothers among a crowd of women and children huddled in a house further up the mountainside. Even here in the primitive villages of the Hindu Kush, opium destroyed everything it touched. The mothers of the babies were nowhere to be found.

DEA Assistant Regional Director Keith Weis, a tall, dark-haired father of two who looked far too young to have been in this dangerous business for more than twenty years was the raid leader and one of the few we are allowed to identify. During the mission Keith said intelligence indicated the site was part of "a significant organization with ties to the Taliban." That allegation was substantiated by documents and records seized from the building. The operator of the lab, who looked much older than his age due to sampling his own product, was identified by an informant, taken into custody, and the drugs and chemicals were wired with explosives by the NATO Special Operations team.

It was an extraordinary haul. We found out later from Afghanistan's deputy interior minister Mohammad Hanif Atmar that the six-hour raid destroyed one thousand kilograms of opium, three hundred kilograms of morphine, thirty kilograms of pure heroin, and more than two hundred kilograms of precursor chemicals and yielded weapons and reams of documents. Estimated street value of the drugs and chemicals in Western Europe or the United States: more than $3 million.

After footage of the raid aired on FOX News Channel, the single greatest inquiry we received wasn't about the drugs, the Taliban or the raiders; it was, "What happened to the little babies who were abandoned at the lab?"

Here's the answer: The DEA informants pointed out the two mothers in the crowd gathered nearby, neither of whom looked to be more than fifteen years old. The NIU officers handed the children back to them along with a tongue lashing for abandoning their children. The DEA unit's intelligence chief, also named Keith, later told me, the NIU officers' anger stemmed from embarrassment—that these wives of a lab operator would rush to save themselves and leave their babies behind. "They wanted to make sure the American news crew understood that's not the way a proud Afghan should act."

As for their husband, if he's convicted, it's unlikely the children will ever get to know their father, but perhaps thousands of other children will be spared the horror of being on the receiving end of the drugs the man produced.

For the men of this special mission unit—though they may not be recognized with awards and decorations, that knowledge is good enough.

Exfil—the skilled pilots of these Mi-17s put these huge aircraft down on postage-stamp-sized terraces below the village.

14 SEPT 09

Special Operators on a capture-kill mission have to walk single file to avoid possible IEDs.

CAPTURE/KILL MISSION

NEAR HERAT, AFGHANISTAN

They only had a matter of hours to plan the mission. After tracking a known Taliban warlord for months, the Special Forces team based in Herat received notice that their target was in a village only a few kilometers away. With no time to spare, the ODA, quickly planned a capture/kill mission for that very night and received approval. Though hastily devised, the plan was designed from mission templates they rehearsed over and over, and the team felt confident they could pull it off.

Assigned to the ODA was Staff Sergeant Rob Gutierrez, the same stocky Combat Controller from San Diego, California, who had already distinguished himself in 2008 and earlier in 2009 on previous deployments to Afghanistan. Rob did a quick map reconnaissance of their objective and drew up some pre-planned "nine-line" fire missions that could be fed to attack aircraft supporting their mission. From aerial imagery available, he marked each building in the target village with a number, with which it would be simple to identify the locations of friendly and enemy forces.

Night-vision view of laser target designator

The other Green Berets scrambled around the base, readying night-vision optics, weapons, and equipment. They ran a quick walk-through with their Afghan commando counterparts so every man would know his assigned place in the mission. Though they all would have preferred to have more men for the mission, they made do with what they had and preparations went smoothly because they had done them all a hundred times before.

As the sun sank over the ancient walls of the fortress built by Alexander the Great in Herat city, the special mission unit mounted up in Ground Mobility Vehicles and rolled out toward the foothills surrounding the city. The village where their target, a Taliban warlord took refuge was in an area proven to be very dangerous for Coalition forces. In these parts of Afghanistan, allegiance to the Taliban was high and attacks and IEDs were a major threat to "friendlies" venturing too far outside the city. So the Americans and their Afghan allies went loaded for bear, knowing their target was known to travel with a large and well-trained personal security detail that would fight to the death. If it came to that, the ODA would be happy to oblige.

The only way to avoid IEDs was to stay off the roads completely. This meant the convoy of Humvees had to pick its way at a snail's pace cross country through the farmland surrounding Herat. With the drivers using NVGs, it was agonizingly slow and painful going, as the vehicles bounced and jostled over the uneven ground.

In order to keep their profile as low as possible, the unit decided to travel the last five kilometers on foot. Leaving a rear guard to watch over their vehicles, the ODA and their Afghan counterparts dismounted at about 2200 hours and crept toward the village, following their GPS devices and doing their level best to avoid detection along the way.

At midnight they reached the outskirts of the small hamlet that was their objective. It was surrounded by farmers' fields, many of which had grown opium poppy earlier in the year but now were dry and barren. Others had a half-grown crop of wheat that would be ready in another month for harvest. Trees lined ancient, hand-dug canals that irrigated the fields. The moon was half full, throwing off enough illumination the men hardly needed their night vision whenever clouds were not blocking its light.

The Special Forces Captain, who went by the call sign "Digger" was smart and methodical and this was his first mission as ODA commander. He split his force, sending half the men to set up an over-watch position where they could provide security for the maneuver element that would enter the village. Once the support element was in place, the rest of the team, made up of six operators including the commander and SSG Gutierrez, left cover and ran for the target building—the place where Intel indicated the HVT would be asleep with one of his wives.

The building was constructed in typical Afghan fashion, high mud walls surrounded the compound at least eighteen inches thick, with flat-roofed rooms built

against the outer walls and a courtyard in the center. The team moved up to the corner of the target building and pressed themselves against the wall.

But the enemy was waiting.

Gunfire exploded above them from three rooftops less than thirty feet away. The Special Operators dove behind a short mud wall jutting from the building, then began to return fire. But the enemy had constructed "spider holes" in the walls around each rooftop that would allow them to fire their AK-47s without exposing themselves in the process. Small arms fire rained down from these concealed fighting positions smacking the wall behind which the operators were crouched. Then, a PKM machine gun opened up on them from ground level, blasting rounds at them from down an alleyway. As the ODA fought to improve their position, a cow appeared in the alley, scared up by the gunfire. Disoriented, it charged the machine gun position, taking the majority of the bullets meant for the Green Berets.

The team took advantage of the diversion caused by the bovine's demise and made for the doorway of the target building. Gutierrez and another man took up positions to draw the enemy's fire and unloaded on the enemy fighters shooting down on them so the rest of the team could get inside. Then the Captain and another Green Beret charged forward so Gutierrez and his partner could move inside. As he moved, Gutierrez was on the radio talking with two Air Force F-16s overhead. The aircraft had visual contact on the objective and warned Gutierrez they identified more enemy reinforcements moving toward their position. This was bad news, but not wholly unexpected, since they knew any fighters in the area would definitely run to the guns as soon as the shooting started. The ODA had been engaged for just a few minutes—and time was already running out.

The support-by-fire element positioned outside the village was trying to engage the enemy and give the assault team some relief, but the height of the walls obstructed their ability to deliver accurate fire. They repositioned to try and get better fields of fire but began taking RPG rounds into their midst. Forced to relocate again, the fire-support element was, for the time being, out of the fight. Inside the compound, the assault team was now on its own.

Then Digger got hit. The bullet made through-and-through holes in his thigh. Two other men caught shrapnel from a grenade as well, both superficial wounds. They were able to reach the relative safety of the target building, however, where the SF medic quickly went to work dressing their wounds. But the enemy began throwing hand grenades onto the rooftop of the room they were in, and the explosions caused mud and debris to cascade on top of them. Then rocket-propelled grenades started slamming into the outside walls, turning the plaster-like mud into shrapnel and blowing holes in the structure.

With the Captain in a mild state of shock from his leg wound, the Team Sergeant took charge of one corner of the compound, sending men to defend the approach from the direction of the alleyway and ordering two men up on the rooftop to discourage the grenade throwers. A warrant officer in front of Gutierrez was firing out the doorway at Taliban fighters on the rooftop across the alley when his weapon jammed. He spun out of the doorway to clear it and change magazines. The battle-hardened

Latino Combat Controller stepped in to replace him and saw two Taliban shooting down on his buddies from the two-story building across the yard. He stepped out and put two well-aimed shots center mass, watching them fall.

Then another man in black pajamas stood up at the corner of the rooftop. Gutierrez snapped his weapon up and pulled the trigger just as the man's AK-47 spat flame. The man dropped his weapon and toppled over, but Gutierrez felt like someone had just punched him in the lower back. He ignored the sensation because another man stood up and took the place of the one he'd just engaged. He shot that man, too, and watched him fall.

Back on the radio, Gutierrez began trying to find a way for the F-16s to help them out of their predicament. With Taliban fighters crawling over the rooftops only a few meters away, there was no way to use the fighter jets' onboard missiles to take them out without killing Americans in the process.

Gutierrez suddenly felt exhausted. Then he coughed and was surprised to taste blood in his mouth. He dropped to his knees and spit blood—too much blood. That was when he realized how badly he'd been shot.

The terrorist's bullet entered just above his armpit and punched a fist-sized hole in the small of his back. In between, it torn up his insides and caused his left lung to collapse. The medic appeared at his side and dragged him into a doorway, rolling him onto his uninjured side so he wouldn't drown in his own blood.

Rob Gutierrez was no stranger to combat and saw plenty of men die. As the medic worked frantically to remove his combat harness and body armor, the wounded Staff Sergeant realized he had about three minutes left to live. Images of Julie, his wife, seven months pregnant with their first child and thoughts of his mother—the Mexican immigrant who realized the American dream when she married his father. A part of him knew they would be okay. It would be sad, but theirs was a strong, close-knit family.

Another part of him, though, was saying "This really sucks!"

An instant later, both sentiments were overcome by one fiery emotion—anger. He wasn't going to let his team down. If this was it and he only had minutes to live, Robert Gutierrez was going to go down fighting, protecting his team. He rolled his head to the side and could see out the doorway into the courtyard. Silhouetted in the moonlight was a Taliban fighter, blazing away with his AK-47. Summoning his remaining strength, Gutierrez raised his rifle and fired.

"Rob! Hey Rob!" It was the medic. He was busy stuffing curlex into the hole in Gutierrez's back. "You've got a sucking chest wound, buddy. Your lung is filling up with fluid. If we don't get you to a hospital, you're not going to make it."

Tell me something I don't already know, Rob thought.

"I've got to stay and call in the aircraft," he wheezed through bloody lips. Just breathing was becoming more and more difficult. It felt like someone was pumping his chest cavity full of concrete.

"I've got to decompress this lung." The medic pulled out a needle the size of a ballpoint pen. "This is gonna hurt like hell, buddy. But it will make it easier to breathe."

It already hurt like hell. How much worse could it get? Gutierrez gave a feeble nod, "Do it."

The medic was right. He lifted Rob's armor plate and jabbed the needle between his ribs. If he could have, Gutierrez would have screamed. But within seconds, the pressure in his chest started to ease, and he could feel breath coming back. He gulped in the sweetest lungful of air he'd ever tasted and said, "Thanks, Doc."

Then he got back on the radio.

The F-16s orbiting overhead were armed with hellfire missiles and five-hundred-pound bombs. But there was no way they could use either weapon system without killing Americans and enemy alike. The two jet pilots had a clear picture on their thermal scopes as the Taliban swarmed in, only feet away from the team of ten Special Operators who were now trapped inside the compound and about to be overrun. And they were almost out of gas.

Gutierrez had an idea. He keyed his radio and said to the fighter pilots, "How about a show of force, over?" If the jets could make a high-speed pass and get low enough, they might just scare the enemy fighters into taking cover.

The jets' fuel tanks were hovering just above "bingo"—the absolute minimum they needed to make it back to base. But the pilots agreed to try. A moment later, they dove their planes to rooftop level and screamed over the target area with full afterburners. The noise was so deafening everyone who wasn't wearing ear protection had

their eardrums blown out as the jets screamed by. Taliban fighters were literally blown off the rooftops by the fiery jet wash and Gutierrez and his mates were sure the building they were in would collapse.

But it didn't slow the enemy for long. The Taliban fighters renewed their attack with a vengeance as soon as the jets turned for home.

Gutierrez heard the handover as the jets left and passed the battle space to two incoming A-10 Thunderbolt aircraft. In addition to missiles like the fighters, the "warthogs" were armed with seven-barrel rotary cannons capable of firing seventy rounds of 30-mm high explosive and incendiary ammunition per second. Regulations said friendlies had to be no less than two hundred feet away from where the aircraft were shooting in order to be safe.

They barely had twenty feet, much less two hundred. But at that point, they didn't have much of an option. Gutierrez discussed it with the captain, who would have to authorize such a "danger close" gun run by the A-10s. The enemy grenades exploding on the roof of their position and RPGs still blasting holes in the walls of their enclave were enough to convince him it was worth the risk.

Gutierrez got on the radio and tried his best to calmly relay the information to the A-10 pilots. When he got to the part about them being thirty feet away from the enemy, the pilot asked him to re-send his transmission. Even if the pilot's aim was perfect, the slightest turbulence could cause the impact to vary as much as sixty feet. There were

Green Berets half that distance from the enemy.

When the pilots finally agreed to the gun run, Gutierrez turned to the men around him and said, "Everyone had better cover up. This is going to get loud."

The operators got into the prone position, huddled together in the corner of the room. The medic draped himself over Gutierrez and they waited for the firestorm.

When it came, it felt like the end of the world. The walls around them imploded and then crumbled, flaming debris was falling everywhere and the sound was something you felt, not heard—like it was raining house-sized meteors. For a moment Gutierrez wondered if any of them would survive.

After the first A-10 made its run, Gutierrez coughed dust and blood and heard the team sergeant checking to see if everyone was alive. Miraculously they were. But there was still some incoming gunfire, though much less than before. So Gutierrez keyed his mike and cleared the second aircraft hot.

Again, it felt like they were inside the apocalypse, and again, they all survived. After that, more Taliban moved in to replace their fallen comrades, so after a few minutes, in anticipation they'd soon be able to pull out, the CCT airman slid his body armor back on over the still-bleeding wound in his back. Then Gutierrez ordered a third pass.

These guys just didn't learn.

The village exploded again in a rain of high-explosive rounds. When the A-10s pulled up and shot skyward at the end of their run, the only sound was the crackling of flames as the destroyed buildings around the team burned. Then the aircraft radioed that a large group of enemy reinforcements was heading their way. There was no time to lose.

The team sergeant dragged himself to his feet. "Lets' get out of here." One by one, the Special Operators got up and moved out, single file, helping the injured along as best they could. They picked their way through the dust, smoke, and burning rubble, sidestepping the bodies of their foes.

A-10C Thunderbolt II

They had to walk almost two kilometers to find a safe extraction point where helicopters could come in and get them. During this movement Gutierrez held onto the harness of the man in front of him, but otherwise walked under his own power. Every step became more difficult, however, as his punctured lung slowly filled with blood once again. Despite his pain and blood loss, he maintained contact over the radio with the A-10 pilots, who prowled the skies above, escorting the team to safety. After he called in the helicopter that would take them home, Staff Sergeant Gutierrez passed out from loss of blood.

The medic performed a second needle-decompression of his lung and started an IV to replenish his fluids. The injured staff sergeant briefly regained consciousness, only to lose it again as they were loading him on the aircraft.

It takes time for awards to make their way through the system and be approved. Had Staff Sergeant Gutierrez died that dark night east of Herat, he might well have been awarded the Medal of Honor his team mates wanted him to receive. As it is, he will likely receive the Air Force Cross, which added to his Silver Star from Bari Kowt in 2008 and Bronze Star from the Shok Valley four months later, will make him one of the most highly decorated airmen alive today.

But Rob Gutierrez doesn't care about any of that. If anything, the accolades and attention are an additional burden as he does his best to heal quickly so he can get back out with his brothers who are still in harm's way.

Staring death in the face has made him a little more philosophical, however. Now the chance to hold his infant daughter and spend time with Julie has a sweeter flavor he appreciates more than he ever thought possible. And he's grateful, too, for the country that allowed him the opportunity to serve with men for whom he would, even today, lay down his life.

Staff Sgt Robert Gutierrez

SSG Damone "D" Brown and his K-9 partner Argus

SPECIAL OPERATIONS K-9

The U.S. Special Forces are some of the most highly specialized soldiers in the world. Each soldier trains for years, cross-training for every job in his unit. There are weapons experts, communications specialists, engineers, and Intel officers. They can train a force of foreign fighters or take down a terrorist network with direct action. Years of combat experience hone their senses to a razor's edge.

But these super warriors rely on one special member who has skills none of them can match. His name is Argus. Most Green Berets wait until after they finish high school to join the military—Argus was hand-selected to be a Special Operator almost from birth. He has years of combat experience and

highly specialized training. He can drop onto a target by parachute, or fast rope in from a helicopter. He can track the enemy across mountainous terrain in freezing weather and take him down without a weapon. In fact, he never carries a gun, because he doesn't need one.

Oh, and one other thing Argus has the other Green Berets don't—four feet and a tail. He's a Belgian Malinois—one of only a handful of Special Operations qualified military working dogs and he's proven his worth as a member of the 7th Special Forces Group on three combat tours in Afghanistan.

Specially trained to find explosives by smell, Argus has been credited with saving dozens of lives by sniffing out IEDs. His handler, Staff Sergeant "D" likes to point out that Argus is as much one of the team as any of the other guys. And most of the time, he swears Argus smells better, too.

Argus has been trained to go anywhere his team goes—whether that means jumping from an airplane at ten thousand feet (albeit connected to his handler with a special harness) or going out on a twenty-five-mile rucksack march. Argus even wears his own kevlar body armor.

Since its inception as an experimental program in 2005, the special operations military working dog program has met with great success, and some of its graduates have even been awarded bronze stars for their work saving lives in the war zone.

It's a program enjoying huge success and is very popular with the soldiers. Argus always trains as a member of the team. Even during medical refresher training—the Green Berets take turns sticking each other with needles, learning to give each other intravenous fluids which might save a life on the battlefield. Argus gets stuck too, and though he obviously doesn't like it, SSG "D" points out that Argus is one of the most likely to be injured, so they need to know how to save him if that ever happens.

The bond between man and dog was never stronger than between these two—they spend nearly every hour of the day together, even sharing a room. "Argus has been there by my side the whole time—it's like taking my son to war—such a huge responsibility. But one that I wouldn't trade for anything in the world. We definitely have a very strong bond."

Argus has found dozens of IEDs, thousands of pounds of explosives, and has even survived an IED attack. So far he's never been injured, but a sizeable percentage of the dogs in this profession will be wounded or killed in the line of duty. It's likely Argus will complete at least one more combat tour before he retires—at which time he'll be put up for adoption if he's deemed not to be too aggressive.

SSG "D" plans to be first in line to take him.

2010

Air Force Pararescuemen jump from an HC-130 aircraft during a training exercise off the coast of Djibouti.

PARARESCUE CREED

It is my duty as a Pararescueman to save life and to aid the injured. I will be prepared at all times to perform my assigned duties quickly and efficiently, placing these duties before personal desires and comforts. These things I do, "That Others May Live."

APR 2010

THE PEDROS

KANDAHAR AIRFIELD, AFGHANISTAN

"We've got one urgent surgical!" The helmeted Air Force Pararescueman shouted over the whine of the two HH-60 Pave Hawk helicopters spinning up on the tarmac. "An auto vehicle accident—a four-year-old local national. It's a ventilated patient and it's worsening, so we don't know what we're going to get when we get there."

Crewmen scurried around the choppers, making quick last-minute checks before we lifted off into the cool morning air over Kandahar. It was to be the first of eight missions flown by this crew today.

When we arrived in Afghanistan in April 2010 for a month-long embed, one of the first units we went to visit was the 41st Expeditionary Rescue Squadron, also known as the "Pedros." The unit boasts some of the most experienced helicopter pilots in the military, because they fly nonstop rescue missions during each four-month deployment to the war zone—and these pilots, aircrews, and PJs have made many trips "in theater."

Pedros crew chief

The Pedros are always in high demand. That's because these "rescue warriors" are willing to go where other medevac units won't to save the lives of Coalition forces and Afghan civilians alike. Red crosses—the universal symbol for medical personnel —are conspicuously absent from their aircraft. That's because the Geneva Convention expressly forbids medical personnel displaying the symbol from carrying weapons. Not that any of that stops the Taliban—they'll shoot at any helicopter regardless its markings.

But the Pedros will shoot back if they are shot at and they happily forego the "protection" of the red cross in exchange for the ability to do so. As is their practice, two Birds were spinning up for the mission.

As the Pave Hawks completed final preparations for takeoff, I watched as the crew chiefs readied their door-mounted weapons—twin GAU-17 miniguns capable of firing four thousand rounds per minute of 7.62 ammunition. If the Taliban planned to disrupt this mission, they had better think twice.

The senior mission crew chief put cameraman Chuck Holton on one Bird and me on the other and asked, "Are you armed?"

"Sure," I said, holding up my camera. "I have a Sony but Chuck is carrying his Canon." He shook his head and grinned as I jumped aboard and slithered into a web belt connected to the floor of the chopper by a five-foot strap. There were no seats, because most of the "passengers" the Pedros transport, take the ride lying down. I wedged myself into a niche between the two door gunners just as the helicopter lifted off.

Moments later we were pounding over the Afghan countryside at over one hundred fifty miles per hour—so low it seemed I could reach out and touch our shadow as it raced along over trees and mud-brick houses below. The combination of speed and extremely low altitude are breathtaking—but essential. The Pedros fly low and fast because it is the safest way to get a wounded patient to a hospital without getting shot down. At treetop level, by the time any enemy saw us, we'd already be gone.

Tech Sergeant Richard Oberstar was one of two Pararescuemen (called "PJ's") on the Bird. Both of them sat with their feet hanging out the doors, scanning the ground below with M-4 assault rifles at the ready. Their faces showed no sign of tension or anxiety—this was their element and it showed. As we swept over the outskits of Kandahar, Bill, the other PJ, reached into a green aviator kit bag and produced a plastic bag. It contained a small stuffed penguin, some pencils, and a little bound notebook. I gave him a look that said, "What's that for?" He flashed a crooked smile that said, "Watch this."

Bill leaned out of the helicopter, scanning the ground ahead of us. Below a small village came into view, with a half-dozen mud-walled compounds. Just before our aircraft flashed over it, Bill tossed the plastic bag down and away from the chopper. Children instantly raced out of the mud-walled huts to retrieve the gifts.

Stuffed animal bombs. Now that's diplomacy—and a whole lot different than the kind the Soviets practiced. They built tiny bombs that looked like children's toys and dropped them over Afghan villages.

TSgt Oberstar grinned and gave Bill a thumbs-up. Oberstar was no stranger to saving lives. After five years as an Air Force dog handler, he decided to try out for Pararescue.

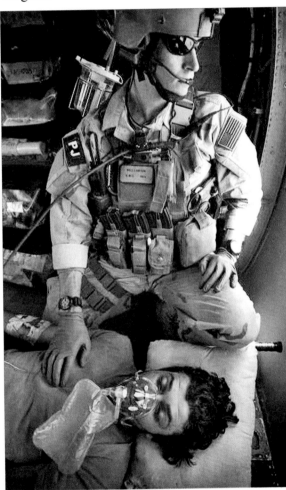

Staff Sgt William Lawson, a Pararescueman with the 129th Expeditionary Rescue Squadron, keeps an eye on the countryside as he cares for a wounded Afghan National Army soldier from the Hemland Province, Afghanistan. Sergeant Lawson will provide care to the injured soldier until he is safely delivered to a hospital.

Though older than the average inductee, he successfully completed the grueling two-year pipeline they call "Superman school," and took his place among fewer than four hundred Air Force Pararescuemen. That was twelve years ago.

The flight of two Pave Hawks pulled up and over the serrated edge of a rocky ridgeline, shooting so close through a mountain pass that for a moment we were looking up at sheer rock walls on both sides of the aircraft. Then, a gut-wrenching drop back down to the valley below. Soon we arrived at a tiny Special Forces firebase tucked away in the mountains of Oruzgan province. The helos set down on a gravel helipad as a camouflaged ambulance raced to meet us. Oberstar and his partner unhooked from the Bird and ran to assist.

The child, strapped to a litter, was carefully lifted out of the ambulance by a team of medics and carried to our helicopter. He already had an IV in his arm and an oxygen tube leading into his tiny nose. Behind them the boy's father followed, his traditional Afghan robe whipped about by the rotor wash from the HH-60. The Pararescuemen escorted him along with his son and put them both on the helicopter with great care. Seconds later they hopped aboard and shut the doors to shield the unconscious boy from the blast of wind as we lifted off.

The boy's father was terrified. We were soon flying along at 150 knots, one hundred feet about ground level. Given the remote neighborhood we just left, it's likely the fastest he'd ever traveled before was at the speed of his old Russian farm tractor. This was completely outside the realm of his experience.

As we flew back to Kandahar, the father alternately reached out to hold his son's hand with a mixture of genuine concern for his boy and then out the Plexiglas door panel—the abject terror at his first flying experience evident on his face. He had probably seen a helicopter before and might even have shot at one. But after this day I was willing to bet he never would again.

The boy was transferred to the level-three trauma facility at Kandahar and was expected to fully recover. Some say I'm naive about events like this, but I'm betting the Pedros' rescue flight made an ally out of the boy's father.

TSgt Oberstar and his crew went on to perform seven more missions that day alone. Just a few weeks later another aircraft from the 41st Expeditionary Rescue Squadron was on a mission to save wounded British soldiers when they were shot down by an enemy rifle grenade. Four men died in the resulting crash, including two Pararescuemen, TSgt Michael Flores and SrA Benjamin White. Flores, a thirty-one-year-old husband and father of two who was on his second tour in Afghanistan, is credited with the original idea of putting toys and goodies in plastic bags and tossing them to children while en route to missions. These four brave men died

while living up to the motto of the Pararescuemen: "That others may live."

HH-60 helicopter, about $16 million dollars. Training for the aircrew, about $4 million dollars. Training for the PJ's in the back, about a million dollars apiece.

Saving the life of a wounded American or Afghan child—priceless.

Honor Guard members of the 305th Air Mobility Wing, McGuire Air Force Base, New Jersey, perform a twenty-one gun salute for the funeral of Master Sgt Michael Maltz of the 38th Rescue Squadron, Moody Air Force Base, Georgia. Maltz was killed when his Pave Hawk helicopter crashed eighteen miles north of Ghanzi, Afghanistan, on the way to rescue Afghan children.

SUPERMAN SCHOOL

Saving lives. That's what being a pararescueman, or "PJ" is all about. But being a professional rescuer means making a living going into places everyone else wants to escape. And that takes a special kind of selflessness and sacrifice. It also takes a tremendous amount of training.

Pararescuemen probably get more real-world experience than any other branch of the military. That's because lifesavers aren't only needed in wartime. Once trained, PJ's regularly perform rescues at sea, on mountaintops, during floods, fires, storms, and earthquakes. In between disasters, they train constantly to keep their skills sharp.

The pararescue "pipeline," is the two-year process by which a man becomes qualified to do this job. Part of the process is as follows:

- **THE PARARESCUE/COMBAT CONTROL INDOCTRINATION COURSE**
  Ten weeks, Lackland AFB, Texas

- **US ARMY AIRBORNE PARACHUTIST SCHOOL**
  Three weeks, Fort Benning, Georgia—learning how to perform static-line parachute jumps out of a perfectly good airplane.

- **US ARMY COMBAT DIVERS SCHOOL**
  Four weeks, Key West, Florida—basic and advanced training in advanced scuba diving, water infil/exfil techniques, and underwater rescue.

- **US NAVY UNDERWATER EGRESS TRAINING**
  One day, Pensacola NAS, Florida—how to escape an aircraft that has crashed in water.

- **US AIR FORCE BASIC SURVIVAL SCHOOL**
  Two and a half weeks, Fairchild AFB, Washington—living off the land, navigation, and how to survive in hostile territory.

- **US ARMY MILITARY FREEFALL PARACHUTIST SCHOOL**
  Five weeks, Yuma Proving Grounds, Arizona—HALO parachuting.

- **SPECIAL OPERATIONS COMBAT MEDIC COURSE**
  Twenty-two weeks, Fort Bragg, North Carolina—extensive training in all areas of trauma medicine, minor surgery, combat trauma management, pharmacology, and combat evacuation procedures.

- **PARARESCUE RECOVERY SPECIALIST COURSE**
  Twenty weeks, Kirtland AFB, New Mexico—how to get into and out of any environment safely. Includes mountaineering, skiing, advanced parachuting, and combat tactics.

One look at the crushing schedule of training, and it's easy to see why they call the process of becoming a pararescueman "superman school."

SCUBA SCHOOL

Some form of "Scuba School" is offered by every branch of the military. Usually around six weeks in duration, they all train Special Operators on the basics of underwater navigation, physiology, and both closed- and open-circuit breathing systems. Believed by many to be the most physically demanding military school, it requires students to learn to swim distances over fifty meters underwater, to share breathing apparatus with a buddy, learn submarine lock in/lock out procedures, long-distance swimming, and deep diving among other skills.

The Army Combat Diver Qualification Course (CDQC) takes place at Key West, Florida. The price of admission: Just to get into the course, each student must be able to tread water for two minutes continuously, with both hands and ears out of the water; swim twenty-five meters underwater without breaking the surface, retrieve a twenty-pound weight from a depth of three meters and perform a surface swim of five hundred meters, nonstop, using only the breaststroke or sidestroke.

Because of the extremely physical nature of the course, there is always some risk involved. While the military takes every precaution to safeguard the lives of the men who enter, students have been killed in training, a fact which underscores the high level of commitment of these Special Operations warriors.

Staff Sergeant Mark Maierson was one of those. A member of the 3rd Battalion, 7th Special Forces Group, Maierson had already proven his mettle many times over, successfully completing the Special Forces Qualification course, Airborne school, and even the grueling Survival Evasion Resistance

Escape course at Fort Bragg. In addition, the stocky engineer sergeant proved himself in combat, earning a Bronze Star in Afghanistan. He was the very picture of health and vitality.

No one knows exactly what caused the twenty-seven-year-old Maierson to black out in the pool during the initial phase of the Army's Special Forces Underwater Operations School on 13 March 2009. Medical professionals standing by immediately pulled him from the water and administered aid, but his heart had stopped. There was nothing they could do.

Maierson dedicated his life to the service of his country and his fellow man. He may not have died in battle, but his sacrifice illustrates just how much courage and commitment it takes even to prepare a Special Operator for the field.

Staff Sgt Mark Maierson in dive school (in forefront)

8 APR 10

CAMP MOGENSON

QALAT, ZABUL PROVINCE, AFGHANISTAN

On 8 April, Chuck Holton—combat cameraman, editor, frequent-flyer friend, and war-zone companion—and I boarded a Black Hawk helicopter in Kandahar Air Base and headed out to Camp Mogenson, a small Special-Operations base outside the city of Qalat, where we were to be embedded with SEAL Team Three.

Camp Mogenson is named after a Green Beret, Staff Sergeant Robert J. Mogenson. He was a weapons sergeant assigned to the third Special Forces group when he was killed by an IED on his way back from a mission here in Zabul province in May 2004. Also killed in that IED strike was Captain Dan Eggers, a Citadel graduate who also had a camp named after him—near the American embassy in Kabul. Having a base named after you is the kind of honor most men seek to avoid, for the same reason few warriors set out to get a Medal of Honor—one normally has to die to get it. If I've learned anything in the years I've spent in and around the military, it is that when bullets are flying, it's love for one's comrades that makes men do valiant things, not the hope of an award.

Our chopper set down on a rudimentary gravel helipad outside the camp, a typical border-land outpost surrounded by "Hesco" barriers—large wire-framed, fabric-lined containers filled with Earth to create quick and effective protection on hastily constructed outposts in the war zone. Living conditions inside the camp were Spartan, but more comfortable than we often found with regular U.S. Army and Marine units in the field.

Like many Special-Operations bases, Camp Mogenson had some creature comforts—like showers, a generator, lights, a chow hall—even bunks to sleep on instead of the dirt. Some Special-Ops bases we have lived in—even in some of the remotest places on the planet have modern creature comforts like refrigeration and air conditioners. On one base the communicators and engineers even found a way to deliver and hook up a large-screen TV. When the Team Chief was asked where it came from, he winked and said, "If you can't get it you aren't trying. And if you get caught, you aren't trying hard enough."

For its part, Camp Mogenson appeared to have been built in stages inside the compound of a former Afghan warlord. Large steel gates served as a portal into a warren of mud-brick buildings. These were modified by Sea-Bees for use as a headquarters building, a small chow hall staffed by a local Afghan family, and a weight

Afghan women in a compound

room. Interspersed among them were shipping containers turned into housing units for additional troops and well-built metal-roofed, plywood buildings like those found at every "temporary" U.S. base around the world.

Chuck and I were graciously shown to the "VIP quarters"—a plywood room next door to the SEAL Team command post. It was the lap of luxury. We not only had electricity to charge the batteries for our equipment—but an air conditioner! It didn't work. We dropped our gear and headed to the headquarters building to meet with the SEAL commander, who briefed us on the mission they planned for the following day.

Later, we accompanied some of the SEALs to the rifle range while they sighted-in their weapons in preparation for the next day's mission. The range looked out on a barren hilltop and the SEALs expertly adjusted their sights and zeroed in on a few metal targets placed in the open ground several hundred yards away. Several times they had to stop shooting while Afghan goat herders ambled through the range, obviously certain the Americans wouldn't fire on them.

That evening we dined with the SEALs and the Afghan soldiers and interpreters who would accompany us on the mission. The XO of the SEAL team explained that the Afghan troops were "fresh"—that this unit had just been established and was "early on" in their tactical proficiency.

After nightfall, we received a call from FOX News in New York, requesting us to

Navy SEAL providing village overwatch

Taking down a Taliban drug lab

"come up" on our satellite gear for a live "hit" from the war zone. Chuck set up our Hughes BGAN satellite transceiver and ran cables while I hung my camouflage poncho liner on the plywood wall behind my bunk. We uploaded a short package about the takedown of a Taliban drug lab we'd been on the day before and went on Fox and Friends to discuss it with the folks back home.

In the U.S., some of the mainstream media outlets were reporting that U.S. troops were chaffing under a "tactical pause" and more restrictive rules of engagement (ROE) ordered by Kabul. On air, I acknowledged some of the Special Operators we'd been traveling with expressed frustration that they weren't being allowed sufficient latitude to take the fight to the enemy. One said he felt "like a meat eater being fed a steady diet of cabbage." What we couldn't reveal at the time was that the mission we were slated to do with the SEALs the following day was supposed to include a high likelihood of enemy contact.

Special Operators in the field told us the slowdown in "op tempo" was intended to give time for additional U.S. and allied troops to surge into the country. Lt Gen. David Rodriguez, the operational commander of the International Security Assistance Force in Afghanistan, called it "repositioning." Others said is was all part of a "realignment" necessary to prepare for a major offensive being planned to secure the former Taliban stronghold in Kandahar.

With SEAL Team 3

The troops I was talking to used slightly more colorful language to describe it.

The story hit a nerve. One junior officer in the group growled, "It's not the ROE. None of us has a problem with reducing the incidence of civilian casualties. But we need to stay on the offensive here if we're going to win." Another Special Operator with long experience in Afghanistan agreed, pointing out that the Taliban hadn't paused in trying to kill them, but U.S. troops were hampered in taking the fight to the enemy. Everyone expressed their hope that the following day's mission to a remote village in the mountains would be a good opportunity to work off their frustration and give the new Afghan unit they were training a chance to show what they could do when confronting the enemy.

Just before midnight we retired to recheck our gear and get some sleep before the 0400 wake-up call for the mission. Just moments later there was a thunderous roar as a USAF V-22 Osprey swept over our billet, coming in for a landing on the LZ less than fifty meters away.

The Big Bird remained on the ground for a few minutes off-loading personnel and equipment, then loading others to take them to a different base. It lifted off, again flying directly over us. And then—tragedy.

A week or so earlier we had interviewed the commander of the Marine V-22 squadron at Kandahar and he said the tilt-rotor aircraft, "will go further, faster, and carry more stuff than anything else out there." He also noted the craft was "easy to fly, but hard to fly well."

The V-22 that went down wasn't his. It was one of the recently arrived craft flown by the 58th Special Operations Wing, based at the airfield in Kandahar.

Inside the downed aircraft, was an assault force of Rangers from A Company 3rd Ranger Battalion on a mission targeting the terrorist network in Zabul Province. The USAF Special Operations crew aboard were killed when the Bird went down. Survivors and others who saw the crash said it appeared as though the pilot became disoriented in the swirl of dust as he took off from Camp Mogenson and it went down outside the base.

Medevac helos quickly lifted the casualties from the crash to the triage hospital at Camp Morgenson and the big Level III trauma hospital at Kandahar Air Base. But before we lifted off on our mission with the SEALs, Taliban "sources" were claiming they shot the craft down.

It wasn't true, but both pilots and a civilian contractor were killed outright, while a fourth man, Army Ranger Michael D. Jankiewicz, was pulled from the rubble alive but died a short time later.

Jankiewicz, a twenty-three-year-old Ranger from New Jersey was on his fourth combat tour. His family said he wanted to be a soldier since he was three years old. Highly intelligent and a voracious reader, he planned to complete a career in the military and then go on to become a history teacher. He was engaged to be married as soon as he returned from Afghanistan. Instead, Corporal Jankiewicz was buried eleven days

V-22 Osprey

later at Arlington National Cemetery with full military honors and was posthumously awarded the Bronze Star.

With the sobering news of the crash fresh in our minds, we followed members of SEAL Team 3 and their fresh Afghan soldiers onto two Russian MI-17 "hip" helicop-

Cpl Michael Jankiewicz

ters for the forty-minute ride to the mountain village which was our objective for the day. Shortly after liftoff, the pilots pointed out the black smudge on the desert floor below, all that was left of the MV-22 Osprey.

We flew the rest of the mission in silence, every man alone with his thoughts inside the old Russian helicopters. The two SEALs sitting in the open rear ramp took pictures as the Birds climbed over stark, craggy peaks on the way to the objective.

One minute out, the inside of the Birds became a study in focused activity. Men readjusted their equipment, charged their weapons, and prepared for a quick exit as soon as the aircraft touched down. We landed a half kilometer from the village, in a tight wadi with a small stream running through it. As the pilots picked their way carefully among boulders in the streambed and landed the huge helicopter with surgical precision, I marveled at their skill. Once we were down, the team wasted no time filing off the bird. As I jumped out behind them, I landed ankle-deep in the

Mi-17 Transport Helicopter

Special Forces soldiers were inserted on mountaintops around the village to overwatch our element.

tiny rivulet flowing down the wadi. *Just like the SEALs,* I thought with a grin. *Always have to start out wet.*

The helos took off again and the team spread out along the hillside and began moving toward the village. So far, there was no sign of the enemy. The SEALs moved swiftly and with all senses on high alert, though their Afghan counterparts—new to the business of countering insurgents in their own land weren't quite as attentive.

During the mission, the green Afghan troops, though led by a capable Afghan sergeant, exhibited only the slightest tactical proficiency. Carrying their AK-47s slung over their shoulders seemed to be standard operating procedure. The platoon's machine-gunner ditched his Kevlar helmet and instead wore a white turban around his head. I noticed that Chuck, a former Army Ranger, spent the day staying as far from the lackadaisical Afghan gunner as he could and so did I. Both of us knew his white turban would make him target number one for a sniper.

Thankfully the Taliban were out to lunch—or went to ground to prevent being spotted on the thermal sights of the Apache helicopters overhead.

The village could have been a scene from the Old Testament. About a dozen mud-walled compounds, the largest of which enclosed at least an acre of ground. All looked to have been built centuries ago. A fertile ribbon of farmland separated it from the river, which ran fast and clear out of the snow-capped peaks on all sides. It was stark but very beautiful.

The people we could see were dressed in traditional Pashtun garb, the men in dark earth-toned robes and the women arrayed in bright colors from head to toe. The only road, if you could call it that, was a dirt track that wound its way up the valley along the river. One of the SEALs immediately took up an over-watch position with a machine gun to guard the approach to the village as the rest of us ventured in.

We moved into the village and began to search each compound. The village men were cool toward the group at first, but when the interpreter explained to them we were there looking for Taliban, they seemed to relax. The elders came out and said the Taliban came to their village every year and demanded food and shelter, but that they had not yet arrived this year. The SEALs pressed their Afghan counterparts to continue searching for weapons, IED-making equipment, and opium while the mission commander and the Afghan sergeant sat down to tea with the head man and the elders. As they sat on the ground and talked outside the headman's home, the rest of the men from the village gathered around to listen.

The village children quickly lost their timidity and began following Chuck around like the Pied Piper. With no electricity in the village, it was clear none of the kids had ever seen a camera and were fascinated by the moving pictures he was capturing.

After a couple of hours in the village, the SEAL team decided they had done all they could and moved out to take up a position on the outskirts and wait for the helicopters to return. The children followed along, prompting one of the special operators to comment that the team had become the world's most expensive day care providers.

But as the men played with the kids that afternoon, it became clear to me that while they may not have found any Taliban, the mission itself was a success. The SEALs quickly identified how far they had to go in preparing this Afghan Army unit for the war they were in. And perhaps more importantly, the village children, who were now delighting themselves by arm wrestling and besting the SEALS at slingshot marksmanship, had at least one very positive experience with U.S. and their own Afghan forces.

Chuck Holton with Afghan children

A Navy SEAL stands watch over Afghan children in the village.

THE FUTURE

FOR AMERICA'S
SHADOW WARRIORS

Through the end of the last century, conventional and strategic nuclear forces were the instruments of national power that received the most resources and attention. The so-called "Powell Doctrine" dictated that our wars would be fought as we did in Operation Desert Storm. Before engaging in combat, we would conduct a massive build-up of conventional forces. The American attack would be preceded by a "shock and awe" air campaign—and then U.S. armored and mechanized forces would rapidly overwhelm the adversary. The one-hundred-hour war to evict Saddam Hussein's Republican Guards from Kuwait seemed to vindicate the strategy.

Then came 9-11-01.

An air campaign alone would be inadequate to unseat the Taliban and destroy al-Qaeda. There were no bases from which the U.S. could stage an attack into the foothills and deserts south of the Hindu Kush. And so the nation called on its shadow warriors.

Since then, the long campaign of "Nation Building" in Iraq and the prolonged conventional fight in Afghanistan have tested the patience and treasure of the American people. Radical Islamic terrorism has proven remarkably resilient to conventional forces—and vulnerable to small teams of highly trained and uniquely equipped unconventional forces—shadow warriors—willing to brave difficult and dangerous terrain and take on an enemy far from other "friendlies" with a minimum of attention. Notably, when the last American "combat units" were withdrawn from Iraq in August 2010, the mainstream media somehow missed the U.S. Special Operators who stayed behind, training, mentoring, and accompanying their Iraqi counterparts on dangerous missions.

U.S. Special Operations Command—and units like the CIA's Special Activities Division and DEA FAST units have proven not only less costly than conventional military force—but in many ways, unexpectedly effective. In some places, like the Horn of Africa, the periphery of the Persian Gulf, and hostile spots like Yemen, unconventional forces are the only option for projecting U.S. power without risking wider hostilities.

A decade from now, unconventional warfare—the art practiced by the American Heroes of Special Operations—is likely to be our nation's first line of defense from those who would do us grievous harm. The shadow warriors in this book are the ones who showed us how.

FREEDOM ALLIANCE

SCHOLARSHIP FUND—Supporting the Children of America's Military Heroes

The Freedom Alliance Scholarship Fund honors the bravery and dedication of Americans in our armed forces who have sacrificed life and limb and provides college scholarships to their children. Through the generosity of the American public, the Scholarship Fund has awarded more than $1 million to the sons and daughters of American heroes.

Many of freedom's brave defenders who have lost their lives fighting terrorism have left behind young children. We believe it is our duty to help their children meet the rising costs of a college education, but more importantly to remind them that their parents' sacrifice will never be forgotten by a grateful nation.

SUPPORT OUR TROOPS—Honoring America's Armed Forces

The Freedom Alliance Support Our Troops program honors and supports our servicemen and women and their families—especially those who are serving on the front lines or who have been wounded and are recuperating at our military hospitals.

Freedom Alliance provides financial assistance and gift packages to these troops. The program also includes events such as Military Appreciation Dinners and special holiday activities. Freedom Alliance sponsors these activities to say "thank you" to our service members and their families.

Freedom Alliance, which was founded in 1990 by Lt Col Oliver North, USMC (Ret.), is a nonprofit 501(c)(3) charitable and educational organization dedicated to advancing the American heritage of freedom by honoring and encouraging military service, defending the sovereignty of the United States, and promoting a strong national defense.

For more information or to donate, contact:
FREEDOM ALLIANCE
22570 Markey Court, Suite 240
Dulles, Virginia 20166-6919
1(800)475-6620
www.freedomalliance.org   *"LEST WE FORGET"*

Meet **FIDELIS**, a bold book imprint dedicated to America's heroes. Whether they serve in our military or as first responders, or are parents, teachers, or lawmakers, these brave men and women stand in defense of the values of faith, family, and freedom we hold dear. Like the Latin word "faithful" from which the name comes, Fidelis books extol the virtues of courage, honor, and self-sacrifice, standing as a rebuke to a world devoid of integrity.

HER ⭐ ES

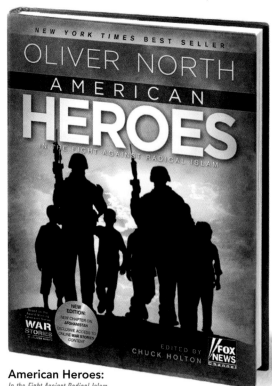

American Heroes:
In the Fight Against Radical Islam
Oliver North and Chuck Holton
Hardcover, $24.99   978-08054-4953-2

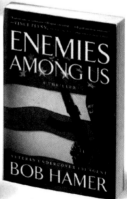
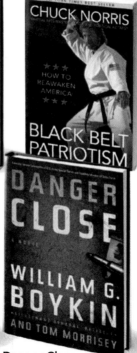
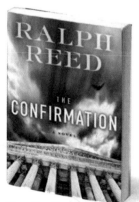

Air Force
15b, 32, 40, 41, 47, 186, 208a, 208b,
  263
SSgt Aaron Allmon: 8
TSgt Steve Elliott: top 9
SSgt James L. Harper Jr.: 13a, 38,
SSgt Nicholas Pilch: 10, 221, 222, 223
TSgt Maria L. Taylor: 16
SSgt Gary Coppage: 24a
SrA Julianne Showalter: 39
SSgt Brian Boisvert: 48
MSgt James M. Bowman: 73
MSgt Cecilio Ricardo: 75a, 278
Kristin Molinaro: 75b
MSgt Gerold O. Gamble: 99
SSgt Stacy L. Pearsall: 135
SSgt Shane Cuomo: 162
SrA Jason Epley: 164
SSgt Jeremy T. Lock: 177a
MSgt Lance Cheung: 178
SrA Stephen Otero: 187
MSgt Andy Dunaway: 195
Capt. Justin T. Watson: 196
TSgt Francisco V. Govea II: 265
TSgt Efren Lopez: 236
SSgt Samuel Rogers: 272
SSgt Shawn Weismiller: 275
SSgt Jason Lake: 276
SSgt Chrissy Best: 277a
Scott H. Spitzer: 277b
A1C Veronica Pierce: 279

AFSOC
185, 192a, 209b

Army
35, 65, 70, 81, 102, 103b, 131a, 131b,
  141a, 142b, 1698, 169, 172, 286a
Javier Martinez: 14b, 114b, 218, 219,
  232, 235
SSG Damone Brown: 15c, 15d,
  268a, 268b, 269, 270a, 270b,
  271a, 271b, 280, 281
PO2 Eli Medellin: 9b
SSG Russell Lee: 36
Capt Nate Self: 49
CPL Sean Harp: 50, 201, 202a, 203a
SSG Gene Vance: 53a
SGT Julie Nicolov: 62, 66,
SGT Keith D. Henning: 64
SSG Rebekah-mae Bruns: 97
SGT Fay Conroy: 98
SGT Jeffrey A. Ledesma: 100b
David Bohrer: 101b
SFC Fred Gurwell: 104, 109

MSG Sarun Sar: 106a, 106b, 107,
  108, 110, 111, 112
SGT Tara Fuerst: 136
SGT Daniel Love: 141b, 143b
SGT Keith D. Henning: 142a, 143a
SPC Melissa Harvey: 149
SPC Henrique deHolleben: 173, 174
Angela E. Kershner: 181
SGT Keith D. Henning: 182
SSG Robert Gutierrez: 183, 209a, 267
SPC Gretel Sharpee: 184
SSG Corey T. Dennis: 188, 189
SGT David N. Gunn: 190, 198, 207a
SSG John Wayne Walding: 193, 206
SGT Jason Carter: 194
SPC Ryan A. Goldsmith: 210, 256
CPL Jory Randall: 214
75th Ranger Regiment Public
  Affairs: 215a, 215b
SGT Debra Richardson: 266
SSG Aubree Clute: 289

Chuck Holton
6, 11b, 13b, 14a, 17, 18, 20, 21, 26b,
  27, 28, 29b, 33, 34b, 37, 43, 44,
  54a, 54b, 55a, 55b, 63, 74, 76a,
  76b, 80, 83, 113, 120, 121, 124,
  125, 128, 129, 130, 132, 134, 137,
  138, 139, 155, 165, 166, 220,
  224, 225, 230, 234, 243, 244, 245,
  246, 247, 248, 249a, 250, 251,
  252, 253, 254, 255, 257, 258, 259,
  273, 274, 282, 283, 284, 285, 286,
  288b, 290, 291a, 291b, 292a,
  292b, 293, 295, 296

Department of Defense (DOD)
68, 69, 175, 176a
Cpl Tyler W. Hill: 60b, 61
PO3 Kaitlyn Rae Vargo: 176b

Google Earth
60, 77, 91, 92a, 179, 191, 197, 217

Marines
85, 96, 103a, 294
SSgt Aaron Holleyman: 4, 114
CWO3 Philippe E. Chasse: 19
Sgt Joseph R. Chenelly: 25b, 92b
PHC Johnny Bivera: 25a, 31
Joe Rippetoe: 71
Sgt Mark Fayloga: 87
Maj Rob Bodisch: 90
Sgt Jose E. Guillen: 93
Sgt Kimberly Snow: 94

Sgt Kevin R. Reed: 95
Cpl Richard Blumenstein: 226, 229
LCpl Jeffrey Cordero: 227a, 227b
Hayne Palmour IV: 228

MISC.
Family of William Carlson: 78a
CIA: 86
USCCPA/Spc. Eric Jungels: 119
AFP/Getty Images/Liu Jin: 133
ABC News/James Hill: 140
Family of Mike Monsoor: 145, 146,
  147a, 147b, 150, 151b
Dimiter Kenarov: 170
John F. Kennedy Special Warfare
  Center & School: 177b
DVIDS: 199
Lori A. Bultman: 211
FOX News/Andrew Stenner: 216
Ken Hackman: 231
militaryphotos.net: 167
Chris Maddaloni: 202c
Family of Ben Kopp: 237, 238, 239,
  240, 241b, 242a, 242b
Judy Miekle: 241a
StoptheDrugWar.org: 251b

Navy
34a, 45, 46, 115, 117a, 117b, 118a,
  118b, 122, 123, 126, 127a, 127b, 144
PhoM2 Michael W. Pendergrass: 12
PhoM2 Robert Houlihan: 23
MC2 Dominique M. Lasco: 56
MC2 Christopher Menzie: 57
MCC Kathryn Whittenberge: 58,
  59a, 59b
Glen Mueller: 78b, 79, 88a, 88b
Michael Fumento: 148
Oscar Sosa: 151a
MC2 Joe Laurel: 213, 261, 262
MC2 Christopher Perez: 260
MC2 Brett Cote: 264
CPO Joe Kane: 287

Public Domain
22, 26a, 29a, 30a, 30b, 38a, 42, 52

USASOC
11a, 15a, 89, 152, 153, 159, 160, 161,
  170, 180, 192b, 200, 203b, 204a,
  204b, 204c, 205, 207b, 207c, 212
Spc Tony Hawkins: 154
Trish Harris: 67, 157, 163
Spc Jennifer J. Eidson: 233